Contestations and Accommodations

Contestations and Accommodations

Mewat and Meos in Mughal India

SURAJ BHAN BHARDWAJ

Oxford University Press is a department of the University of Oxford. It furthers the University's objective of excellence in research, scholarship, and education by publishing worldwide. Oxford is a registered trademark of Oxford University Press in the UK and in certain other countries.

Published in India by
Oxford University Press
YMCA Library Building, 1 Jai Singh Road, New Delhi 110001, India

First Edition published in 2016

ISBN-13: 978-0-19-946279-7
ISBN-10: 0-19-946279-8

Typeset in ScalaPro 10/13
by The Graphics Solution, New Delhi 110 092
Printed in India by Rakmo Press, New Delhi 110 020

To my parents

CONTENTS

TABLES

ACKNOWLEDGEMENTS

IN CHILDHOOD, I WAS EXPOSED to an extremely rich oral tradition of folk tales (*sang/svang*), popular in and even integral to the rural society and culture of Haryana. One of these tales, a musical rendition of the medieval legend of a bandit named Jyani Chor, composed by Pandit Lakhmi Chand, made a deep impression on me. It encapsulates the notions of justice, ethics, and class conflict current in the medieval rural society of the region. Jyani Chor was the son of a poor Meo peasant who was often imprisoned for non-payment of revenue to the state. His family's dire economic circumstances and his father's mistreatment at the hands of the oppressive state officials forced him to become a bandit in his youth. A Robin Hood–like character, Jyani used to rob the rich landlords and redistribute the wealth so acquired among the peasants. Even today villagers in Haryana can be found listening to the musical enactment of this tale with rapt attention. Later, as a student of history, I saw in this tale a vivid picture of the medieval peasant's socio-economic and moral world. As I delved deeper into this world while conducting my MPhil research on the agrarian history of Mewat, a region spread across Haryana and eastern Rajasthan, at Jawaharlal Nehru University (JNU), New Delhi, I realized the immense potential of the Rajasthani archival sources for reconstructing the history of the Meo community in late medieval India (late 17th and early 18th centuries), then a relatively untapped area. It was this subject that subsequently fashioned my doctoral research. This book is, therefore, a revised and substantially enlarged version of my PhD thesis.

In preparing this book, I have been helped by many individuals and institutions in numerous ways. First, I acknowledge the deep intellectual debt that I owe to Professor Dilbagh Singh, my research guide at JNU. His command over Rajasthani language and Rajasthan's archival sources helped me to progressively refine my understanding of both. On his insistence I regularly visited the Rajasthan State Archives in Bikaner and spent days tapping into the veritable gold mine of revenue and other official records pertaining to the region. He also gave me complete academic freedom to develop my arguments, while gently offering his useful comments and suggestions. I am also obligated to Mrs Singh for the affection and concern that she has shown for me since the days of my doctoral research. Professor Satish Chandra, under whose guidance I wrote a seminar paper on Mewat, brought to my attention several important points that I subsequently incorporated in my work. Professor Harbans Mukhia's seminal works on the character of peasantry and agricultural production in medieval India have, over the years, enhanced my historical understanding of these areas so intrinsic to my work. Besides, his comments on the final draft of this book have been extremely helpful. I am thankful to Professor Muzaffar Alam for his generosity in discussing with me at length issues pertaining to my work on several occasions; these discussions as well as the new perspectives that he apprised me of have been, perhaps unbeknownst to him, very enriching for me. Professor Yogesh Sharma of JNU, despite his busy academic schedule, always took out time to read the draft chapters of this book with extreme care and offer his editorial advice. I am also indebted to Mayank Kumar and Dipankar Das, without whose help at different stages of the work it would not have been possible to put this book together.

Shail Mayaram's book *Against State, Against History*, which explores the construction of community identity and contestation of state in the Meo oral tradition, provoked me into formulating more incisive arguments about the role of succession of states in inducing crucial changes in the social, economic, and cultural life of the Meo community. Though I do not agree with several of her conclusions, especially about the interface of the community and the state, and though the historical credibility of the oral tradition that she analyses to bring forth a supposedly 'subaltern' perspective on community and state demands scrutiny when juxtaposed with the information from the archival sources of late medieval Rajasthan, her work is a welcome addition to the limited literature on this area insofar as it presents a new framework for reconstructing the history of the Meo community. It has, therefore, turned out to be an intellectual stimulus to my own research. Indeed, some of my arguments have been shaped in direct response to hers.

I thank Professor R. P. Rana of Delhi University who is among the first few to encourage me to explore the socio-economic history of Mewat. Professor R. P. Bahuguna of Jamia Millia Islamia, New Delhi, has been a friend, advisor, and teacher to me throughout the course of my intellectual development from my doctoral research till the preparation of this book. I am also grateful to the staff of the Rajasthan State Archives for the help and hospitality they unfailingly extended to me in the course of my visits there for over two decades. In particular, I acknowledge the invaluable help I received in learning the Rajasthani language from Chuni Lalji at the Archives, who, unfortunately, is no longer alive to see the fruits of my labour. Professor G. S. L. Devra of Kota Open University, Rajasthan, has always taken pains to arrange for my accommodation during my frequent visits to Bikaner and to make my prolonged stay comfortable and pleasurable. Besides, I have always benefitted from his deep knowledge of the State Archives. I am also thankful to the staff of Nehru Memorial Museum and Library (NMML), JNU library, and Central Secretariat library in New Delhi for helping me locate the much-needed references. Mahesh Rangarajan, former director, NMML, encouraged me to continue with my research and enquired about it on several occasions.

In my long teaching career at Delhi University, I have had the privilege of associating and forming friendships with individuals who are too numerous to mention here and have helped me in many ways, academically and otherwise. In particular, I would like to thank Subhash Chandra Sharma, Daksh Lohia, Prakash, R. Gopinath, Mumtaz Khan, Manoj, Rohtas Singh Kharab, Chetna, Mahavir, Rajeshwari, Anil, Dhananjay, Renu, Bhupendar, Rajashri, Pragyan Chowdhary, Mukul Manglik, Prem Kumar, Rajesh, and Dinesh. Thanks are also due to my colleagues at Motilal Nehru College: Vipul Singh, Netrapal Singh, Kalpana Malik, Padma, Anand, Atul, Iliyas, and Sakul. I am grateful to Surendar Sharma for typing the entire manuscript with impeccable proficiency. I acknowledge the strong emotional support and confidence that I have consistently received from my family: my wife, Sushila, and my sons, Rahul and Madhulak. They have witnessed the long and arduous journey that I have made to prepare this book. Finally, I am grateful to the editorial team of Oxford University Press, Delhi, for facilitating the fruition of my research in the form of this book.

New Delhi Suraj Bhan Bhardwaj

A NOTE ON SPELLING AND TRANSLITERATION

I HAVE AVOIDED THE USE OF diacritical marks in Rajasthani and Persian words in the book for the ease of reading. However, diacritical marks have been used in the text of the 16th-century Mewati ballad 'Hasan Khan ki Katha', which, to the best of my knowledge, is being reproduced for the first time in Roman script. Since the text is in an old dialect with a mix of Persian and Mewati words, the marks would serve as an aid to correct pronunciation.

INTRODUCTION

THE CONVENTIONAL IMAGE OF COMMUNITIES in medieval India as self-sufficient and autonomous entities has come under scrutiny in recent times. Contemporary studies have successfully challenged these stereotypes and argued that communities have regularly undergone profound socio-economic changes, and such transformations have been an integral part of their histories. A dominant corollary to this stereotype has been the argument that these communities were averse to the state as a centralized polity, as any negotiation with the state would have diluted their autonomy and control over their own affairs. The Meos of the Mewat region have also been portrayed as believers in and practitioners of '*pal* polity' or autonomous community. In this book, the oft-repeated idea of 'autonomy of communities' in medieval India has been challenged in the course of investigating the evolution of the social identity of Meos.

In the Indo-Persian chronicles of the early Sultanate period, the Meos were broadly represented as tribes inhabiting the Aravali hills, valleys, and dense forests of the Mewat region, and notorious for cattle-lifting and plundering. In a similar vein, the British administrators-cum-ethnographers, such as Alexander Cunningham and Major P. W. Powlett, clubbed the Meos with the Meenas, portraying them as predatory and criminal social groups. However, one witnesses major transformations in their identity with the passage of time: they were not only peasantized by taking to sedentary plough-based agriculture and largely abandoning their predatory activities, but were also able to emerge as the region's landed elite by establishing their zamindaris all over the region. Further, they were gradually but continuously Islamized. During the Mughal period, we also find them engaged in several other important occupations. For instance, they became trusted post carriers for the Mughal state and came to be known as Dak Meoras. They were also employed as the emperor's personal bodyguards and palace guards, and came to known as *khidmatiyyas*. It is the crucial role of the Dak Meoras in the Mughal postal and espionage system that Irfan Habib has pointed out in his essay.[1]

The recent writings of Shail Mayaram have evoked a good deal of interest in the history and folk traditions of the Meos. In an earlier work, *Resisting Regimes: Myth, Memory and the Shaping of a Muslim Identity*, Mayaram provided a rich account of the relation of the Meos with the Rajput state of Alwar and the Jat state of Bharatpur. But it is in her latest book, *Against History, Against State*, that she draws upon the Meo folklore to delineate the Meo *pal* polity. She argues that they were socially organized on the basis of *pals* (lineages) which traditionally enjoyed the status of autonomous self-governing communities, and that their *pal chaudharis* acted like sovereign kings in taking decisions related to their respective *pal* communities. She further contends that the Meo *pal* polity was hostile to monopolistic sovereignty and favoured decentralization of power, and that the *pals* retained this pristine character of theirs without undergoing any change over a long period of time. She holds engaging in raid and plunder and opposing the powerful Mughal and Rajput states as integral to this *pal* polity. The very nature of their *pal* polity implicitly rendered them incapable of state formation. Mayaram's arguments on the Meos are similar to those of the British East India Company officers on the village communities in Mughal India in that they were perceived as 'independent' and 'autonomous' entities.

However, as the evidence suggests, during the medieval period, the Meos underwent unprecedented social, economic, and cultural changes in the wake of their peasantization. As the Meos largely adopted agriculture as their means of subsistence, they were culturally and socially transformed from a tribal into a settled agricultural community. Like the caste Hindus, they also received *gotra*

1 'Postal Communication in Mughal India', *Proceedings of the Indian History Congress*, 46th session (Amritsar, 1985), 236–52.

identities and emerged as the dominant community in Mewat. In this context, it must be pointed out that Mayaram's thesis on the changeless, autonomous *pal* polity is ahistorical because no records of the Mughal period, Rajasthani or Persian, prove her argument, and the sources used by her are largely the folk traditions of the late 19th century. Further, given that the Meos inhabited the area between Agra and Delhi, the twin cities that became Mughal capitals in succession, it would not have been possible for them to remain unchanged and retain the allegedly traditional pristine character of their *pal* polity, unaffected by state interventions. Thus, the *pal* system, too, underwent certain changes. The power of the *pal chaudharis* diminished and their role and character also underwent changes, as Mewat came under the rule of the Delhi Sultanate and the Mughal state that controlled Mewat and collected land revenue from there. During the Mughal period in particular, as Mewat was brought under the Mughal land revenue administration, the role of the *pal chaudharis* was reduced to collecting land revenue from the peasants and for the state, and their position became that of small zamindars, not 'sovereign' rulers. Rajasthani documents reveal that the Meo peasants approached the *amil* (revenue officer) of the Mughal state, not the *pal chaudharis*, to resolve their local disputes pertaining to engagement, marriage, theft of grain and cattle, and so on. Clearly, the Meo community had not been enjoying 'autonomy' under the Mughal rule, as Mayaram suggests.

Further, Mayaram's argument that the Meos were perpetually and uncompromisingly against the state, whether Mughal or Rajput, is untenable, as it ignores the multiple forms of negotiations and interactions between the Meo peasants and the state. Historically, no peasant community, however defiant and rebellious, could survive on resistance against the state alone; in times of peace, it could find ways and means of negotiating with the state and expressing its grievances to get concessions and relief. Petitioning, for one, was an important 'weapon of the weak' in the hands of the Meo peasants. The Rajasthani documents inform us that the Meo peasants presented a large number of petitions before the Mughal emperors and their *diwans* (chief ministers) from time to time, complaining against the high-handedness of the Amber officials and the non-customary taxes imposed by them. They would repeatedly remind the Mughal emperors and the authorities that they were the *raiyat* (revenue-paying subjects) of the Mughal *padshah* and not the Raja of Amber, and hence the latter had no legitimate right to impose non-customary taxes upon them.

The present study is largely based on Indo-Persian chronicles; various village- and *pargana*-level revenue records and reports preserved and catalogued in the Historical Section of Jaipur Records, at the Rajasthan State Archives, Bikaner; and other works of local (Mewati) origin. All these sources provide rich information about the political, social, and economic conditions prevailing during the late 17th and early 18th centuries in the Mewat region.

Given the dearth of information on the history of Mewat during the period of the Delhi sultans and the early Mughal rulers, the Indo-Persian chronicles are helpful in understanding the nature of state formation under the sultans and Mughals and the relationship of the Khanzada chiefs of Mewat with the Delhi Sultanate, the Mughal state, and other regional potentates. These chronicles, however, only record the political events involving the chiefs of Mewat in the form of narratives. Nevertheless, they foreground the strategic importance of Mewat for the Delhi Sultanate, the Mughal state, and other regional potentates.

As most of the *parganas* of Mewat were held by the rulers of Amber as *tankhwah jagir* in their capacity as imperial *mansabdars* or *ijaradars* at various points of time during the period under study, various categories of surviving records illumine the revenue administration and agrarian conditions at the *pargana* and village levels, but they have not been extensively utilized so far. The information contained therein sheds light not only on the revenue administration and the mechanism of surplus extraction, but also on the various aspects of the rural society and economy, such as the patterns of production and distribution of agricultural produce among the peasants and the various constituents of the ruling class; the relationship between production, prices, and land revenue; and the nature of administrative control. Linkages between the nature of agrarian economy and the social relations and the impact thereof on the agrarian administration can also be discerned from these records. The statistical data given in the revenue records are crucial to ascertaining the magnitude of land revenue demand, and the trends in agricultural production and crop prices.

These records, available from the second half of the 17th century, are *arsattas*, *arzdashts*, *chithis*, reports of the Amber *vakil*, *dastur-al-amals*, *yaddashtis*, Amber records, *dehai ferhashtis*, *jamabandis*, *khatoot ahalkarans*, and *dastur komwars*. As most of these records pertain to those *parganas* that were held by the Amber rulers as *jagirs* and on *ijara*, they do not provide any information about the *parganas* assigned as *jagirs* to other imperial *mansabdars*. Unfortunately, records pertaining to the latter have not survived. Nonetheless, the records left by the Amber rulers give us valuable insights into the conditions obtaining in the areas in the immediate vicinity of their own *tankhwah jagirs*.

The *arsattas* constitute the most important category of revenue records. They furnish a good deal of information on various aspects of the economy of Mewat, such as the total number of villages in each *pargana*; the number of villages assigned to the troopers and those held by the Amber Raja; the estimated income, arrears, and revenue realized as well as the expenditure under various heads in each *pargana*; and the area under the cultivation of *zabti* and *batai-jinsi* crops for each *pargana* and also separately for each village within a *pargana*. By and large, it is the record of the amount of *mal* (tax on crop) and various other cesses contained in the *arsattas* that provides useful information on cropping patterns and revenue receipts of a *pargana* and thus has been extensively used in this study. Besides, information about expenditure in the *parganas* is useful for the purpose of analysing the claims of the holders of superior rights to income from land in the rural society.

Although the information provided by the *arsattas* is extremely valuable, this category of records has its own limitations. The *arsattas* do not cover the whole region and the period under study. For instance, we do not get *arsattas* for more than five years for *parganas* other than Khohri, Pahari, Gazi ka Thana, Jalalpur, Mojpur, Wazirpur, Atela Bhabra, Piragpur, Pindayan, and Harsana. Therefore, long-term trends in prices and cropping patterns across all *parganas* cannot be determined with the help of the *arsattas*. Further, the *arsattas* pertaining to a *pargana* are not available for successive years, there being long time gaps between two nearest dated *arsattas*.

Another category of records is the *arzdashts* written by the *amils*, *faujdars*, and other officials of Amber, posted in various *parganas*. These *arzdashts* are addressed to the Amber Raja and each contains details of political, social, and economic conditions prevailing in a particular *pargana*. Hence, they are of great importance in reconstructing the political, social, and economic conditions of Mewat. They also contain the Amber Raja's directives to his officials, reflecting the attitudes of the *jagirdars*/*ijaradars* with regard to their territorial jurisdictions. As they are available for the entire period of our study, they are a more reliable source of information on the long-term trends in the social relations, political developments, and economic conditions in the *parganas* of Mewat.

The *chithis* are letters written by the *diwan* of Amber to its officials, particularly *amils* and *faujdars*. Each *chithi* contains the substance of a complaint received by the *diwan* and his instructions for its redressal. These complaints, lodged by various aggrieved parties including peasants, throw considerable light on social conflicts and tensions as well as customary practices in the rural society. We get a large number of *chithis* pertaining to the *parganas* of Mewat but the majority are dated to the 18th century.

The reports addressed to the Amber Raja by his *vakil* posted at the Mughal court are in the form of *arzdashts*, written in Hindi but incorporating Rajasthani and Persian vocabulary. These reports contain details of political developments at the Mughal court that the Amber Raja was regularly informed about. As an imperial *mansabdar*, the Amber Raja had to depend on the goodwill of the emperor for various favours, that is, the grant of *mansabs*, the fixation of salary, the assignment of *jagirs*, postings, promotions, and so on. In view of the factional rivalries among the nobles at the imperial court, it was the duty of the *vakil* to keep a watchful eye on various developments at the court and inform his master regularly. In fact, the *vakil* was the official representative of the Amber Raja at the Mughal court and served as an intermediary between the Raja and the Mughal emperor. Being the representative of the Raja, he was directly responsible to him and, therefore, worked in consultation with him in all matters that affected his interests directly or indirectly. The *vakil*'s reports throw considerable light on the petty interests of the various groups of nobility at the Mughal court and their mutual conflicts, as also their attitude towards rebel zamindars such as the Naruka Rajputs and the Jats.

The *dastur-al-amals* are schedules of revenue rates prepared by local revenue officials in conformity with the rules laid down by the central authority. We come across many such *dastur-al-amals* for various *parganas* of Mewat. Each *dastur-al-amal* mentions the respective shares of the state and the cultivators in the produce of land, as also the differential rates of revenue applicable to various categories of cultivators. Some also state the amount of other cesses and *zabti* rates. The *dastur-al-amal*s are extremely useful for computing the magnitude of revenue demand on the peasants.

The *yaddashti* is a kind of memorandum or a document of remembrance. The *yaddashti*s were written by village-level revenue officials such as *chaudhari*s, *qanungo*s, *patel*s, and *patwari*s. They provide rich information about such aspects as arable and fallow land, livestock, and bullocks owned by peasants of a village or a *pargana*. They also contain information about the availability of agricultural implements and other assets with the various categories of cultivators. However, the number of *yaddashti*s pertaining to Mewat is limited, and as such, they cannot be used extensively for the study of this region.

The Amber records contain letters written by the officials to the *diwan* of Amber. From these documents, we get good deal of information about the day-to-day functioning of the administration at the *pargana* level. The economic and political dimensions of the local administration are a recurrent theme of most of these letters. These documents are as important as the *arzdasht*s. In fact, both these categories of documents provide ample scope for mutually corroborative evidence.

The *dehai-ferhashti*s are descriptive lists of villages in each *pargana*, prepared by village-level officials such as *patel*s and *patwari*s. They provide us village-wise information about the categories of land—arable and fallow—as also details of crops under the *zabti* and *batai-jinsi* systems of land revenue assessment. They mention whether a village was given on *ijara* or held as *jagir* or *khalisa*, and also reveal the names of *ijaradar*s and *jagirdar*s. Although we have only few *dehai-ferhashti*s pertaining to *pargana* Khohri in Mewat, they are an important source of information about various aspects of the village economy and society.

The *jamabandi* documents were prepared *pargana*-wise by the *amin*. They contain information about the methods of revenue assessment and the magnitude of land revenue demand in the form of *mal*, *jihat*, and *sair-jihat*. They provide details of land revenue for each village under *khalisa*, but do not include the revenue figures of villages held in *ijara*. Nevertheless, they are of immense value in measuring the magnitude of land revenue demand on those crops that were assessed under the *batai-jinsi* system.

The *khatoot ahalkarans* are written in Rajasthani in the form of *arzdashts* and cover the period from 1633 to 1769. They provide useful information on various aspects of the internal administration of the *jagirs* in Mewat whose *ijara* was obtained by the Amber chiefs, as also the reaction of the peasantry against the non-customary taxes imposed by the Amber chiefs.

The non-archival records of the Alwar state, preserved at the Rajasthan State Archives of Bikaner, are very useful for understanding the perceptions of people in the Mewat region, although some of this information is based on local folk traditions.

The other important works used in this study are: 'Hasan Khan ki Katha', a historical ballad written by Narsingh Meo of Kajhota village in Mewat in the late 16th century, illumining the perceptions of the Meos about the First Battle of Panipat (1526) and the Battle of Khanwa (1527); and *Arzang-i-Tijara* (1873) written by Sheikh Muhammad Makhdum, *tehsildar* of Tijara, narrating the history of the Khanzada chiefs of Mewat and their relation with the Delhi Sultanate and the Mughal state. Being of local provenance, these sources are very important for understanding the socio-cultural history of the Meos and the Khanzadas during the medieval period. Besides, Abdul Shakur's *Tarikh Mev Chatri* (1919) in Urdu gives mythical genealogies (*vamshavalis*) of the Meos, connecting them with the Rajput clans. The work thus reveals the early 20th-century perceptions on the social origins of the Meos. Muhammad Habibur Rahman Khan's *Tazkirah-i-Sofiya-i-Mewat* betrays a clear Islamic orientation insofar as it seeks to chiefly argue that the Meos were the oldest community of the region to be converted to Islam, during the Sultanate period—a point belied by the Indo-Persian sources of the period itself. A useful compilation of scholarly articles on the Meo folklore can be found in G. D. Gulati's *Mewat: Folklore, Memory, History* (2013), although certain folk traditions, as discussed in this book, are in the want of corroboration by historical sources and can be seen as attempts to reinforce and legitimize certain self-perceptions of the Meos.

Mewat, the focus of this study, comprised parts of two important *subas* of the Mughal empire, that is, Delhi and Agra. A major part of Mewat was assigned as *tankhwah jagirs* to a number of imperial *mansabdars* including the Kachhwaha chiefs of Amber who also obtained the *ijara* of some *parganas*. The strategic geographical location of the region, particularly its close proximity to Delhi and Agra, made control over it crucial for the Mughal state. The economic significance of the region lay in the fact that the trade routes connecting north Indian plains with the sea ports of Gujarat passed through it.

Chronologically, the study concerns the period when the Mughal empire was faced with a growing crisis of both agrarian and *jagirdari* systems which had serious socio-economic and politico-administrative ramifications. The implications of the weakening control of the imperial administrative authority on economy and various constituents of the society are yet to be fully assessed. The analysis of the relationship between political and agrarian changes, therefore, assumes significance in view of the fact that the politico-administrative structure evolved under the Mughals was aimed at systematizing the pattern of production and distribution, and the redistribution of surplus produce extracted from the peasants.

The book is divided into five chapters that examine the social, economic, and political history of Mewat from 13th to early 18th centuries. In the first chapter, the nature of state formation under the Delhi sultans and Mughals and their relationship with the Khanzadas (Jadon Rajputs converted to Islam) have been discussed. The chapter focuses on how the Khanzadas formed their own chiefdom with the help of the former slaves of the deceased Sultan Firozshah Tughlaq in the periphery of Tijara from late 14th to early 16th centuries, but could not develop their chiefdom into a full-fledged state due to either the lack of resources, the region's proximity to Delhi and Agra, or the nature of the Mughal polity.

The second chapter focuses on the region's ecology and its impact on economy. It discusses the region's physiography; soil types; sources of ground and surface water; and agricultural and pastoral practices, particularly the cropping pattern of both harvests, *kharif* and *rabi*, and the cropped area under each crop, as well as the area under the cultivation of *kharif* and *rabi* crops by both rich and poor peasants. The third chapter explains how the Meos transformed themselves from tribal groups into a peasant caste and got converted to Islam. The fourth chapter works out the magnitude of land revenue and various cesses extracted from the village as a unit or the peasant as a unit. It also analyses the total burden of land revenue demand from the different strata of peasantry and their resentment against the non-customary taxes imposed by and other excesses committed by the Mughal state and the Amber chiefs, resulting in massive revolts. Besides, it analyses the movement of the prices of food and cash crops, and discusses the non-agricultural, that is, artisanal, production in the region and the role of the *mahajans* (moneylenders) and *qasbas* (towns) in local trade.

The final chapter focuses on the emergence of a new class of zamindars, namely the Rajputs and the Jats, at the cost of the old zamindars, namely the Khanzadas and the Meos—a phenomenon that generated agrarian turmoil in the rural society at large. The oppression of peasantry resulting from conflicting claims staked by different sections of the ruling class, that is, the Amber Raja and the Jats, over the surplus produce, as also the misery caused by the incidence of droughts and famines in the villages of Mewat at regular intervals, ultimately provoked peasant protests in various forms in Mewat.

1

STATE FORMATION IN MEWAT

RELATIONSHIP OF THE KHANZADAS WITH THE DELHI SULTANATE, THE MUGHAL STATE, AND OTHER REGIONAL POTENTATES

THERE IS A POPULAR PERCEPTION AMONG the Meos that lands were allotted to them by the Mughal emperor Akbar. This perception seems to be grounded in historical reality, as Abul-Fazl observes in the *Ain-i-Akbari* that for the first time the Mewat region was brought under direct Mughal administration during the reign of Akbar. The whole of Mewat was divided into four *sarkar*s comprised within the two Mughal *suba*s of Agra and Delhi.[1] These *sarkar*s were further divided into 70 *parganas*[2] and the Meos established their zamindari rights over 12, 14, and 4 *pargana*s of Alwar, Tijara, and Sahar *sarkar*s respectively.[3] The preponderance of Meo zamindaris in the region and their recognition

[1] Abul-Fazl, *The Ain-i-Akbari*, vol. 2, trans. Col. H. S. Jarrett; corr. and ann. Sir Jadunath Sarkar, 3rd ed. (Calcutta: Royal Asiatic Society, 1978), 202–6; these *sarkar*s were Alwar (43 *parganas*), Tijara (18 *parganas*), Sahar (7 *parganas*), and Rewari (2 *parganas*).

[2] Abul-Fazl, *The Ain-i-Akbari*, vol. 2, 202–6.

[3] Abul-Fazl, *The Ain-i-Akbari*, vol. 2, 202–6.

by the Mughal administration under Akbar gradually gave birth to the myth that land was allotted to each Meo lineage group (*pal*) by Akbar.[4] By the end of the 16th century, the Meos had not only been transformed into a landed peasantry but had also established their zamindari rights in the Mewat region. However, other cultivating classes such as the Jats, Gujjars, Ahirs, Rajputs, Brahmins, and Malis also lived—and still live—in the region.[5]

Mewat is situated approximately 64 kilometres south-west of Delhi, roughly corresponding to Alwar and Bharatpur districts of present-day Rajasthan, and Nuh district of present-day Haryana. Presently, it comprises nine *tehsils*: Tijara, Kishangarh, Alwar, and Lachhmangarh in Alwar district; Deeg, Nagar, and Kama in Bharatpur district; and Nuh and Firozpur-Jhirka in Nuh district.

Mewat is the popular name for the region inhabited by the Meos or Mevs. The Meos believe that the term 'Mewat' is derived from 'Mev', and 'Meo' or 'Mev' from 'mewas' which means a hiding place for robbers. Therefore, in the Indo-Persian court chronicles and colonial records, the term 'Mev' became synonymous with robber, ruffian, or rogue.[6] The topography of Mewat is varied due to a combination of Aravali hill ranges, plains, and dense forests. The Aravali hills have served as a habitat for wild animals such as tigers, panthers, wolves, hyenas, foxes, jackals, and deer. Sultan Firozshah Tughlaq had a keen interest in hunting wild beasts; therefore, he constructed a fortress near a lake at Kotla in the Kala Pahad (black mountain) ridge for

4 Pratap C. Aggarwal, *Caste, Religion and Power: An Indian Case Study* (New Delhi: SRC, 1971), 24–5. The territory of Mewat has been subdivided into 13 geographical units. Twelve of these are referred to as *pals* and one as *palkra*. However, in practice, all of them are equal in status. There is no record of when and why Mewat was divided. According to a legend, however, the various *pals* were demarcated in Akbar's time. The different clans of the Meos often fought with each other over territory. Because of these feuds, it was realized that their collective strength against external adversary was adversely affected, and an assembly was convened in which leaders of all the clans participated. After a good deal of deliberation, Mewat was divided into these units.

5 Abul-Fazl, *The Ain-i-Akbari*, vol. 2, 202–6.

6 *Rajasthani-Hindi Sangshipt Shabdakosh*, vol. 2, ed. Sita Ram Lalus (Jodhpur: Rajasthan Oriental Research Institute, 1988), 415.

the purpose of undertaking royal hunts.[7] The Kala Pahad ridge is at the centre of Mewat and demarcates Haryana from Rajasthan. It rises abruptly to more than 300 metres at some places and is remarkable for its uninterrupted stretch. In the words of O. H. K. Spate, 'All the hills are dissected by generally dry but at times torrent-field nullahs, and surrounded by pediment fans.'[8] According to F. C. Channing, parts of the plains were rendered waste because the torrents at the foothills of Kala Pahad formed deep gorges and caused erosion.[9] In the medieval times, Mewat was dotted with lakes, seasonal streams, springs, and dams, which played an important role as a source of irrigation for agricultural production.[10] The main lakes were Kotla, Chandeni, Siliserh, and Deoti. Some channels were cut from these lakes when the waterbed was full, in order to support the cultivation of food and cash crops.[11] Later, when these lakes dried up, their fertile beds served to grow superior crops such as cotton, wheat, and sugarcane. Abul-Fazl mentions that Meo peasants cultivated not only food crops but also indigo, cotton, sugarcane, mustard, and pulses.[12] The Kala Pahad and other hills of the Aravali range have been a source of food, water, shelter, and protection to a number of tribal communities since the pre-Sultanate period. There is a popular saying about the Kala Pahad which also describes the geographical setting of Mewat:

इत दिल्ली उत आगरा, इत मथुरा और बैराठ
मेरो कालो पहाड़ सुहावणों, जाके बीच बसे मेवात ।

[The geographical setting of Mewat is such that one of its sides is bordered by Delhi and others by Mathura, Agra, and Bairat. The stretches of

7 Siraj Afif, 'Tarikh-i-Firozshahi', in *History of India as Told by Its Own Historians*, vol. 3, ed. H. M. Elliot and John Dowson (New Delhi: Low Price Publications, 2001), 354.

8 O. H. K. Spate, *India and Pakistan: A General and Regional Geography* (London: Metheun, 1957), 572.

9 F. C. Channing, *Land Revenue Settlement of the Gurgaon District* (Lahore: Central Jail Press, 1882), 2–5.

10 Channing, *Land Revenue Settlement of the Gurgaon District*, 4–5; P. W. Powlett, *Gazetteer of Ulwur* (London: Trubner & Co., 1878), 28–9.

11 Abul-Fazl, *The Ain-i-Akbari*, vol. 2, 76–8.

12 Abul-Fazl, *The Ain-i-Akbari*, vol. 2, 76–8.

> Kala Pahad pass through the centre of Mewat whose beautiful ranges and ravines enhance the beauty of Mewat.][13]

This popular saying is significant, since both sides of the Kala Pahad have densely populated villages and agriculturally fertile tracts. There has also been an old popular perception that Kala Pahad is a blessing for the Mewat region, as from time immemorial it has provided food, shelter, water, and immense benefits to various tribal communities and wild animals.

The strategic location of Mewat had manifold advantages for the Mughal state. First, from the economic point of view, its suitability for the cultivation of rich cash crops such as indigo and cotton made it an extremely viable source of revenue. Second, its proximity to Agra and Delhi facilitated the transport of agricultural commodities to feed the urban population. Third, through the region passed a vital trade route that linked western India to Agra and Delhi. That Mewat was a crucial link between the ports of Gujarat and its upcountry hinterland has also been stressed upon by scholars.[14] Hence, any political disturbance in the region would perhaps be reflected in the disruption of trade between Gujarat and the Gangetic Doab. Finally, control over Mewat was crucial for the Mughal state, since a hostile power based in Mewat could threaten the safety of Delhi and Agra, the seats of imperial power. These considerations were, to a great extent, responsible for shaping the Mughal policy towards the chiefs of Mewat.

According to Minhaj Siraj's *Tabakat-i-Nasiri*, the attitude of the Meos ever since the establishment of Turkish rule had been one of hostility.[15] They had conflict with the Mughal state that continued intermittently till the downfall of the empire, although its intensity varied over time. The nature of the Mughal–Meo conflicts—and their impact on the fortunes of the people of Mewat—forms a key subject

[13] Bhagwan Das Morwal, 'Mewati Lok Sahitya Mein Jeevan Darshan', in *Shrijan*, ed. Changa Ram Mina (Alwar: Babu Shobharam Arts Government College, 2005–6), 96–8.

[14] Ashin Dasgupta, 'Trade and Politics in 18th Century India', in *Islam and the Trade of Asia: A Colloquium*, ed. D. S. Richards (Pennsylvania: University of Pennsylvania, 1970).

[15] Minhaj Siraj, *Tabakat-i-Nasiri*, trans. H. G. Raverty (New Delhi: Oriental Books Reprint Corp., [1881] 1970), 864.

for the study of political history of medieval north India. Here, a preliminary examination of the nature of political and administrative structures of the region would be relevant in assessing its impact on the society and economy of the region.

I

The most conspicuous phenomenon in the polity of early medieval India was the rise of independent and semi-independent principalities, one of which was Mewat. The topographical features of Mewat influenced the course of its political history. The hilly region not only offered considerable protection against external attacks but was a veritable stronghold too. Although Mewat was often prone to invasions due to its proximity to Delhi and Agra, a striking fact is that up to the beginning of the 16th century, the chieftains of Mewat could not be brought under total subjugation for any considerable length of time.[16]

A brief survey of the political events in Mewat from the establishment of the Turkish rule in India to the beginning of the reign of Akbar is necessary in order to understand the nature of state formation in the region, as well as the relationship between the Khanzada chiefs (the ruling class of Mewat) and the Mughal authority. The earliest references to the Meos can be traced in the Indo-Persian chronicles of the Sultanate period. Both Minhaj Siraj and Ziauddin Barani describe the Meos as lawless, plunderers, raiders, robbers, and assaulters who had become a serious threat for the sultans of Delhi.[17] Minhaj Siraj writes:

> Balban (Ulugh Khan) and other nobles, with the royal troops and their own followers suddenly resolved upon a campaign in the hills and made

[16] Babur, *Baburnama*, vol. 2, trans. A. S. Beveridge (London: E.J.W. Gibb Memorial Trust, 1921; Reprint, New Delhi: Low Price Publications, 1995), 368–9. Babur, referring to the Mewat rulers, admitted, 'The Sultans of Hind, whether from the extent of their territories, from want of opportunity, or from obstacles posed by the mountainous nature of the country, had never subdued Mewat. They had never been able to reduce it to order and obedience as was tendered to them' (Babur, *Baburnama*, 368–9).

[17] Minhaj Siraj, 'Tabakat-i-Nasiri', in *The History of India as Told by Its Own Historians*, vol. 2, ed. H. M. Elliot and John Dowson (New Delhi: Low Price Publications, 1990), 380–3; Ziauddin Barani, 'Tarikh-i-Firozshahi', in *The History of India as Told by Its Own Historians*, vol. 3, 104–5.

> the first march in advance on Monday, 4th Safar 658H (Jan. 20, 1260 A.D.). They retreated to the summits of the mountains, the defiles, to deep gorges and narrow valley, but they were all taken and put to the swords. For twenty days, the troops traversed the hills in all directions. The villages and the habitations of the mountaineers were on the summit of the loftiest hills and rocks and were of great strength, but they were all taken and ravaged by the order of Ulugh Khan, and the inhabitants who were thieves, robbers and highwaymen were all slain.[18]

One hundred years later, Ziauddin Barani writes in 'Tarikh-i-Firozshahi' about the Meos:

> The daring of the Mewatis in the neighborhood of Delhi was carried to such an extent that the Western gates of the city were at afternoon prayer, and no one dared to go out of the city in that direction after that hour, whether he travelled as a pilgrim or with the display of a sovereign. At afternoon prayer, the Mewati would often come to the girls who were fetching water; they would strip them and carry off their clothes. These daring acts of the Mewatis had caused a great ferment in Delhi.[19]

The aforementioned Indo-Persian writings project the Meos as robbers, plunderers, and dacoits who disrupted trade and travel and became a great source of trouble to the people of Delhi and its neighbourhood. However, on the basis of their lifestyle and occupational pursuits, it appears that the Meos had to struggle a lot to eke out their living. On the other hand, their geographical and social isolation enabled them to lead a life of relative socio-political freedom. Nevertheless, being in the vicinity of Delhi and Agra, Mewat remained within the reach of the sultans of Delhi who undertook military campaigns to control the lawlessness and marauding activities of the Meos. For instance, in January 1260, Balban marched from Delhi to Mewat with a big force to punish the Mewati rebels who used to conduct organized plunder in the villages of Haryana, Siwalik, and Bayana regions. They used to rob the property of the Muslims and harass the common people. Three years ago, the Meos had so much courage that under the leadership of Malka, they took away the camels from the royal camp of Balban near Hansi and distributed

[18] Siraj, *Tabakat-i-Nasiri*, vol. 2, 380–3.

[19] Barani, 'Tarikh-i-Firozshahi', 104–5.

these camels among the Chauhan Rajputs of Ranthambore.[20] Balban personally led a campaign against the Meos, and for 20 days, the royal army remained in the Mewat region.[21]

It appears from the above descriptions of Minhaj and Barani that along with the Meos, the Rajputs were also involved in committing dacoities in the Mewat region. The Meo–Rajput nexus of looting and robbery has also been pointed out by A. B. M. Habibullah. He writes that the frequent mention of Ranthambore in connection with the operations of the Meos in Mewat may imply a link between the Mewati rebels and the Chauhan Rajputs of Ranthambore.[22] This is corroborated by the instance of Kutlug Khan, a rebel noble of Sultan Nasiruddin Mahmud Shah, seeking refuge at Santur, Rana Ran Pal's capital situated in the Aravali hills of Mewat. Rana Ran Pal, the descendant of Jadon Rajputs of Karauli, had carved out a principality at Santur in the Aravali hills during the early Sultanate period and must have accepted the overlordship of Balban. As the chief of Mewat, he enjoyed a high reputation among the Meos. Balban reached Santur with a big military contingent and destroyed the fortress of Santur, thereby forcing Kutlug Khan to leave Mewat.[23]

In 1266, Balban, again, took severe action against the Meos. He devoted a whole year to suppressing the Meos and clearing the forests around Delhi; he constructed a fort to guard the south-western side of Delhi against the incursions of the Mewatis. Subsequently, Mewat was brought under the direct administrative control of the sultan and 3,000 Afghan soldiers were posted in the neighbourhood of Delhi to closely watch the activities of the Mewatis. A number of military posts (*thanas*) were established in Mewat, manned by the Afghan soldiers.[24] These postings helped the Afghans considerably in establishing and consolidating their base in the region. In order to terrorize the Meos, Balban ordered the reward of one silver *tanka* for a head, and two for every living prisoner. Minhaj even states that the

[20] Barani, 'Tarikh-i-Firozshahi', 380.

[21] Barani, 'Tarikh-i-Firozshahi', 383.

[22] A. B. M. Habibullah, *The Foundation of Muslim Rule in India* (Allahabad: Central Book Depot, 1961), 153–4.

[23] Siraj, *Tabakat-i-Nasiri*, vol. 2, 375–6.

[24] Barani, 'Tarikh-i-Firozshahi', 104–5.

Afghan section of the imperial army was particularly active and each of them brought at least 100 prisoners. The rebel chief Malka was arrested along with his entire family and 250 other leading men of the Meo tribes. They were brought to Delhi and cruelly put to death near Hauz Rani in front of the Badaun gate of the city. Besides, 142 horses were captured and 60 cotton bags containing 30,000 *tankas* of loot seized by the army.[25] It was during these campaigns that Balban captured Santur, the capital city of Mewat. Alexander Cunningham identified Santur as Indore, which was situated 6 miles to the north of Kotla Lake and about 70 miles to the south of Delhi. The foundation of the fort is attributed to the Nikumbha Rajputs about whom no historical records, however, exist. It seems that the fort was actually founded by the Jadon Rajputs, a branch of Yaduvanshi Rajputs who ruled over Karauli–Bayana regions.[26]

Amir Khusrau informs us that when Sultan Alauddin Khalji launched his military expedition against Ranthambore, he went through the Mewat region. However, it may be noted that he does not mention the lawlessness and predatory activities of the Meos, although he remarks that the Mewat region was surrounded by high Aravali hills and infested with wild animals.[27] Alauddin Khalji continued Balban's policy of suppressing the turbulent chiefs in the vicinity of Delhi. He made the trade route between Delhi and Gujarat reasonably secure after thoroughly subjugating the Meos. Therefore, it may be assumed that Alauddin Khalji had full administrative control over Mewat.

According to the oral tradition of the Khanzadas, Adhanpal, a Jadon Rajput descended from Tahanpal who was the Jadon chief of Bayana, had carved out his settlement in Sarheta near Tijara hills. It is possible that the Jadon Rajputs may have shifted their principality from Sarheta to Santur (Indore) during the reign of Nasiruddin Mahmud Shah. The point that needs to be highlighted is that there, indeed, existed a Meo–Rajput nexus in plundering; otherwise, it was

25 Siraj, *Tabakat-i-Nasiri*, vol. 2, 381–2.

26 Alexander Cunningham, *Report of a Tour in Eastern Rajputana in 1882–83*, Archaeological Survey of India Reports, vol. 20 (Varanasi: Indological Book House, [1885] 1969), 13.

27 Amir Khusrau, 'Khazaina-i-Futuh and the Kiranu-i-Sadain (The Poem of Amir Khusrau)', in *History of India as Told by Its Own Historians*, vol. 3, 540.

not possible for the Meo tribes to possess huge amounts of currency and horses captured at Santur by Balban's army during his campaign against the Meos. Therefore, the complex relationship between the Meos and the central authority may be understood in the light of a combined Meo–Rajput struggle for their survival in the thick forests and Aravali hills of the Mewat region till the reign of Firozshah Tughlaq.

However, during the Tughlaq period, the Mewatis went back to their old habit of plundering, as reflected in the contemporary writings. Firozshah Tughlaq posted a force at Firozpur Jhirka for controlling the depredations of the Mewatis,[28] and constructed a fortress at Indore in the Aravali hills for the purpose of hunting as well as military expeditions.[29] It appears that during the reign of Firozshah Tughlaq, the Meos and a section of the Jadon Rajputs actively indulged in plundering activities. The Urdu work *Arzang-i-Tijara* informs us that a branch of Jadon Rajputs and the Meos were notorious for plunder, arson, and lawlessness in the Mewat region, and had created a serious law-and-order problem for the sultan of Delhi.[30]

According to *Tarikh-i-Mubarakshahi*, in 1379–80, Firozshah Tughlaq invaded Mewat and reached Santur and forced the Rai of Mewat to pay regular tributes.[31] The name of the Rai is not mentioned, but it appears that Bahadur Nahar may have been the Rai of Santur at that time. It appears from Firozshah Tughlaq's *Futuhat-i-Firozshahi* that he had paid much attention to Mewat. He writes:

> In the village of Malúh [Malab],[32] there is a tank which they [the Hindus] call *kund* (tank). Here they had built idol-temples, and on certain days the Hindus were accustomed to proceed thither on horseback, and wearing arms. Their women and children also went out in palankíns and carts.

[28] Cunningham, *Report of a Tour in Eastern Rajputana*, 14.

[29] Afif, 'Tarikh-i-Firozshahi', 354.

[30] Sheikh Muhammad Makhdum, *Arzang-i-Tijara* (Urdu) (Agra: Agra Akhbar, H. 1290/1873 CE, trans. [Hindi] Anil Joshi, Alwar, 1989), 3–4.

[31] Yahya Bin Ahmad Bin 'Abdullah' Sirhindi, *Tarikh-i-Mubarakshahi*, trans. H. Beveridge (New Delhi: Low Price Publications, 1990), 141.

[32] The village Malab is situated on the main road between Nuh and Firozpur Jhirka. The water pond and old structure of the mosque are still extant.

> There, they assembled in thousands and performed idol worship. This abuse had been so overlooked that the *bázár* people took out there all sorts of provisions, and set up stalls and sold their goods. Some graceless Musulmáns, thinking only of their own gratification took part in these meetings. When intelligence of this came to my ears my religious feelings prompted me at once to put a stop to this scandal and offence to the religion of Islám. On the day of the assembling I went there in person ... [and] I destroyed their idol temples, and instead thereof raised mosques. I founded two flourishing towns (*kasba*) one called Tughlikpúr, the other Sálárpúr. Where infidels and idolaters worshiped idols, Musulmáns now, by God's mercy, perform their devotions to the true God. Praise of God and the summons to prayer are now heard there, and that place which was formerly the home of infidels has become the habitation of the faithful, who there repeat their creed and offer up their praises to God.[33]

Further, he adds, 'Information was brought to me that some Hindús had erected a new idol temple in the village of Sálihpúr, and were performing worship to their idol. I sent some persons there to destroy the idol temple, and to put a stop their pernicious incitements to terror.'[34]

The history of the Khanzadas of Mewat begins with Bahadur Nahar, who embraced Islam during the reign of Firozshah Tughlaq. His ancestors were Jadon Rajputs, who had ruled over Bayana and Thangir before the invasions of Muhammad Ghori. During the 14th century, Jadon Rajput Lakhanpal was the chief of a small tract of Mewat around Tijara. Lakhanpal had two sons, Sambharpal and Sanparpal. The former took the name of Bahadur Nahar and gained control over Sarehta situated 4 miles to the east of Tijara, while the latter took the name of Chhaju Khan and got possession of Jhirka. The two brothers embraced Islam in order to save their estates from annexation by Firozshah Tughlaq. The name of the town was also changed from Jhirka to Firozpur Jhirka.[35] The author of *Arzang-i-Tijara* has given two reasons for the conversion of Bahadur Nahar: the first was his deep faith in the Sufi saint Hazrat Nasiruddin Chirag-Delhvi; and second was his and his brother's arrest and imprisonment in Delhi by Firozshah's troops their depredations in the

33 Firozshah Tughlaq, 'Futuhat-i-Firozshahi', in *The History of India as Told by Its Own Historians*, vol. 3, 380–1.

34 Tughlaq, *Futuhat-i-Firozshahi*, 381.

35 Cunningham, *Report of a Tour in Eastern Rajputana*, 15–16.

neighbourhood of Delhi that posed a serious law-and-order problem for the Sultanate of Delhi.[36]

Historical evidence shows that after embracing Islam, Bahadur Nahar was enrolled into the Sultanate nobility and given the title of Khanazad by Firozshah. The title 'Khanazad' or 'Khanazadun' was also given to those Firozi slaves who happened to be very close and loyal to the sultan.[37] Many of the Firozi slaves were appointed to high positions in the military and administrative departments of the government by the sultan. Afif mentions 36 *karkhanas* (workshops) under Firozshah run by these slaves in different capacities.[38]

As a succession struggle broke out in Delhi after Firozshah's death (1389), Bahadur Nahar became a staunch supporter of Abu Bakr Shah, son of Fateh Khan, grandson of Firozshah and the leader of one of the factions of the Firozi slaves. But another son of Firozshah, Muhammad Shah became the sultan of Delhi with the help of another faction of the Firozi slaves. Abu Bakr fled to Kotla, Bahadur Nahar's fortress in Mewat.[39] The Firozi slaves supporting Abu Bakr were ordered to vacate their official positions in the government and asked to leave Delhi within a short period as their loyalty to the new sultan was suspect. One of the first acts of Sultan Muhammad was to seize the royal elephants from the Firozi slaves and hand them over to their old keepers. It is said that many innocent persons were killed at the order of the new sultan. In order to distinguish between the Firozi slaves of foreign and Indian origins, he ordered that everyone pronounce 'Khara Khari

36 Makhdum, *Arzang-i-Tijara*, 15–16.

37 A. M. Husain, *Tughluq Dynasty* (Calcutta: Thacker Spink, 1963), 336. After being given the title of Khanazadar Khanazadun by Firozshah, Bahadur Nahar became a powerful and respectable chief of Mewat. Later, the word 'Khanazad' changed to 'Khanzada' (Makhdum, *Arzang-i-Tijara*, 3).

38 Afif, 'Tarikh-i-Firozshahi', 444–5. Some of the slaves were appointed to high positions by Firozshah. One such slave was Bashir-i-Sultani who was awarded the title of Imad-ul-Mulk. He was appointed the *mufti* of Rapri and, later, the commander-in-chief of the army (*sar-lashkar*). Another slave was made the superintendent of hunting; yet another one was appointed the auditor (*mustaufi*) of Gujarat with the title of Iffikhark-i-Mulk. A slave by the name of Malik Shamsuddin Abu Rija was so favoured by Firozshah that he was able to grab the positions of *wazir*, *naib wazir*, and the controller of accounts (Afif, 'Tarikh-i-Firozshahi', 444–5).

39 Sirhindi, *Tarikh-i-Mubarakshahi*, 153–4.

Kara Jana'. In course of this test, many Firozi slaves, whose pronunciation of the phrase supposedly revealed their local origin, were disgraced and put to the sword. This story was supposedly well known throughout Hind and Sind and is recounted in the *Tarikh-i-Mubarakshahi*.[40] Sirhindi narrates in detail the blood war that subsequently took place between the Firozi slaves and Sultan Muhammad Shah. Many Firozi slaves whose loyalty to the new sultan was suspect were killed while many others fled with their families to Kotla, seeking refuge with Bahadur Nahar.[41] On 31 August 1390, a decisive battle was fought at Kotla, in which Abu Bakr Shah and the Firozi slaves were defeated. Abu Bakr Shah and Bahadur Nahar came out of the Kotla fortress and asked for amnesty. Muhammad Shah's son, Humayun Khan, gave a robe to Bahadur Nahar and sent him back to Mewat, but imprisoned Abu Bakr and sent him to Meerut where he later died.[42] However, after the death of Muhammad Shah in January 1394, Bahadur Nahar managed to re-enter the arena of court politics, taking advantage of the civil war that now ensued between Muhammad Shah's successors. His friend Mukarrab Khan, who was the leader of one of the rival groups, called him from Kotla and put him in charge of the fortress of old Delhi.[43] In the wake of the general confusion that followed Timur's occupation of Delhi at the close of 1398, Bahadur Nahar withdrew to Kotla from where he watched the subsequent developments.[44]

[40] Sirhindi, *Tarikh-i-Mubarakshahi*, 158–9. Firozshah took interest in buying both foreign and Indian slaves. Among the former, his favourites were those who hailed from Hazara (present-day Pakistan); Afif describes them as mounted on Arab and Turkish horses and bearing standards and axes. It appears that the Firozi slaves of Indian origin called Hindustanis may have created trouble for Muhammad Shah during his struggle with Abu Bakr. Upon becoming the sultan, Muhammad Shah thus sought to eliminate the dissident Hindustani slaves. The test was thus meant to distinguish them by having them pronounce the phrase 'Khara Khari Kara Jana'. See Athar Ali, 'Ethnic Character of the Army during the Delhi Sultanate (13th–14th Centuries)', in *Medieval India 2: Essays in Medieval Indian History and Culture*, ed. Shahbuddin Iraqi (Delhi: Manohar, 2008), 165–72.

[41] Sirhindi, *Tarikh-i-Mubarakshahi*, 159.

[42] Sirhindi, *Tarikh-i-Mubarakshahi*, 159–60.

[43] Sirhindi, *Tarikh-i-Mubarakshahi*, 168.

[44] Timur, 'Malfuzat-i-Timuri', in *The History of India as Told by Its Own Historians*, vol. 3, 449. When Timur occupied Delhi, he came to know that

Bahadur Nahar's position vis-à-vis the Delhi Sultanate further suffered a setback with the Sayyid rulers coming to power. When the Sayyids claimed the throne of Delhi, they were opposed by Bahadur Nahar. Sultan Mubarak Shah, the founder of the Sayyid dynasty, led military campaigns against the Mewati chiefs in 1421, 1422, and 1425–6, but could not achieve much success due to the natural defence provided by the Aravali hills and the thick forests of Mewat.[45]

Bahadur Nahar's successors, Kadar Khan (Khadu) and Jalal Khan (Jallu), were equally hostile to the Sayyids and refused to pay tribute to the Sayyid rulers. Mubarak Shah personally led his army into Mewat in order to subdue the Mewati chiefs.[46] Malik Kadar Khan was captured and executed on the charge of exchanging presents and envoys with the Sharqi ruler of Jaunpur who were the arch rivals of the Sayyids. Sarwar Malik was sent with a big force to suppress the Mewatis, and he destroyed many *qasbas* and villages of Mewat. Realizing the gravity of the situation, Jalal Khan and other Mewati nobles assembled at the fortress of Indore and decided not to offend the sultan any further. He also agreed to pay tribute.[47]

When Bahlul Lodi became the sultan of Delhi, the whole of India was divided into provinces governed by petty rulers. The Meo

---

Bahadur Nahar Khanzada had been held an important position in the court of Delhi. Timur sent two messengers—Alauddin and Naib Karkari—to Bahadur Nahar at Kotla. Bahadur Nahar courteously replied, 'I am one of the most insignificant servants of the great Amir, and will proceed to his court to wait upon him.' Bahadur Nahar sent two white parrots to Timur, which could talk well and pleasantly. These two parrots had belonged to Sultan Tughlaq Shah, and they had lived at the courts of the sultans ever since. Timur writes that the sight of these parrots and the sound of their voices gave him great satisfaction. Bahadur Nahar and his son came to Timur to pay their respects. As Timur writes, '[T]hey brought rare and suitable presents from Hindustan, but I looked upon the two parrots as the best of their gifts. After I had ascertained their sincerity from their words and actions, I honoured them with my royal favour and bounty, and having raised their dignity, I removed all doubt and apprehension from their minds' (Timur, 'Malfuzat-i-Timuri', 449).

45 Sirhindi, *Tarikh-i-Mubarakshahi*, 29.

46 Sirhindi, *Tarikh-i-Mubarakshahi*, 19.

47 Sirhindi, *Tarikh-i-Mubarakshahi*, 221.

chief Ahmad Khan Mewati ruled the area extending from Mehrauli to Lado Sarai,[48] near the city of Delhi. As Bahlul consolidated his position, he sought to expand his authority. He forced Ahmad Khan Mewati to submit to his rule and deprived him of seven *parganas* including Tijara, but allowed him to retain the rest of Mewat and rule as a tributary chief. These *parganas* were bestowed upon Tartar Khan Lodi who retained them till the reign of Sikandar Lodi. This was an important event in the history of Mewat insofar as the Mewati chief was dispossessed of the core *parganas* of his chiefdom and his political autonomy stood compromised. Thereafter, the Mewati chiefs had to shift their capital from Tijara to Alwar. Ahmad Khan appointed his uncle Mubarak Khan to be perpetually in attendance at the court in Delhi. He soon won the confidence of the sultan which he and his descendants continued to enjoy till the end of the Lodi rule. His son Alwal Khan and grandson Hasan Khan governed their ancestral state during the reigns of Sikandar Lodi and Ibrahim Lodi respectively. It appears that they had to pay only a nominal sum of money as annual tribute to the Lodi sultans.[49] Ahmad Khan Mewati figures in the list of 34 nobles of Bahlul Lodi, provided by *Tabaqat-i-Akbari*.[50] During the reign of Sikandar Lodi, Alam Khan Mewati held an important position at the Delhi court.[51] This cordial relationship between the Lodis and the Mewati chiefs continued till the end of the reign of Ibrahim Lodi. Ahmad Khan's grandson, Hasan Khan Mewati, even fought for Ibrahim Lodi in the First Battle of Panipat,[52] but later joined hands with Rana Sanga against Babur and fell in the Battle of Khanwa.[53]

48 The village Lado Sarai was/is situated to the north-east of Mehrauli.

49 Naimutulla, 'Tarikh-i-Khan-Jahan Lodi', in *History of India as Told by Its Own Historians*, vol. 5, ed. H. M. Elliot and John Dowson (New Delhi: Low Price Publications, 1990), 74, 79.

50 Khwajah Nizamuddin Ahmad, *Tabaqat-i-Akbari*, 3 vols, ed. and trans. B. De and M. Hidayat Hossain (Calcutta: Bibliotheca Indica, 1913–35), 202–3.

51 Naimutulla, 'Tarikh-i-Khan-Jahan Lodi', 97.

52 Naimutulla, 'Tarikh-i-Khan-Jahan Lodi', 97; Babur, *Baburnama*, 273–4.

53 Babur, 'Tuzuk-i-Baburi', in *History of India as Told by Its Own Historians*, vol. 4, ed. H. M. Elliot and John Dowson (Allahabad: Kitab Mahal, 1975), 273.

II

As discussed in the previous section, a large number of the Firozi slaves, along with their families, had fled from Delhi to Kotla in Mewat, to save their lives from Sultan Muhammad Shah. Bahadur Nahar, in all probability, inducted the former Firozi slaves into his aristocracy by giving them important positions. Subsequently, the former Firozi slaves merged with the local elite of Mewat, that is, the military-cum-land-proprietors. This can be inferred from the fact that they were also called Khanazads[54] and later commonly spoken of as Khanzadas. On account of their military skills and past administrative experience, the former Firozi slaves were able to carve out a place for themselves in the Khanzada chiefdom.

The social organization of the Khanzadas as the political elite of their evolving state in Mewat was rather loose and fluid, and they absorbed new groups such as the Firozi slaves within their ranks. Once the former Firozi slaves joined the state, their social identity became one with that of the ruling Khanzada class. The state assigned them villages in lieu of remuneration, but eventually they claimed hereditary rights over these villages. This can be inferred from the *Ain-i-Akbari*, which states that by the end of the 16th century, the Khanzadas had acquired zamindari rights over 18 *parganas* out of a total of 61 *parganas* in Alwar and Tijara *sarkars*.[55]

As many of the former Firozi slaves inducted into the Khanzada state had acquired administrative knowledge and experience of the *iqta* system during the reign of Firozshah Tughlaq, they directed much of their attention towards the expansion of agricultural production in order to increase the state's financial resources. They militarily coerced the Meo and other tribal communities living in the Aravali hills (Kala Pahad) to practise agriculture. This is borne out from a Meo folk tale that five Meo *pals*, namely Chhiraklot, Duhlot, Pundlot, Daimrot, and Nai (Jadon Vamshi), living in the Kala Pahad, once used to harass people, but when the traders and citizens lodged several complaints against them with the king, the state pressurized them

54 Makhdum, *Arzang-i-Tijara*, 3.

55 Abul-Fazl, *The Ain-i-Akbari*, vol. 2, 202–6.

to give up their old predatory habits and they settled down in the plains. The Jagga records[56] also reveal that by the end of the 15th century these five Meo *pals* settled down in the plains of Nuh-Firozpur-Jhirka, Ramgarh, and Lachhmangarh regions in the vicinity of Kala Pahad.

That the Khanzadas exercised considerable pressure on the Meos to leave their old occupations and shift to agriculture in order to strengthen the economic base of the state is evident from another folk tale about the reign of Ahmad Khan Mewati. The Meos of Sonkh village, situated between Nuh and Palwal, were arrested by Ahmad Khan Mewati's army on account of the non-payment of land revenue to the state. They were imprisoned and deployed as labourers in the construction of the fortress at Indore. Ladh Begam, the daughter of Ahmad Khan Mewati, lost her heart to a young and handsome Meo boy named Santhal who also worked as a labourer. Finally, Ahmad Khan Mewati had to submit to his daughter's wishes and marry her to Santhal. After the marriage, they were assigned an *iqta* where they founded a village and named it Ladhpuri after the name of Ladh Begam.[57] The folk tale also conveys that matrimonial relations with the Meos were essential for Ahmad Khan Mewati in order to expand the social base of the Khanzadas among the Meos.

It appears that the Khanzadas of Mewat adopted a very pragmatic approach towards the Meos because the Meos formed the majority of peasants in the Mewat region. Whatever little information we have about the relationship between the Khanzadas and the Meos suggests that the Khanzada chiefs enjoyed the support of the Meos. An early 16th-century ballad, 'Hasan Khan ki Katha', by Narsingh Meo of Kajhota village of Mewat reveals that not only did the Meos constitute the majority of peasants, but the army of Hasan Khan Mewati also had a large number of Meo soldiers. Moreover, he enjoyed the full support and cooperation of all the 12 chiefs of the Meo *pals* in the Battle of

56 Jagga records, *pothi* no. 1, in the personal possession of Jagdish, son of Shri Ghasi Ram Jagga, village Kuteta Kalan, *tehsil* Ramgarh, district Alwar, Rajasthan. The Jagga caste maintained the genealogical records of the Meos and Khanzadas since the colonization of the villages by them. These records are divided on the basis of the *gotras* and *pals* of the Meos.

57 *Bandhak* no. 4, *granthank* no. 83, Non-archival Records of Alwar State, Rajasthan State Archives, Bikaner.

Khanwa.[58] The Khanzada chiefs established their matrimonial relations not only with the Meos but also with the Meenas. 'Hasan Khan ki Katha' tells us that Hasan Khan lost his life in the Battle of Khanwa along with his two sons who were born to his wife from the Meena caste.[59] A large number of Meena peasants inhabited the Alwar *sarkar* where the Khanzada chiefs had shifted their capital from Tijara during the reign of Bahlul Lodi, as mentioned earlier. This explains Hasan Khan's efforts to establish matrimonial alliance with the Meenas in order to extend his social base.

The foregoing discussion shows that many new villages and *qasba*s were founded and settled, particularly in the periphery of Tijara, by the Khanzadas in the wake of the assignment of land grants to the former Firozi slaves who were absorbed into the ranks of Khanzadas. Following this, the second stage of expansion of the Khanzada state set in during the Lodi period with the shift of its capital to Alwar in eastern Rajasthan.[60]

The expansion of the Khanzada state was partially guided by their political ambition, but the cession of important *pargana*s to Bahlul Lodi, as mentioned earlier, mainly forced the Khanzadas to move towards eastern Rajasthan. The land in eastern Rajasthan was more fertile than their heavily forested and hilly ancestral land of Mewat. Thus, more land was brought under plough, leading to further

58 Narsingh Meo, 'Hasan Khan ki Katha', *Shodh Patrika*, vol. 4 (October–December) (Udaipur: Rajasthan Vidyapeeth, 1970), 53–62, couplet no. 86.

59 Meo, 'Hasan Khan ki Katha', couplet no. 114.

60 Makhdum, *Arzang-i-Tijara*, 26. A popular local legend attributes the defeat of the Nikumbha Rajputs of Alwar at the hands of the Khanzadas to the practice of human sacrifice by the former. They used to offer men and women of lower castes to Durga Devi, their patron goddess. When a young boy was sacrificed, his mother, a widow *domani* (i.e., a woman of the *dom* caste) sought revenge. She went to the Khanzada chief of Kotla and disclosed to him the way to defeat the Nikumbha Rajputs. She told the Khanzadas that the Rajputs could be attacked suddenly at a time when they worshipped the goddess and had laid down their arms. Accordingly, the Khanzadas attacked the disarmed Nikumbha Rajputs and slayed them. The story, whether true or not, suggests the maltreatment of the lower castes by the Nikumbha Rajputs and their decline as a consequence of provoking their hostility. For the legend, see Powlett, *Gazetteer of Ulwur*, 155.

peasantization of the Meos and the Meenas. The folk tradition of the Khanzadas has it that they controlled 1,484 *kheras* (villages and towns) of Mewat.[61]

In his memoir, Babur has also described the political conditions of Mewat under the rule of Hasan Khan Mewati:

> The country of Mewât lies not far from Delhi and yields a revenue of three or four krors. Hassan Khan Mewâti had inherited the governant [*sic*] of that country from his ancestors, who had governed it, in uninterrupted succession for nearly two hundred years. They had yielded an imperfect kind of submission to the Sultan of Delhi. The Sultan of Hind, whether from the extent of their territories, from want of opportunity, or from the obstacles posed by the mountainous nature of the country, had never subdued Mewât. They had never been able to reduce it to order, and were content to receive such a degree of obedience as was tendered to them.[62]

Condemning Hasan Khan for his hostility to Babur, Zain Khan, Babur's secretary, writes:

> Mewat, one of the most fortified towns in Indian land, was under Hasan Khan Mewāti, who had put it in a strong defensive position. He was the prime mover of all the insurrections, and had become the chief of the agitators and leaders of the many pagans and infidels. Having thrown down the banner of faith (of Islam) at his feet, he had associated himself with, joined and submitted to the refractory wicked people and thus he supported their hostile cause.[63]

Accounts of both Zain Khan and Shaikh Rizqullah Mustaqi inform us that after the death of Ibrahim Lodi in the First Battle of Panipat, Hasan Khan Mewati, who had fought for Ibrahim Lodi, invited Rana Sanga of Chittor, Rai Silahdi, and the Khan of Nagore and persuaded them to make Mahmud, the son of Sikandar Lodi, the sultan of Delhi and fight against Babur at Khanwa.[64]

61 Powlett, *Gazetteer of Ulwur*, 7.

62 Babur, *Tuzuk-i-Baburi*, 273.

63 Zain Khan, *Tabaqat-i-Baburi*, trans. S. Hasan Askari (New Delhi: Idarah-i Adabiyat-i Delli, 1982), 138.

64 Shaikh Rizqullah Mustaqi, *Waqiat-e-Mustaqi*, ed. and trans. I. H. Siddiqui (New Delhi: Northern Book Centre, 1993), 116; Khan, *Tabaqat-i-Baburi*, 138.

Offering a regional perspective on these events, the 16th-century Mewati ballad 'Hasan Khan ki Katha' criticizes the role of Hasan Khan in the Battles of Panipat and Khanwa, arguing that there was no reason for him to fight against Babur. In the beginning of the ballad, the author, Narsingh Meo, pays his respect to Narayana and Paigambar (the Prophet) and assures the audience that whatever he has written in the ballad is absolutely based on facts and hearsay. He states that in the ancient times there were many kings and kingdoms, but only a few of them are remembered for their right judgements and thoughts about the masses. He then goes on to cite instances of supposedly 'good' and 'bad' mythical and historical rulers. Ravana, the king of Lanka, possessed a great kingdom, but his irrational thinking and excessive pride brought ruination to his kingdom at the hands of Rama and his army of monkeys. King Vikramaditya, on the other hand, was known for his just treatment of the masses. Ibrahim Lodi, the king of Hindustan, remained in his palace all the time and used to play *chaupar* (a board game). He was neither bothered about the masses nor about his state. On the other hand, Babur came to India fully prepared for the Battle of Panipat. It was a known fact to every man of Babur that Rana Sanga, the king of Chittor, also wanted to destroy the kingdom of Ibrahim Lodi.[65] Ibrahim Lodi fought against Babur in Panipat till afternoon, but thereafter never came back alive from the battlefield. The war was over, and the battlefield was full of dead soldiers and horses. The traders (*banias* and *baqqals*) were making profits, while the other artisans such as tailors (*darjis*) and goldsmiths (*sunars*) were being harassed and looted. The Turks, Kolis, and Malis were completely decimated in the battlefield of Panipat.[66]

According to Narsingh Meo's account, after Ibrahim Lodi's defeat at the Battle of Panipat, his son Mahmud Lodi came to Hasan Khan Mewati at Alwar seeking refuge and help against Babur. Hasan Khan, son of Alawal Khan Mewati, was a man of his word and a great warrior. He summoned Karam Chand Khatri, the commander-in-chief of his army, to discuss the strategy for the imminent Battle of Khanwa. He brought Sher Khan Nagori to his side and invited all the chiefs of the Meo *pals* to his palace to discuss the war strategy. Among them, the

[65] Meo, 'Hasan Khan ki Katha', couplet nos 15–22.

[66] Meo, 'Hasan Khan ki Katha', couplet nos 49–50.

Duhlot and Singhal Meo *pals* held the front position in Hasan Khan's army.[67] Hasan Khan sent two messengers, Harna Meo and Sukhna Meo, with a letter to Rana Sanga at Chittor asking for his support in the war. In the letter, he promised that if they won the Battle of Khanwa, the entire middle region (Madhya desh) of Ibrahim Lodi's regime would be part of the Rana's dominions. In his response, the proud Rana declared that he would push back Babur from the battlefield of Khanwa all the way to Kabul.[68] Both rulers gave assurances to each other that they would stick to this alliance. Hasan Khan then ordered Karam Chand Khatri to proceed with the army towards the battlefield of Khanwa.

Eventually, as Narsingh Meo recounts, Hasan Khan and his two sons lost their lives in the battle and his kingdom was ruined by Babur. In the ballad, Narsingh Meo accuses Hasan Khan for bringing about the destruction of his kingdom. He invited unnecessary trouble for himself twice, first, by joining forces with Ibrahim Lodi in the First Battle of Panipat against Babur and then, by inviting Rana Sanga for the Battle of Khanwa against Babur for the cause of Sikander Lodi's son even when Babur had shown clemency by releasing his son, Nahar Khan, from captivity.[69] According to the author, Rana Sanga was untrustworthy and thoroughly dishonest; he had committed the heinous crime of killing some Brahmins in his own state and thereby incurred a great curse. Nevertheless, the author held Hasan Khan responsible for his own and his kingdom's tragic end, since he sided with the sinner and dishonest.[70] While criticizing Hasan Khan's role in the two battles, the author of the ballad, perhaps, implicitly projects

[67] Meo, 'Hasan Khan ki Katha', couplet no. 86.

[68] Meo, 'Hasan Khan ki Katha', couplet no. 72.

[69] This is also corroborated by Babur who writes,

> I advanced four marches, and after the fifth encamped six kos from the fort of Alwâr, which was the seat of the government, on the bank of river Manisni ... A person named Kermchand, one of Hassan Khan's head men, who had come to visit. Hassan Khan's son while he was a prisoner in Agra, now arrived from the son, commissioned to ask a pardon. I sent him back, accompanied by Abdal-i-rahîm Shaghâwel, with letters to quiet his apprehensions, and promising him personal safety; and they returned along with Nâhar Khan, Hassan Khan's son. I again received him into favour, and bestowed on him a Perganna of several laks for his support (*Tuzuk-i-Baburi*, 273–4).

[70] Meo, 'Hasan Khan ki Katha', couplet nos 115–17.

the perceptions of some sections of the Meo community about these battles.

Ahmad Yadgar, in his 'Tarikh-i-Salatin-i-Afghana', an account of Lodi and Afghan dynasties, describes the aforementioned events in the following words:

> Hasan Khan Mewati was a man of royal descent from several generations and his family had possessed regal power until the reign of Fíroz Sháh. Ráná Sánká, who was at that time a powerful chief, sent a message to Hasan Khán saying, 'The Mughals have entered Hindustan, have slain Sultán Ibráhím and taken possession of the country; it is evident that they will likewise send an army against both of us; if you will side with me, we will be allies, and not suffer them to take possession'. Hasan Khán, carried away by the vanity which the possession of so large a force produced, and by the Ráná's message, did not send the presents which he had prepared for the Sultán, and the King's *vakíl* returned home without accomplishing his purpose. These things came to the King's hearing in Ágra, and Mírzá Hindál and Muhammad Mahdí Khwája, the king's son-in-law, were sent with an immense army, which was shortly afterwards followed by Bábar himself. When Hasan Khán was informed of the approach of the victorious army, he send to tell Ráná Sánká of it. Upon this the Ráná left his home, and assembled an army of Hindús with the intention of making war. He marched and joined Hasan Khán and prepared for action in the plains near Fírozpúr Jharka. Ráná Sánká placed Hasan Khán on right, and took up his own post on the left. As he was secretly displeased with Hasan Khán, he determined to ensnare and ruin him. He, therefore, privately sent a *vakíl* to Mírzá Hindál and Khwája Mahdí, to say that he was the slave and obedient servant of the King, and that he consented to the reading of the *khutba* and the coining of money in His Majesty's name; that Hasan Khán had compelled him to go to war, but that he would not fight the royal troops, but retire early; and that they should make arrangements so that Hasan might be either captured or slain, as in the event of his death they would obtain country of Mewát.[71]

III

The consequences of the Battle of Khanwa affected the fortunes of a number of Indian chiefs, though in varying degrees, but the

[71] Ahmad Yadgar, 'Tarikh-i-Salatin-i-Afghana', in *The History of India as Told by Its Own Historians*, vol. 5, 36.

Khanzadas of Mewat were the worst hit. The territory of Mewat, which yielded revenue amounting to three to four crore *dams*, was annexed by Babur and this shifted the control of Mewat from the Khanzadas, who had enjoyed it for over 175 years, to the Mughals. Babur assigned only a few *parganas* of Mewat to Nahar Khan.[72] A *jagir* worth 50 lakh *dams*, including Tijara, was assigned to Chin Timur Sultan, one of Babur's nobles. Amir Tardika, who in the battle with Rana Sanga had commanded Tulughma on the right, was given the charge of Alwar fort, along with a *jagir* worth 15 lakh *dams*. The treasure of the fort was given to Humayun.[73] Thus, the Khanzadas remained no longer a regional political entity of any great significance, although the Mughal emperors tried to cultivate them by either forging matrimonial relations or co-opting them into the *mansab* system. For instance, when Humayun regained his lost power (1555), he tried to consolidate his position vis-à-vis the Khanzadas by marrying the elder daughter of Jamal Khan Mewati, nephew of Hasan Khan; his powerful Turkish noble Bairam Khan married the younger one.[74] In fact, Jamal Khan presented himself before Humayun at Delhi and offered his daughters in marriage.[75] According to *Arzang-i-Tijara*, Akbar married the daughter of Hasan Khan's brother,[76] although this event is not recorded in the Persian chronicles. However, Akbar did marry Bairam Khan's widow, daughter of Jamal Khan and mother of Abdur Rahim Khan-i-Khana.[77] The mother of Aman-ullah 'Khan Zaman', son and heir of Mahabat Khan Zaman Beg and a noble of Shahjahan, belonged to the Khanzadas of Mewat.[78]

72 Babur, *Tuzuk-i-Baburi*, 274.

73 Babur, *Tuzuk-i-Baburi*, 274.

74 Abul-Fazl, *The Ain-i-Akbari*, vol. 1, trans. H. Blochmann, 3rd ed. (Calcutta: Royal Asiatic Society, 1977), 354; Abul-Fazl, *The Akbarnama*, vol. 2, trans. H. Beveridge (New Delhi: Low Price Publications, [1902–39] 1993), 76. Jamal Khan Khanzada was a famous zamindar of Mewat (Nawwab Samsam-ud-daula Shah Nawaz Khan and Abdul Hayy, *The Maathir-ul-Umara*, vol. 1, trans. H. Beveridge, revised, annotated, and completed by Baini Prasad [Patna: Janaki Prakashan, 1979], 50).

75 Abul-Fazl, *The Akbarnama*, vol. 2, 76.

76 Makhdum, *Arzang-i-Tijara*, 13.

77 Khan and Hayy, *The Maathir-ul-Umara*, 50.

78 Khan and Hayy, *The Maathir-ul-Umara*, 212.

It appears that Akbar must have paid some attention to Mewat, since a revenue document of his reign dated *rabi-ul-awal*, H. 970 (1592 CE) contains an imperial order for the *chaudharis*, *qanungos*, and *muqaddams* of Alwar *sarkar* to assist certain Khanzadas of the Indore family who had been commissioned to put down an insurrection in that *sarkar*.[79] Further, the conduct of the Khanzadas must have satisfied Akbar during his military campaigns. Nonetheless, the Khanzadas' relations with Akbar can be broadly understood as a part of his policy towards nobility, which was aimed at maintaining a balance of power among the different groups of nobles.[80] Abul-Fazl specifically mentions in the *Akbarnama* that Akbar cultivated the Khanzadas of Mewat on account of their military background.[81] Powlett, too, cites an account of Akbar's visit to Alwar on his way to Fatehpur Sikri.[82]

In the context of the discussion on the relations of the Mewati chiefs with the Delhi sultans and the Mughal emperors, it is important to foreground their relationship with the other regional chiefs during the Sultanate period. Mubarak Sayyid's suppression of the Mewati chiefs Kadar Khan and Ahmad Khan on account of the latter's relations with the Sharqi rulers of Jaunpur who were in conflict with the Sayyids, as mentioned earlier, points to a brief alliance between the chiefs of Mewat and the Sharqis during the Sultanate period. Hasan Khan's alliance with Rana Sanga, Khan of Nagore, and Rai Silahdi against Babur for the Battle of Khanwa[83] points to his ability to influence the neighbouring chiefs.

During the reign of Akbar, there were Rajput converts to Islam settled in Mungana, a few miles to the south of Alwar city, and known for their plundering activities. Akbar gave orders to punish them. In the ensuing punitive campaign, many of them were killed and captured, the entire fortress town of Mungana was destroyed, and a new *qasba*

79 Powlett, *Gazetteer of Ulwur*, 135.

80 Iqtidar Alam Khan, 'The Nobility under Akbar and the Development of His Religious Policy, 1560–1580', *Journal of the Royal Asiatic Society of Great Britain and Ireland* (1968): 29–36.

81 Abul-Fazl, *The Akbarnama*, vol. 2, 76.

82 Powlett, *Gazetteer of Ulwur*, 10.

83 Meo, 'Hasan Khan ki Katha', couplet nos 63–72.

named Akbarpur was founded on the site of the destroyed town.[84] This is corroborated by the non-archival records of the Alwar state, according to which this incident took place in 1578. Akbar received reports that the notorious Meos of Mungana and Binak villages had not paid their land revenue for past several years to the Mughal state, but no official had the courage to go to these villages and forcibly collect revenue. Therefore, Akbar personally led a military campaign against these Meos who fled out of fear to the Aravali hills. With the help of a local Brahmin, the Mughal forces found them out, and captured and punished all of them. The two villages were completely destroyed and a new village, Akbarpur, was founded on the site.[85] The Khanzada nobles must have played a supportive role in the Mughal campaign. Whatever may have been Akbar's reasons for their inclusion in the Mughal nobility, the fact is that we come across many references to the Khanzadas posted in different capacities by successive Mughal emperors, from Akbar to Muhammad Shah. *Arzang-i-Tijara* tells us that Akbar deployed the best talent from the Khanzadas in the service of the empire, and they, too, proved loyal to the emperors.[86]

84 Powlett, *Gazetteer of Ulwur*, 11. In 1579, Akbar visited Alwar on his way to Fatehpur Sikri (Powlett, *Gazetteer of Ulwur*, 11).

85 *Bandhak* no. 13, *granthank* no. 1.

86 Makhdum, *Arzang-i-Tijara*, 13. The Khanzadas of Indore were appointed *chaudhris* in Alwar *sarkar*. Mohabat Khan and Daulat Khan, Khanzadas of Guwalla village, were appointed as imperial *mansabdars*. Khalil Ulugh Khan, Vaki Khan, Wajehdi Khan, Sukrala Khan, and Nusaratyar Khan Khanzadas were appointed as *fauzdars* of Mewat, following each other in succession (Suraj Bhan Bhardwaj, 'Socio-economic Conditions in the Mewat Region, c. 1650–1750' [PhD thesis, Centre for Historical Studies, Jawaharlal Nehru University, 1990], 199). Firoz Khan Mewati, who was very close to Dara Shukoh, sided with him in the war of succession during the reign of Shahjahan, but was later appointed by Aurangzeb as an imperial *mansabdar* (Khafi Khan, 'Muntakhab-ul-Lubab', in *History of India as Told by Its Own Historians*, vol. 7, ed. H. M. Elliot and John Dowson [Delhi: Low Price Publications, 1993], 240). Purdil Khan, son of Firoz Khan Mewati, was also an imperial *mansabdar* during the reign of Aurangzeb and was sent with other *mansabdars* to crush the Satnami revolt at Narnaul (Saqi Mustad Khan, *Maasir-i-Alamgiri*, trans. Jadunath Sarkar, 2nd ed. [New Delhi: Munshiram Manoharlal, 1986], 71–2). Khan-i-Zaman Mewati was a learned man and received many titles, such as Kartabah Khan, Ali Askar Khan,

IV

During Akbar's reign, Mewat became an integral part of the Mughal empire. It was brought under direct imperial administration and divided into five *sarkars*—Alwar, Tijara, Sahar, Rewari, and Narnol—within the two *subas* of Agra and Delhi.[87] With the absorption of Mewat by the Mughal empire, the Mewati chiefs lost their political autonomy, as is evident from the fact that no Mughal chronicles made any reference to them as rulers. Nevertheless, they continued to hold on to dominant positions in the rural society as zamindars of varying statures. On the other hand, the Meos were accommodated in the lower rungs of the administration. Akbar employed about 1,000 Meos as post carriers (Dak Meoras).[88] The Amber rulers, too, appointed many Meos as messengers or post carriers because of their reputation as good runners.[89] The disintegration of the Mughal empire in the 18th century led to many political changes in the Mewat region. Many *parganas* of Mewat were taken by the Kachhwaha state of Amber (later known as Jaipur), while all the *parganas* of Sahar, Alwar, and Tijara *sarkars* were occupied by the emergent Jat state of Bharatpur and the Naruka Rajput state of Alwar.

Here, the question that arises is why the Khanzada chieftains were not conceded relative autonomy by the Mughals, as the Rajput chieftains were. Akbar had a specific policy towards the Rajput chiefs. Not only were their principalities protected as *watan jagir*, but they were given autonomy to manage their home affairs. Thus, the Rajput states survived even the decline of the Mughal empire. The Khanzadas, on the other hand, lost their political importance after the Battle of Khanwa. Most of Mewat was annexed by Babur and parcelled out among his nobles. Nahar

---

and Khan Zaman Bahadur, during the reign of Bahadurshah. His father, Sheikh Gulam Mustafi Kartalab Khan, was the bodyguard of Bahadurshah (Khan and Hayy, *The Maathir-ul-Umara*, vol. 1, 808).

87 Abul-Fazl, *The Ain-i-Akbari*, vol. 2, 202–6. The *sarkars* of Tijara and Narnaul were transferred from the province of Agra to Delhi just before the end of Shahjahan's reign (Irfan Habib, *The Agrarian System of Mughal India, 1556–1707* [Bombay: Asia Publishing House, 1963], 8).

88 Abul-Fazl, *The Ain-i-Akbari*, vol. 1, 262.

89 *Arzdasht*, Chait Sudi 1, VS 1740/1683 CE, Historical Section, Jaipur Records, Rajasthan State Archives, Bikaner.

Khan (son of Hasan Khan Mewati) was given a few *parganas* for the maintenance of his own family, according to the author of 'Hasan Khan ki Katha'. During the rule of Sher Shah Suri, Mewat remained an administrative unit of the Sur empire. On the accession of Islam Shah (1545), the *parganas* of Tijara *sarkar* were assigned as a *jagir* to Khawas Khan, Sher Shah's slave and general who established his headquarters at Firozpur Jhirka.[90] During the reign of Islam Shah Sur, a water tank was constructed in Alwar by Chand Qazi, the in-charge of Alwar fort.[91] It appears that by the time of the Sur empire, the position of the Khanzada chiefs of Mewat had become insignificant. However, when Humayun returned to India in 1555, he decided to develop his political relations with the regional chiefs through matrimonial alliances. To quote Abul-Fazl:

> When Humayun was at Delhi, he, in order to soothe the minds of the zamindars, entered into matrimonial relations with them. Among these, Jamal Khan, the cousin of Hasan Khan of Mewat, who was one of the great zamindars of India, came and paid homage. He had two beautiful daughters. Humayun himself married the elder sister, and gave the younger in marriage to Bairam Khan. At the time the standards of the Shahinshah [emperor] were directed towards the suppression of Hemu.[92]

According to the *Ain-i-Akbari*, Jamal Khan Mewati came from the Khanzada family of Mewat and happened to be a 'great zamindar of Hindustan', by which Abul-Fazl meant the image of Hasan Khan Mewati who had fought against Babur. Therefore, Abul-Fazl states that

[90] Abdullah, 'Tarikh-i-Daudi', in *History of India as Told by Its Own Historians*, vol. 4, ed. H. M. Elliot and John Dowson, 482–4. Khawas Khan revolted against Islam Shah on account of his treachery against his brother Adil Khan, but was defeated in a battle near Agra. Thereafter, he fled to Firozpur Jhirka in Mewat, but Islam Shah sent a powerful force in pursuit of Khawas Khan. A battle was fought between the army of Islam Shah and Khawas Khan at Firozpur Jhirka in which Khawas Khan found it difficult to continue the war and fled to the outskirts of Kumaun hills (Abdullah, 'Tarikh-i-Daudi').

[91] An inscription on a tank in the Alwar fort states that it was constructed by Chand Kazi (Hakim Killa) at the order of Islam Shah; the construction was completed in H. 958 /1550 CE (*bandhak* no. 6, *granthank* no. 71).

[92] Abul-Fazl, *The Akbarnama*, trans. H. Beveridge, vol. 3 (New Delhi: Low Price Publications, [1902–39] 1993), 76.

although the political position of Jamal Khan Mewati may not have been very significant during the reign of Humayun, he belonged to a family that had acquired a great political importance in the past.[93] However, it was very clear to Akbar that the Khanzada chiefs of Mewat had lost their erstwhile political power and, if absorbed into his nobility, might not be able to play as important a role as the Rajputs or the Sheikhzadas would. Further, Mewat, lying on the trade route between Agra and Delhi, was close to these two centres of Mughal power, and therefore, the formation of a Khanzada state there could have become a serious threat to the consolidation of the Mughal state. In 1560, when Akbar sacked Bairam Khan from his position, the latter revolted from Mewat. It was the Khanzadas who not only provided him protection, but were also sympathetic to his cause.[94] This might have caused Akbar's annoyance at the Khanzadas. Finally, state formation required a strong material base which the Khanzadas of Mewat lacked. All the aforementioned factors, if present, might have contributed to the formation of the Khanzada state of Mewat.

93 Abul-Fazl, *The Ain-i-Akbari*, vol. 1, 426. The military fame of the Khanzadas of Mewat even overshadowed the renown of the Sayyids of Amrohah and Manikpur.

94 Abul-Fazl, *The Ain-i-Akbari*, vol. 1, 349. When Bairam Khan incurred the displeasure of emperor Akbar, he left Agra and proceeded towards Alwar. Khan Jahan brought Bairam Khan's insignia from Mewat to Akbar, and as he was a near relation of the rebel Bairam Khan, he was detained and left under the charge of Asaf Khan, the commander of Delhi.

2

NATURAL SETTINGS

POTENTIAL AND CONSTRAINTS

THE SYSTEM OF AGRICULTURAL PRODUCTION in a region is largely influenced by its ecological conditions. The nature of soil and climatic conditions, including the quantity of rainfall, determine the area under cultivation and cropping patterns to a large extent. Similar has been the situation in Mewat. On the basis of soil quality and rainfall pattern, the region is categorized as a semi-arid zone. The geographical location and the level of technology employed in raising crops have had a direct bearing on the output per unit of area (*bigha*) in the region. The chapter discusses the impact of ecology on the pattern and organization of agricultural production in this region.

I

One of the most distinguishing features of the region is its physiography. The soil is light in texture, particularly sandy, sandy loam, and clay loam. The upper hills are mostly barren. The region is characterized by the presence of several types of rocks belonging to the Archean, pre-Cambrian, and Pleistocene ages. The most conspicuous geomorphological feature is the ancient Aravali range, with its rocky and precipitous hills. The Aravali hills emerge in the west in

Rajasthan and, passing through this part of Haryana, reach up to central Delhi. Throughout their course, flat hilltops are found to have formed some kind of plateau-like structures. In between the Aravali hills, there are enclaves of fertile valleys and alluvial plains. Mewat is one such zone between such hilly tracks.[1]

Mewat comes under the subtropical, semi-arid zone with extremely hot summers. May and June are the hottest months of the year with temperature ranging from 30°C to 48°C, while January is the coldest month with temperature ranging between 4°C and 25°C. Strong dusty winds are conspicuous during summer. The average annual rainfall varies from 336 millimetres to 440 millimetres, but mainly occurs during the monsoon season (June–September) when the region receives about 80 per cent of its annual rainfall; it experiences peak rainfall in July. Humidity is considerably low during the greater part of the year and dryness of air is a standard feature. Thus, dry weather conditions, coupled with erratic annual rainfall, have not historically allowed it to be prosperous and consistent in agricultural production.[2] But in terms of mineral wealth, the region has been very rich, as will be discussed later in the chapter.

The Alwar *sarkar* that covered more than half of the Mewat region during the medieval period was/is occupied by the ranges of Aravali hills, the highest of which rises to an elevation of nearly 2,400 feet above the sea level and about 1,600 feet above the general level of the surrounding country, formed of wide sandy alluvial plains. The direction of the range varies considerably: generally it is from north and south to north-east and south-west, but in many places the ridge makes a complete semicircle. The rock quality throughout is similar, although at many places the soft and hard rocks have been partially removed by denudation resulting in the formation of valleys between the hills.[3]

The geology of the region was/is dominated by Quaternary sediments and Delhi supergroup of rock formations. The Quaternary sediments include alluvium deposits consisting of a sequence of interlayered clay/silt and sand with occasional *kankar* formations in case

[1] Powlett, *Gazetteer of Ulwur*, 177–83; Channing, *Land Revenue Settlement of the Gurgaon District*, 1–2.

[2] Channing, *Land Revenue Settlement of the Gurgaon District*, 6.

[3] Powlett, *Gazetteer of Ulwur*, 177.

of older alluvium formations and coarse to fine aeolian sand in case of aeolian deposits. These are largely distributed over areas of 1135.27 square kilometres and 166.69 square kilometres respectively. The Delhi supergroup rock formation is dominated by quartzite, phyllite, and slate in the south-eastern part (51.05 square kilometres), and by quartzite and schist in the western edges (130.99 square kilometres).[4]

The gazetteer of Alwar state prepared by P. W. Powlett, a British ethnographer and settlement officer of the Alwar state, divides the Aravali hills of Alwar *sarkar* into four main groups: the Mandan group, the Ajabgarh group, the Kushalgarh group, and the Alwar group.[5] The rocks of the Mandan group form a ridge on the north-west corner of the state, mainly on the left bank of Sabi River at Mandan, Bahrod, and Tasing, as well as a double ridge at Mandaor, 30 miles to the south-east of Alwar town. The group consists of schists abounding in crystals of andalusite, staurotide, garnets, and actinolite, and some bands of quartzite interbedded with them. Near Bahrod, however, there is a long hill formed of the Kushalgarh limestone and breccia between two ridges of schist, and separated from them about half a mile of alluvium. In the south-east corner of the state, at Mandaor, the double ridge of Mandan schists occurs between two ridges of Alwar quartzites converging towards the south, and both dipping towards the schists, apparently forming a synclinal in which the schists lie. Mineralogically, there is a little difference between the Mandan rocks and those of the known Aravali series, and therefore, the Ajabgarh rocks in the hills east of Alwar are mainly quartzites and are very similar to those of the Mandan group.[6]

The Ajabgarh group contains a considerable thickness and a great variety of rocks, principally limestones, quartzite, hornstone breccia, and slates. The rocks of this group occupy the synclinal troughs formed by the quartzites of the Alwar group, and in some of the ridges east of the town of Alwar. These valleys are the Delawas, Kushalgarh, Ajabgarh, and Narainpur. There is a continuous section of the Ajabgarh group in the valleys, but the rocks above, being only exposed in the isolated ridges east of Alwar town, are consequently

4 Powlett, *Gazetteer of Ulwur*, 177–8.

5 Powlett, *Gazetteer of Ulwur*, 177.

6 Powlett, *Gazetteer of Ulwur*, 181.

difficult to place in the section. The ridge, extending south from the Moti Dungri hill (near Alwar town) and composed of alternations of calcareous and quartzite bands, is higher in the section than the Berla quartzite, and the Goleta ridge, which is located about 6 miles east of Alwar city, is still higher in the section.

At the head of the Delawas valley, the rocks are much contorted, and the Kushalgarh limestone is repeated in the two little valleys east of the Serawas, near Siliserh (4 miles south-west of Alwar town). There is a large spread of the limestone in the Kushalgarh valley. It covers the whole of the bottom of the valley, nearly 2 miles wide, and extends from 2 or 3 miles east of the Kushalgarh town to the head of the valley at Tabbrich. Beyond this point it passes round the quartzites into the Narainpur valley. In the southern branch of the Narainpur valley, it extends to near Indok, where it becomes covered by the higher rocks of the group. A unique feature of this sub-zone is that the whole of the centre of the Ajabgarh valley is occupied by the black slates. These rocks extend into the Narainpur valley as far as Gazi ka Thana, but north of that there are only a few small hills of the slates in the centre, and some of the limestone and breccia on either side of the valley. The slates are entirely covered by the alluvium, which extends to the Moti Dungri ridge, nearly the highest member of the group. Of the ridges on the eastern side of the state, many of them are formed of the rocks of the Ajabgarh group.[7]

The Alwar group is the most important group of the types of rocks found in Aravali ranges, as not only the highest, but the greater part of the hills are formed of it. In fact, nearly the whole of the group of hills extending from Mandawar to Rajgarh on the east and Pratapgarh on the west, as well as the Tijara ridge, are formed of it. The important component of this group is the quartzite, of which there is a great variety. The greater part of it is regularly bedded, compact, and light grey in colour, but in places it is course in texture, and even conglomeratic. Ripple marking and sun cracks are very common in the quartzites, and are particularly well seen in Alwar Fort hill. Arkose rocks frequently occur at the base of the quartzites, where the group rests upon the gneiss.

7 Powlett, *Gazetteer of Ulwur*, 179–80.

In an east and west section about the latitude of Ajabgarh, the quartzites are repeated at least a dozen times in a series of anticlinals and synclinals in which the rocks both above and below them are exposed. The Alwar group overlaps the Raialo group and rests upon the gneiss. Sections of the junction of the two series are scarce, as it generally takes place near the base of a high scarp and is mostly covered by debris. Near Bhadokar, there is another junction in which the gneiss, composed principally of white feldspar, very little quartz, and plates of mica, forms a band about 12 feet across surrounded by the quartzites. In places, the arkose rocks have been metamorphosed to such an extent that, but for their connection with the gneiss below or the quartzites above, it would be difficult to tell them from the true gneiss. The arkose rocks are well developed north-west of the Alwar town at Dadikar, where they form a circle, filled with alluviums, blown sand, and so on, covering the rocks below. The arkose rocks at base, particularly at the south-west corner, are highly crystalline, but getting up the hills they pass gradually into the quartzites.

Such hills of the arkose rocks passing into the quartzites are met with at Palpur, Bagheri, Khairthal, and Palari. At Dariba, a thin band of black slates occurs below the quartzites. Similar black slates run through the series and are largely developed in the Ajabgarh group. The Dariba mines are in these black slates. In places such as near Rajgarh and Kirwari, the quartzites become very micaceous and have a schistose structure. Near the base of the quartzites, several bands of hornblende are intercalated with them. Some of these bands are of considerable thickness and form hills several hundred feet high; near Kankwari and south-east of Pratapgarh, they are quite numerous and attain a great thickness. The thickness of the Alwar group varies in different sections; thus, near Alwar and in the hills west of Rajgarh, an enormous thickness of quartzites is exposed, but towards the southern boundary of the state, the thickness is reduced to a few hundred feet.[8]

According to Powlett's report, the useful minerals in Alwar were more numerous than abundant. They consisted of copper pyrites, argentiferous galena, nickel, rutile, manganese, and iron. The report mentions the existence of several old copper workings in Alwar, from

[8] Powlett, *Gazetteer of Ulwur*, 178–9.

which a considerable amount of ore had been extracted during the medieval period. Further, it lists several localities in which copper ore had been worked or traces of it were observed. The most important of these was Dariba, situated in a sharp anticlinal bend in the black slates and quartzites, the lowest beds of the Alwar group. The copper there occurred in the form of copper pyrites, mixed with arsenical iron. Another copper mine was reported to be in the Indawas hills from which copper ore had been extracted. Besides, small quantities of copper were also extracted from the Bhangarh and schist hills near Tasing, as also from Baghani, Kushalgarh, and Pratapgarh.[9]

Powlett's report points to the occurrence of iron—which is considered to be historically a more democratic metal in terms of its wider distribution throughout the globe—in large quantities in the hills of Rajgarh and Bhangarh. Besides, a number of building materials, some of a very superior quality, were reportedly found in abundance in the Aravali hills of Alwar. Limestone, capable of making good lime, was found to exist throughout the state. The report remarks that ordinary quartzite was useful for constructing rough buildings, walls, and so on, but pearly grey and durable Berla quartzite made an excellent building stone and was largely quarried at Berla, Doroli, and Bharkol. Schistose quartzites, used for roofing, flags, and so on, were largely quarried near Rajgarh, Kirwari, and Mandan. The Ajabgarh slates, used for roofing most of the railway stations, were not quarried at Alwar, although some of the hills in Ajabgarh could produce equally good slates. The Talcose limestone, found at the base of the black slates, was used for ornamental purposes in the form of carved doorposts, and so on. Capital marble produced by the Raialo group of rocks was quarried at Jhirri, whereas coloured marbles could be had near Kho and Baldeogarh, and black marble from the Moti Dungri ridge.[10]

II

Three types of soils are found in Mewat, namely the fertile sandy loam, clay loam, and clay soils. The hilly areas that form a major part of the region extend from Firozpur Jhirka to Sohna, and comprise parts of Nuh, Taoru, Tapukara, Tijara, Kishangarh, Alwar, Ramgarh,

9 Powlett, *Gazetteer of Ulwur*, 182.

10 Powlett, *Gazetteer of Ulwur*, 183.

and Govindgarh. This area is also part of the Aravali range and its soil is, therefore, known as hilltop soil. The hilltop soil is broadly divided into three categories, namely clay, matiyar, and sandy. About 15 per cent of the area falls in the first category and 62 per cent in the second category. The third category of soil accounts for only 23 per cent of the total cultivated area.[11]

In *pargana* Taoru, the land is characterized by the prevalence of inferior sandy soils that are suitable for producing chiefly *bajra* and pulses. The area of *pargana* Kotla with clay and sandy loam was known as Dahar; it comprised 116 villages and was a low-lying area. During the rainy season, flood water accumulated in the three basin-like depressions of Khalilpur, Chandeni, and Kotla Lakes. The soil of this *pargana* was suitable for raising crops such as cotton, barley, wheat, and gram.[12]

Pargana Firozpur Jhirka consists of a valley, in length 24 miles and in breadth gradually increasing from 5 miles in the south to 11 miles in the north, bounded on east and west by two ranges of low hills. The lands in the centre of the Firozpur valley are low and liable to inundation from the Landoha stream, which sweeps up the valley from the south, where it opens on Alwar, and from the Jhirr, Darur, and other torrents, which in the rains bring down the collected drainage of the hills on either side. However, most of these streams deposit sand, but wherever the original soil has escaped the deterioration from this factor, it is generally of good quality. Thus, the majority of villages have this good soil. In the north and north-east of *pargana* Firozpur, there occurs a tract of depression marked by the prevalence of a strong black clay and by the saltiness of its wells, both of which characteristics it possesses in common with the adjacent part of Nuh. *Pargana* Punahana, except the part immediately under the hills dividing it from Firozpur, consists of a broad plain of good soil.[13]

The geographical distribution of the aforementioned three soil types in different *parganas* of Mewat is described in Table 2.1:

[11] Pratibha Mishra, *Soil Productivity and Crop Potentials: A Case Study (District Alwar-Rajasthan)* (New Delhi: Concept, 1984), 35; Channing, *Land Revenue Settlement of the Gurgaon District*, 110.

[12] Channing, *Land Revenue Settlement of the Gurgaon District*, 133–5.

[13] Channing, *Land Revenue Settlement of the Gurgaon District*, 109.

Table 2.1 Soil types in Mewat

Zone	Soil type	*Pargana*-wise
(a)	Light sandy to sandy loam soils of deep origin	Northern and western parts of Kot-Qasim, northern and western parts of Tijara, and southern part of Taoru, Firozpur Jhirka, Nuh, and Kotla
(b)	Light-textured, moderately deep soils	Mandawar and Ramgarh
(c)	Fertile soils of alluvial origin	Kishangarh, Lachhmangarh, eastern part of Tijara, northern part of Umarni, Firozpur Jhirka, and Punhana
(d)	Heavy clay to clay loam soil	Southern and western parts of Lachhmangarh, Gazi ka Thana, and Rajgarh
(e)	Hilly tract with poorly drained clay loam to clay soils of recent origin	Hilly areas of Gazi Ka Thana, Rajgarh, and Umarni

Source: Mishra, *Soil Productivity and Crop Potentials*, 35.

Loam soil retains and conserves moisture and constitutes a valuable plant nutrient. This retentive quality of the soil makes it suitable for the cultivation of most crops. Sandy loam soil has lesser water retention capacity and its importance to agriculturists depends on the availability of irrigation facilities. Sandy soil, capable of retaining very little water, is of lesser utility to cultivators. Clay loam soil is difficult to plough, especially when it is either too wet or too dry. Clay loam soil is suitable for raising crops such as gram, wheat, cotton, sugarcane, and maize, while loam is conducive for the growth of vegetables. On sandy loam soil, wheat, barley, green gram, mustard, and vegetables can be grown. The sandy soil is suitable for growing *bajra*, *moth* (kidney bean), *urad* (black gram), and *chola* (chickpea).

In the hilly plains, water table is about 20–21 metres deep with an overlying subtract of hard *kankar* and brown to yellow clay. In the sandy areas such as Tijara, water table is generally at the depth of 7–7.3 metres. The colour of soil there varies from brown to black. Water content has a marked effect on the colour: it becomes deeper in the regions with still waters, for example, reservoirs. The quality of water found beneath the soil is very important for the increase in agricultural production. It is more so in the areas where cultivation largely depends on well irrigation. In *parganas* Firozpur Jhirka and Nuh, three types of water—sweet, brackish, and salty—are found. A proper combination of water and soil is crucial for determining the productivity of land. According to tradition, salty water is found beneath sandy soils. In areas of clay soil, sweet and brackish types of water are available. These types of water help peasants to raise better crops.[14] In *parganas* Alwar and Tijara, several types of water are found. In local parlance, these are known as *matwala, malmala, rukalla, mitha, khara, telia,* and *banar telia.* The *malmala, rukalla,* and *mitha* are considered inferior in quality as compared to *matwala,* but could be used for irrigating certain crops. Other varieties of well water are of no use in agriculture.[15]

III

The level of rainfall, to a large extent, determines the area under cultivation and cropping patterns. About 80 per cent of annual rainfall is received during the monsoons (June to September) with the maximum quantum in July. The remaining 20 per cent is more or less uniformly distributed over the rest of the months, particularly January and February, when the probability of getting good rains is comparatively higher. The normal rainfall during the winter months of December, January, and February is 3.7 millimetres, 14.7 millimetres, and 0.5 millimetres respectively. The average rainfall for these three months is 7 per cent of the total precipitation. Thus, it appears that Mewat does not get a reasonable share of the monsoon rains, which has led it to be designated as a semi-arid zone.[16]

Geomorphologically, the region has a certain potential to retain water in the ground below the rocky surface. Piedmont plain with a gentle slope and low drainage density possesses good to very good potential for water retention, while aeolian plain with coarse to fine aeolian sand has good to moderate potential. Structural hills and

[14] Channing, *Land Revenue Settlement of the Gurgaon District*, 8.

[15] Powlett, *Gazetteer of Ulwur*, 91.

[16] Mishra, *Soil Productivity and Crop Potentials*, 14.

linear ridges with steep slopes have a high drainage density, but due to the presence of high lineament density, they possess poor to moderate potential. Residual hills and parts of structural hills with low lineament density, very steep slopes, and very high drainage density have very poor potential for water retention. Even if seen historically, irrigation was the most vital input in agricultural production in the region. However, the documents suggest that there were limited irrigation facilities available in the form of wells, tanks, *nullahs*, lakes, and rivers. The wells were the main source of irrigation in the region. They were of two types: non-masonry (*kucha*) and the brick-lined (*pucca*), the former being more numerous than the latter. The *kuccha* wells were dug in large numbers during the years of famine. The most common means for lifting water from wells and supplying it to the fields was the bucket (*charas*), attached to a rope (*lao*) and drawn over a pulley wheel (*chak*) by a yoke. This method of irrigation was quite cumbersome and costly, as it involved immense use of manual and animal power.[17]

The second most common method was the use of *dhenkli* (wooden scoop) where water level was high. The *dhenkli* consisted of a pole working on a pivot with a weight at one end and a suspended bucket at the other. The British settlement officers Powlett and Channing noticed 92 *dhenkhlis* being operated in *pargana* Kotla.[18]

We do not have any information about the number of wells in different *parganas*. The climatic condition of the region necessitated the expansion of a well irrigation network. The importance of well irrigation in stabilizing and expanding the agricultural economy can be discerned from the *yaddashtis* and *arzdashts*. A *yaddashti* dated 1727 CE furnishes the details of wells in *pargana* Pahari. Out of 33 villages, only three villages had wells.[19] Crop failure in the *rabi* season was owing to the lack of well irrigation in most villages. Hence, in order to stabilize agricultural production and minimize the adverse effects of famines, the state endeavoured to encourage the construction of new wells by providing monetary loans and other incentives. Special

17 Channing, *Land Revenue Settlement of the Gurgaon District*, 110–1.

18 Channing, *Land Revenue Settlement of the Gurgaon District*, 135; Powlett, *Gazetteer of Ulwur*, 91.

19 *Yaddashti Hal Bail*, *pargana* Pahari, *mauza* Darobastki, VS 1784/1727 CE.

efforts were made to dig masonry or at least non-masonry wells. For instance, in 1685, in the wake of a raging famine, 100 new wells were constructed in one *pargana* by the peasants with the financial support of the administration. Those peasants who dug new wells were also offered concessions in the rate of land revenue. In another *pargana*, 150 new wells were constructed with a view to increasing the area under cultivation.[20] Thus, the importance of wells in expanding and improving agriculture was fully realized by the state and the loans were provided for their construction.

According to Channing's report, in *pargana* Taoru 63 out of 91 villages had wells catering to 9.6 per cent irrigated land of the total cropped area, while the remaining 18 villages had no wells due to their proximity to the hills where the water level was very considerable low.[21] Similarly, in *pargana* Kotla the well-irrigated area was small, constituting 3.4 per cent of the total cropped area, partly due to the saltiness of water and partly due to the abundance of natural irrigation.[22]

The land of *pargana* Kotla was called Dahar (Chiknot), formed by three lakes, namely Kotla, Chandeni, and Khalilpur. In the entire area, most of the villages had salty water; therefore, wells could not be dug. In many villages, water was so salty that peasants dug wells not for the purpose of irrigation but for salt manufacture.[23] In some villages, peasants used to make *dhenkhlis* for irrigation. However, this device could be useful for only those villages that were situated around the lakes. The region of Firozpur Jhirka, which consisted of 229 exclusively Meo villages, had the maximum number of wells for irrigation due to the sweetness of water; 198 out of 229 villages had a staggering 1,225 wells. In this *pargana*, peasants constructed *pucca* wells in large numbers.[24] The wells were the main source of irrigation in many villages of Alwar *sarkar* as well, and Powlett, too, mentions the presence of 16,074 wells, the majority of which were unbricked.[25]

[20] *Arzdasht*, Kartik Vadi 3, VS 1742/1685 CE; *Arzdasht*, Kartik Vadi 9, VS 1742/1685 CE.

[21] Channing, *Land Revenue Settlement of the Gurgaon District*, 133.

[22] Channing, *Land Revenue Settlement of the Gurgaon District*, 135.

[23] Channing, *Land Revenue Settlement of the Gurgaon District*, 134.

[24] Channing, *Land Revenue Settlement of the Gurgaon District*, 110.

[25] *Chithi* to the *amil*, *pargana* Piragpur, Kartik Vadi 4, VS 1782/1725 CE; Powlett, *Gazetteer of Ulwur*, 90.

IV

The Mewat region is characterized by an inland drainage system. While most of the streams emerging from the Aravali hills are lost after covering a short distance because of seepage and evaporation, a few streams carry water into depressions that form small pockets of water supply. Almost all streams are incised into the upland tract. The main rivers and streams of the region are Sabi or Sahibi, Ruparel, Chuharsidh, Landoha, Indori, and Banganga. All these, along with others, are seasonal rivers—there is no perennial river in the region—and have water for only about a month in a year. Some of them were useful for irrigation. For instance, Powlett reported that the Ruparel and Chuharsidh were the most important irrigating *nallahs* in Alwar *tehsil*,[26] and peasants of a few villages of *pargana* Khilohra utilized the water of Chuharsidh by raising dam on it.[27] However, during rains, the torrential flow of these rivers from the hills spreads over the low-lying plains and heavily erodes the topsoil on the plains.

The Indori River rises from the hills of Indore near Nuh and gets divided into two streams. They are mainly torrents running for a few hours after the rains. One stream enters the Nandrampurbas village and falls into the Sabi River opposite Jarthal. The other flows northward near Taoru and is joined there by a number of other small *nullahs*. Finally, these streams eventually join the Sabi River near Bohara. Another important river is Landoha, formed by the union of two streams near Alwar. Running towards Firozpur Jhirka, it falls into the Kotla Lake.[28]

The Ruparel River, also known as *baranallah*, is the most important seasonal stream of the region, which carries its flow of water into the villages of *parganas* Khohri, Mojpur, and Ghat Khuteta in Alwar *sarkar*. Earlier, it was popularly known as Manisni. Rising from the Alwar hills, it passes up the Firozpur valley along the Landoha channel and falls into the Kotla *jheel* (lake).[29] Babur has mentioned in his

[26] Powlett, *Gazetteer of Ulwur*, 154.

[27] Powlett, *Gazetteer of Ulwur*, 144.

[28] Channing, *Land Revenue Settlement of the Gurgaon District*, 3.

[29] Channing, *Land Revenue Settlement of the Gurgaon District*, 3–4; Kotla Lake was situated in the vicinity of Kala Pahad between Nuh and Firozpur Jhirka.

memoirs that he took rest for some time on its bank during his march towards Khanwa against Rana Sanga.[30] The Rajasthani documents, too, refer to some disputes over the utilization of its waters in the early 18th century. For instance, the peasants belonging to seven villages of *pargana* Khohri complained that a levy was being imposed on them on account of the construction of a *bandh* on Ruparel, but they were not utilizing the water of the *bandh* for irrigating their fields.[31] In another instance, the peasants of *tappa* Ramgarh in *pargana* Khilohra complained that for past several years they had been utilizing the waters of the stream coming from the hills, but now the Panwar Rajput *patels* belonging to the villages of the valley were forcefully carrying away the water to their own villages.[32]

Lakes and dams, too, played an important role as sources of irrigation in the region. The main lakes were Kotla, Siliserh, and Deoti. Some channels were cut from these lakes when the water level was full, to support the cultivation of food and cash crops in the region. Even when these lakes dried up, their beds remained very fertile and, hence, suitable for growing superior crops, such as cotton, wheat, and sugarcane. Babur extensively describes the Kotla *jheel* and remarks on its utility for irrigation.[33] However, the area that could be irrigated by these lakes was not substantial. The peasants, with the help of the state, used to block the waters by making dams on the drains and streams. Powlett reported seeing dams in many *parganas* of the region.[34] The non-archival records of the Alwar state mention a total of 69 old dams and streams in Alwar *sarkar* which were very useful for the cultivation of crops.[35]

30 Babur, *Baburnama*, vol. 2, trans. A. S. Beveridge, 580.

31 *Chithi* to the *amil*, *pargana* Khohri, Asadh Vadi 7, VS 1782/1725 CE; *Chithi* to the *amil*, *pargana* Khohri, Vaishakh Vadi 4, VS 1790/1733 CE.

32 *Chithi* to the *amil*, *pargana* Khilohra, Kartik Sudi 5, VS 1789/1727 CE. There were six villages, namely Godhana, Samroch, Gopalgarh, and so on.

33 Babur, *Baburnama*, vol. 2, 580.

34 Powlett, *Gazetteer of Ulwur*, 92; these dams were mainly found in Tijara, Lachhmangarh, Bagheri, Babria, Reni, and so on. When the water was drained off, the land of the dam was called *talahi*, that is, fertile for the crops.

35 *Bandhak* no. 11, *granthank* no. 112, Non-archival Records of Alwar State, Rajasthan State Archives, Bikaner.

V

The arid climate of the region forced the people to develop their own adaptive pattern of agriculture—characterized, for instance, by crop rotation and cultivation of climate-resilient crops—distinct from those in the adjoining regions during the medieval period. Nevertheless, because of its ecological limitations, medieval Mewat remained economically underdeveloped as compared to the neighbouring regions of Malwa, Gujarat, Delhi, and Agra, although its geographical location made it strategically important to any ruling authority. During the Mughal period, its close proximity to the heartland of the Mughal empire made the control over it crucial for the Mughal state. Further, the economic significance of the region lies in the fact that the trade routes connecting the upper Gangetic plain with the seaports of Gujarat passed through it. Its integration with the Mughal administration and economic processes at work during the 17th century could bring about only a limited growth in its economy, although it remained politically very significant region throughout the period of our study.

Medieval sources do not shed much light on the nature of agricultural tools and practices in the region, forcing us to depend on the 19th-century colonial settlement reports and district gazetteers. Despite the gap of about a century between the period of our study and the publication of these reports, the tools and practices recorded in them seem to have been in use during the medieval period as well.

According to Powlett's report, to prepare land for the *kharif* crops in unirrigated land, one or two ploughings before the rains were usually undertaken by the peasants so that the rain water may be more readily absorbed. For the cultivation of sugarcane, preparations began in November when the land was first ploughed, an operation that was repeated six or seven times, before the seeds were planted in February. Cotton was sown in March; sowing was preceded by one ploughing after the beginning of rains. *Bajra* and pulses required two ploughings, whereas *jowar* needed three. Among the *rabi* crops, wheat required five ploughings and barley, four. Gram required one or two ploughings.[36]

[36] Powlett, *Land Revenue Settlement of the Gurgaon District*, 88.

The agricultural implements used by the peasantry in the 19th century remained almost the same as those in the 18th century. Ploughs were made up of both wood and iron. Iron seed drillers were used for drilling. Hand hoes with long bamboo handles were used for horticulture. *Daranti* (sickle) was the principal harvesting implement. *Manjha*, pulled by a pair of bullocks, was used for levelling the soil and making ridges or bendings in order to irrigate the uneven land. *Datali*, made of iron with a long wooden handle and driven manually, was used for preparing ridges and bendings of plots, and for spreading and mixing manure or compost fertilizer with soil. *Jeli*, a fork of wood with a long handle, was a multipurpose agricultural instrument, used particularly for collecting and winnowing the reaped crops, and fencing. *Gandasi*, made of a foil of iron attached to a wooden handle, was used for clearing bushes and weeds and thereby preparing the field for ploughing and sowing. It was also used for reaping and cutting straws of *bajra*.[37]

The system of crop rotation (*pher*) was commonly practised on irrigated lands capable of bearing more than one crop in a year.[38] It helped in soil conservation, improved the texture and permeability of soils, checked pests and crop diseases, reduced weed infestation, and helped in maintaining soil fertility. Further, rotation of crops from season to season and year to year helped change the immediate environment in the fields. Better crop yields, too, were obtained from the same field by practising crop rotation than cultivating the same crop for years in succession. In the Mewat region, the usual two-year rotation was cotton in the *kharif* season, followed by tobacco in the *rabi* season, then *bajra* in the *kharif* season, and finally barley in the *rabi* season. On good irrigated double-cropped lands, cultivation of *kharif* crops, namely *bajra* and *guwar*, was followed by that of *rabi* crops, namely barley, gram, or wheat. On inferior and unirrigated lands where cultivation of more than one crop was impracticable, cultivation of drought-resistant crops such as *moth* and *bajra* followed one another, although they were often grown together. *Jowar*, *bajra*,

37 Powlett, *Land Revenue Settlement of the Gurgaon District*, 89; Lallanji Gopal and V. C. Srivastava, eds, *History of Agriculture in India upto c. 1200 AD*, *History of Science, Philosophy and Culture in Indian Civilization*, vol. 5, part 1 (Delhi: Concept Publishing, 2008), 856–79.

38 Powlett, *Land Revenue Settlement of the Gurgaon District*, 89.

and *urad* were also considered suitable alternative crops for rotation in some *parganas* of the region.[39]

Powlett also recorded the quantity of seeds required to be sown per *bigha* for different crops. For *bajra*, 1 *ser* or a little more was required; for Jowar, three *sers*; for *chari*, 10–20 *sers*; for wheat and barley, 20 *sers*; and for gram, 15 *sers*.[40]

The village- and *pargana*-level records such as *arsattas*, *yaddashtis chithis*, and *arzdashts* amply illumine the system of agricultural production in Mewat, although they are not available in a continuous series for the entire period under study. A number of *parganas* of the region were held by the rulers of Amber state as their *tankhwah jagir* or taken by them on *ijara* (revenue farming) from other imperial *mansabdars* in the region. Of these, 10 *parganas*, Khohri, Pahari, Jalalpur, Gazi ka Thana, Atela Bhabra, Piragpur, Pindayan, Mojpur, Harsana, and Wazirpur, have been chosen for the analysis of the nature and pattern of agricultural production. The *arsattas*, being a ledger of receipts and expenditure under different heads of taxation, contain detailed information on the system of taxation on crops: the total land revenue demand; the proportion of revenue demand from the *kharif* and *rabi* output; the area under the *zabti* system (wherein the revenue was assessed and realized in cash) and the amount realized under the *batai-jinsi* system (wherein the revenue was realized in kind); the distribution of different crops over the area; revenue rates per *bigha*, and so on. But all this information pertains to those villages that were held by the Amber rulers as part of their *khalisa* land. No information is available for the villages given in *jagir* or *ijara*. Moreover, the number of villages under *khalisa* used to fluctuate. However, the pattern of production discernible in the *khalisa* villages can be taken as representative of the entire region.

As revenue figures are recorded in the *arsattas* in largely two non-comparable sets of crops assessed under the *zabti* and *batai-jinsi* systems, these have been converted into one form by adopting the method suggested by S. Nurul Hasan, K. N. Hasan, and S. P. Gupta.[41]

39 Powlett, *Land Revenue Settlement of the Gurgaon District*, 89.

40 Powlett, *Land Revenue Settlement of the Gurgaon District*, 88; Gopal and Srivastava, eds, *History of Agriculture*, 856–79.

41 S. Nurul Hasan, K. N. Hasan, and S. P. Gupta, 'The Pattern of Agricultural Production in the Territories of Amber (c. 1650–1750)', *Proceedings*

Fortunately, some of the *batai-jinsi* crops were at times partly assessed according to the *zabti* system and their *zabti* rates are available for some years. It is, therefore, possible to convert the revenue demand in cash per *bigha* into demand in kind per *bigha* on the basis of the prevailing crop prices. By this method, the area under cultivation of different *kharif* and *rabi* crops (the revenue from which was assessed according to *zabti* and *batai-jinsi* systems) in different *parganas*, the proportion of the acreage under each crop to the total cropped area, and the average yield per *bigha* for each crop have been worked out. The estimates obtained may not be entirely accurate, since the method is based on the assumption that the *zabti* rates were calculated taking one-third of the average produce as the state's share. Yet, it is the only possible and relatively reliable method for determining the cropping pattern and changes therein during the period under study.

Mewat was characterized by a significant level of agricultural productivity in consonance with the ecological and topographical constraints of the region. The somewhat rocky terrain of the region was irrigated by a number of seasonal streams to raise a large number of food and cash crops. The *arsattas* give us details of about 32 *kharif* and 24 *rabi* crops cultivated in almost all the *parganas* under study. In every *pargana*, the total number of crops cultivated in a year varied from 40 to 57 and included all the major food and cash crops. A considerable variety of food grains, pulses, and oil-yielding crops provided subsistence to the regional populace. Thus, a multiplicity of crops was an important feature of agricultural production. This crop diversity was, in turn, made possible by a variety of soils conducive to the growth of a variety of crops.

The principal crops of the *kharif* and *rabi* seasons were a mix of major cereals, pulses, vegetables, and cash crops. Some were raised by the peasants chiefly for domestic consumption, while others were produced for the market. The most important cereal crops of the *kharif* season were *bajra*, *jowar* (sorghum), *makka* (maize), *dhaan*

---

of the Indian History Congress, 28th session, Mysore, 1966, 244–64; S. Nurul Hasan and S. P. Gupta, 'Prices of Foodgrains in the Territories of Amber (c. 1650–1750)', *Proceedings of the Indian History Congress*, 29th session, Patiala, 1968, 345–68.

(paddy), *mandwa* (ragi), *kodon* (kodo millet), *kuri, sai, varti, kaguni, rotiko, ralo,* and so on. The chief cash crops were *kapas* (cotton), *baar/ganna* (sugarcane), *tilhan* (oilseed), *neel* (indigo), tobacco, and *san* (hemp). In addition to these, *dodi* or *masino* (opium) was cultivated in *parganas* Pindayan, Mojpur, and Harsana. Among the pulses, the main crops were *moth, moong* (green gram), and *urad.* A large number of vegetables, namely *torai, baingan* (brinjal), *aryia, gajar* (carrot), *pyaaz* (onion), *shakarkandi* (sweet potato), *tarbooz* (water melon), *kharbooza* (musk melon), *chola,* and *cheena* (common millet), were also raised in most *parganas*. Besides, fodder crops were cultivated in all *parganas*. In the *rabi* season, wheat, barley, and gram as well as cash crops, such as *sarson* (mustard), *ajwain* (carom seeds), tobacco, *dhania* (coriander), *bhangi,* and so on, were grown in all the *parganas*. A large number of vegetables, such as *gajar, muli* (radish), *torai, baingan,* and *pyaaz* were also grown in most *parganas*.

Another prominent feature of the *rabi* season agriculture was the cultivation of mixed crops, such as *gochani* (mixture of wheat and gram), *gojaro* (mixture of wheat and barley) and *bejhari* (mixture of gram and barley), in both seasons. Mixed cropping had some advantages. First, given the limited means of irrigation due to the uneven and rocky terrain, mixed cropping was practised as a safety mechanism against the possibility of failure of a particular crop. Second, it is evident from the *arsattas* that the state charged the land revenue on mixed crops at a lower rate under the *batai* system than under the *zabti* system. Thus, mixed cropping enabled the peasants to avoid disclosing all the cultivated crops to the revenue officials and thereby pay taxes lower than what he would be required to pay in case of single cropping.

The following tables (2.2a–2.2m) show the percentage of area under the cultivation of different food and cash crops of both seasons (*kharif* and *rabi*) out of the total cropped area in the 10 *parganas*:

It can be observed from the tables that *bajra* and *jowar* were the main *kharif* crops, covering a larger area than other crops. While chiefly raised as food crops, they were also used as fodder for cattle. They were cultivated just after the first rain of monsoon. Among the *rabi* crops, barley and gram require less water than wheat and therefore are/were grown on a larger area than other crops. Among the pulses, *moth* was grown in all the *parganas* except Pindayan, followed

Table 2.2a Percentage of total cropped area under wheat cultivation

Year (CE)	Jalalpur	Wazirpur	Gazi ka Thana	Atela Bhabra	Piragpur	Pindayan	Mojpur	Harsana	Khohri	Pahari
1666	–	–	–	0.15	–	–	–	2.34	–	–
1689	1.2	–	–	–	–	–	–	–	–	–
1711	2.05	–	–	10.44	–	–	–	–	–	–
1714	–	15.87	–	–	–	–	8.75	–	14.6	–
1718	1.64	10.7	–	–	–	–	–	–	8.87	–
1720	4.48	10.22	–	–	–	27.35	–	39.5	–	–
1722	–	6.43	–	2.37	–	1	5.57	12.8	–	–
1730	–	–	3.7	7.26	16	16.13	15.15	20	–	5.96
1733	–	–	9.2	10.07	14.3	7	11.96	15.5	18	0.66
1735	2.58	–	9.1	10.37	18.15	8.3	14.31	13.3	–	8.09
1737	0.77	–	5	15.32	19.4	–	–	–	–	7.08
1740	3.55	–	4.4	16.61	13.3	–	–	–	–	–
1741	–	–	7.7	1.6	19.1	–	–	–	15.33	1.73
1742	–	–	5.3	11.68	15.9	–	–	–	–	–
1743	–	–	4.6	–	–	–	–	–	–	0.55
1744	–	12.56	–	–	–	–	–	–	27.04	1.58
1745	–	6.3	–	–	–	–	–	–	–	–
1746	–	–	–	–	–	–	–	–	–	–
1747	–	5.48	3.8	–	–	–	–	–	–	–
1748	–	7.34	2.4	–	–	–	–	–	18.3	–
1749	–	3.66	–	–	–	3.76	7.59	6.31	–	–

Source: *Arsattas* of years mentioned.

Table 2.2b Percentage of total cropped area under *bajra* cultivation

Year (CE)	Jalalpur	Wazirpur	Gazi ka Thana	Atela Bhabra	Piragpur	Pindayan	Mojpur	Harsana	Khohri	Pahari
1666	20.35	–	–	51.03	–	–	–	20.01	–	–
1689	4.82	–	–	–	–	–	–	–	–	–
1691	1.12	–	–	–	–	–	–	–	–	–
1711	10.37	–	–	31.87	–	–	–	–	–	–
1713	–	–	–	–	–	–	3.3	–	13.6	–
1714	–	7.18	–	–	–	–	–	–	–	–
1716	–	6.14	–	–	–	–	–	–	4.63	–
1718	18.54	14.31	–	–	–	–	–	–	–	–
1720	13.34	16.45	–	–	–	4.27	–	0.6	–	–
1722	–	23.27	–	–	–	1.02	5.22	16.1	–	–
1730	–	–	3.9	14.8	1.5	1.02	1.15	0.8	–	3.01
1731	–	–	2.73	1.55	4.8	1.04	0.04	–	–	–
1733	–	–	–	6.37	2.4	–	–	8.09	8.11	3.03
1735	1.75	–	1.5	5.24	2.1	4.5	3.52	11.1	–	18.28
1737	21.63	–	5.01	4.6	1.6	–	–	–	–	41.81
1739	5.5	–	–	6.87	–	–	–	–	–	18.43
1740	–	–	3.6	1.42	1	–	–	–	–	–
1741	–	–	1.5	0.8	3.9	–	–	–	15.18	23.76
1742	–	–	1.8	6.96	4.65	–	–	–		4.14
1743	–	–	2.8	–	–	–	–	–	32.79	24.31
1744	–	–	–	–	–	–	–	–	19.2	–
1745	–	12.93	–	–	–	–	–	–	–	17.34
1746	–	17.25	–	–	–	–	–	–	–	–

Source: *Arsattas* of years mentioned.

Table 2.2c Percentage of total cropped area under *jowar* cultivation

Year (CE)	Jalalpur	Wazirpur	Gazi ka Thana	Atela Bhabra	Piragpur	Pindayan	Mojpur	Harsana	Khohri	Pahari
1666	14.74	–	–	0.15	–	–	–	11.04	–	–
1689	18.07	–	–	–	–	–	–	–	–	–
1711	24.62	–	–	7.04	–	–	–	–	–	–
1714	–	25.83	–	–	–	–	6.44	–	7.2	–
1716	–	24.8	–	–	–	2.34	–	–	7.03	–
1718	11	–	–	–	–	–	–	–	–	–
1720	13.19	15.8	–	–	–	6	4.26	–	–	–
1722	–	17.14	–	–	–	24.73	29	5.5	–	–
1730	–	–	3.4	2.15	2.02	36.6	4	3.7	–	–
1731	–	–	0.6	0.56	3.1	–	–	–	–	1.07
1733	–	–	–	2.81	–	21.17	13.54	3.01	4.84	10.23
1735	11.56	–	1.09	1.18	2.08	16.32	6.1	1.03	–	19.91
1737	18.02	–	2.33	0.68	5.6	–	–	–	–	5.08
1740	8.58	–	6.2	1.33	8.5	–	–	–	–	–
1741	–	–	1.5	0.67	11.6	–	–	–	4.73	12.5
1742	–	–	1.65	0.75	5.6	–	–	–	–	5.73
1743	–	–	5.6	–	–	–	–	–	20.26	33.64
1744	–	–	–	–	–	–	–	–	2.6	–
1745	–	23.54	–	–	–	–	–	–	–	7.13
1746	–	13.55	–	–	–	–	–	–	–	–
1747	–	15.18	10	–	–	–	–	–	6.97	–
1748	–	14.81	3.4	–	–	–	–	–	–	–
1749	–	22.15	–	–	–	36.11	21.13	3.1	–	–

Source: *Arsattas* of years mentioned.

Table 2.2d Percentage of total cropped area under barley cultivation

Year (CE)	Jalalpur	Wazirpur	Gazi ka Thana	Atela Bhabra	Piragpur	Pindayan	Mojpur	Harsana	Khohri	Pahari
1666	3.51	–	–	22.57	–	–	–	9.35	–	–
1689	9.64	–	–	–	–	–	–	–	–	–
1711	2.14	–	–	22.86	–	–	–	–	–	–
1713	–	–	–	–	–	–	13.18	–	4.7	–
1714	–	17.9	–	–	–	–	–	–	–	–
1716	–	13.22	–	–	–	–	–	–	2.16	
1718	7.67	23.49	–	–	–	51.56	–	–	–	–
1720	16.03	11.76	–	–	–	29.91	–	46.6	–	–
1722	–	12.52	–	–	–	–	5.72	15.1	–	–
1730	–	–	18.8	21.85	30.8	3.12	5.75	11.5	–	–
1731	–	–	39.4	33.01	25.7	3.58	–	15.3	1.2	28.57
1733	–	–	–	27.97	30.9	3.62	7.67	–	–	1.8
1735	7	–	18	–	23.4	5.15	7.18	10.9	–	0.98
1737	4.52	–	18	32.81	38.1	–	–	–	–	0.75
1739	7.69	–	–	–	–	–	–	–	–	14.12
1740	–	–	13.9	36.76	28.1	–	–	–	–	0.42
1741	–	–	19.9	4.41	45.7	–	–	–	1.62	3.27
1742	–	–	25	44.84	36.2	–	–	–	–	3.94
1743	–	–	24.1	–	–	–	–	–	5.18	4.25
1744	–	–	–	–	–	–	–	–	5.74	–
1745	–	19.97	–	–	–	–	–	–	–	2.68

(*Cont'd*)

Table 2.2d *(Cont'd)*

Year (CE)	Jalalpur	Wazirpur	Gazi ka Thana	Atela Bhabra	Piragpur	Pindayan	Mojpur	Harsana	Khohri	Pahari
1746	–	27.94	–	–	–	–	–	–	–	–
1747	–	15.81	20.6	–	–	–	–	–	–	–
1748	–	10.69	–	–	–	–	–	–	–	–
1749	–	9.45	18.6	–	–	4.52	10.46	16	1.68	–

Source: *Arsattas* of years mentioned.

Table 2.2e Percentage of total cropped area under gram cultivation

Year (CE)	Jalalpur	Wazirpur	Gazi ka Thana	Atela Bhabra	Piragpur	Pindayan	Mojpur	Harsana	Khohri	Pahari
1666	18.25	–	–	0.45	–	–	–	7.5	–	–
1689	21.69	–	–	–	–	–	–	–	–	–
1691	22.01	–	–	–	–	–	–	–	–	–
1711	15.34	–	–	–	–	–	–	–	–	–
1713	–	–	–	–	–	–	1.37	–	3.72	–
1714	–	7.07	–	–	–	–	–	–	–	–
1716	–	16.24	–	–	–	–	–	–	9.87	–
1718	0.64	3.85	–	–	–	–	–	–	–	–
1720	2.54	1.51	–	–	–	–	–	–	–	–
1722	–	5.29	–	–	–	0.92	–	2.2	–	–
1730	–	–	8.3	–	13.3	8.66	3.06	9.4	–	–
1731	–	–	–	–	–	–	14.03	8.8	–	13.16
1733	–	–	–	1.05	8.06	10.49	–	11.6	–	10.74
1735	18.2	–	6.5	0.47	8.2	25.57	15.9	–	7.98	–
1737	–	–	–	–	0.01	–	20.5	–	–	4.72
1739	17.08	–	–	0.09	–	–	–	–	–	–
1740	–	–	1	2.06	5.85	–	–	–	–	13
1741	–	–	1	–	2.3	–	–	–	11.89	7.98
1742	–	–	0.5	–	–	–	–	–	–	–
1743	–	–	0.1	0.02	0.03	–	–	–	–	2.55

(Cont'd)

Table 2.2e *(Cont'd)*

Year (CE)	Jalalpur	Wazirpur	Gazi ka Thana	Atela Bhabra	Piragpur	Pindayan	Mojpur	Harsana	Khohri	Pahari
1744	–	–	–	–	–	–	–	–	13.46	–
1745	–	7.27	–	–	–	–	–	–	–	26.7
1746	–	2.03	–	–	–	–	–	–	–	–
1747	–	17.67	0.2	–	–	–	–	–	8.91	–
1748	–	6.8	1.48	–	–	–	–	–	–	–
1749	–	9.04	–	–	–	1.53	1.92	–	–	–

Source: *Arsattas* of years mentioned.

Table 2.2f Percentage of total cropped area under *urad* cultivation

Year (CE)	Jalalpur	Wazirpur	Gazi ka Thana	Atela Bhabra	Piragpur	Pindayan	Mojpur	Harsana	Khohri	Pahari
1666	1.75	–	–	–	–	–	–	1.34	–	–
1689	3.61	–	–	–	–	–	–	–	–	–
1691	0.96	–	–	–	–	–	–	–	–	–
1711	2.83	–	–	–	–	–	–	–	–	–
1713	–	–	–	–	–	–	–	–	7.27	–
1714	–	1.77	–	–	–	–	–	–	–	–
1716	–	6.24	–	–	–	–	–	–	17.99	–
1718	0.67	0.99	–	–	–	–	–	–	–	–
1720	1.68	1.1	–	–	–	1.7	0.34	–	–	–
1722	–	2.24	–	–	–	–	4.4	2	–	–
1730	–	–	4.2	–	0.1	0.3	–	–	–	–
1731	–	–	0.4	–	0.2	–	0.1	–	–	2.2
1733	–	–	–	–	–	–	–	–	2.6	–
1735	4.8	–	1.21	–	0.2	–	–	–	–	0.47
1737	2.42	–	1.7	–	–	–	–	–	–	3.21
1739	1.76	–	–	–	–	–	–	–	–	10.73
1740	–	–	3.4	–	–	–	–	–	–	–
1741	–	–	1.6	–	–	–	–	–	3.63	2.8
1742	–	–	0.82	–	0.5	–	–	–		1.58
1743	–	–	2.4	–	–	–	–	–	0.57	1.64

(*Cont'd*)

Table 2.2f (*Cont'd*)

Year (CE)	Jalalpur	Wazirpur	Gazi ka Thana	Atela Bhabra	Piragpur	Pindayan	Mojpur	Harsana	Khohri	Pahari
1744	–	–	1.6	–	–	–	–	–	0.44	–
1745	–	0.3	–	–	0.2	–	–	–	–	3
1746	–	0.3	–	–	–	–	–	–	–	–
1747	–	0.19	–	–	–	–	–	–	2.51	–
1748	–	0.2	2.9	–	–	–	–	–	–	–
1749	–	–	–	–	–	–	–	–	–	–

Source: *Arsattas* of years mentioned.

Table 2.2g Percentage of total cropped area under *moth* cultivation

Year (CE)	Jalalpur	Wazirpur	Gazi ka Thana	Atela Bhabra	Piragpur	Pindayan	Mojpur	Harsana	Khohri	Fahari
1689	27.71	–	–	–	–	–	–	–	–	–
1691	14.9	–	–	–	–	–	–	–	–	–
1711	16.9	–	–	5.6	–	–	–	–	–	–
1713	–	–	–	–	–	–	11.48	–	9.16	–
1714	–	10.38	–	–	–	–	–	–		–
1716	–	5.67	–	–	–	–	–	–	9.46	–
1718	1.25	10.63	–	–	–	–	–	–	–	–
1720	3.21	22.89	–	–	–	–	0.68	–	–	–
1722	–	18.76	–	–	–	–	–	–	–	–
1730	–	–	3	11.96	5.7	–	15.54	2.21	–	–
1731	–	–	0.4	–	–	–	–	–	–	0.48
1733	–	–	–	0.49	5.6	–	–	–	16.21	–
1735	11.65	–	1.15	6.16	7.3	–	2.9	–	–	6.21
1737	6.83	–	1.7	1.64	9.2	–	–	–	–	24.17
1739	4.34	–	–	–	0.2	–	–	–	–	–
1740	–	–	4.3	4.73	0.2	–	–	–	19.32	34.13
1741	–	–	1.4	–	9.7	–	–	–	–	20.16
1742	–	–	0.5	–	6.1	–	–	–	–	–
1743	–	5.22	2.7	1.87	–	–	–	–	12.84	4.5
1744	–	9.82	–	1.55	–	–	–	–	9.72	1.51

(*Cont'd*)

Table 2.2g *(Cont'd)*

Year (CE)	Jalalpur	Wazirpur	Gazi ka Thana	Atela Bhabra	Piragpur	Pindayan	Mojpur	Harsana	Khohri	Pahari
1745	–	6.74	–	–	–	–	–	–	–	–
1746	–	8.05	–	–	–	–	–	–	–	–
1747	–	–	4.1	–	–	–	–	–	21.94	–
1748	–	–	4	–	–	–	–	–	–	–
1749	–	9.27	–	–	–	–	6.4	–	–	–

Source: *Arsattas* of years mentioned.

Table 2.2h Percentage of total cropped area under cultivation of other food crops (*gojaro, gochani, bejhari, mandwa, kodo, rolo, kuri-varti*)

Year (CE)	Jalalpur	Wazirpur	Gazi ka Thana	Atela Bhabra	Piragpur	Pindayan	Mojpur	Harsana	Khohri	Pahari
1666	5.25	–	–	7.36	–	–	–	5.2	–	–
1689	6	–	–	–	–	–	–	–	–	–
1691	15.06	–	–	–	–	–	–	–	–	–
1711	9.7	–	–	6.9	–	–	–	–	–	–
1714	–	7.18	–	–	–	–	40.8	–	24.52	–
1716	–	8.08	–	–	–	17.9	–	–	–	–
1718	46.93	7.12	–	–	–	–	–	–	29	–
1720	32.3	9.5	–	–	–	15.3	44.1	4.1	–	–
1722	–	5.66	–	–	–	11.8	12.3	15.4	–	–
1727	–	–	–	26.8	–	–	–	–	–	–
1729	–	–	–	–	–	15.4	–	–	–	–
1730	–	–	34.8	23.45	15.8	16.8	18.4	11	–	24.11
1732	33	–	28.1	36.3	–	17.3	26.4	18.6	31.6	15.98
1735	–	–	34.8	35.4	24.4	13.7	31.9	13.9	–	7.76
1737	31.23	–	38.5	37.5	24.8	–	–	–	–	13.7
1740	40.26	–	41	22.4	25	–	–	–	–	7.34
1741	–	–	40.4	60.5	20	–	–	–	17	–
1742	–	–	37.9	14.5	3.9	–	–	–	–	12.41
1743	–	–	46.3	–	21	–	–	–	14.8	9.5

(*Cont'd*)

Table 2.2h *(Cont'd)*

Year (CE)	Jalalpur	Wazirpur	Gazi ka Thana	Atela Bhabra	Piragpur	Pindayan	Mojpur	Harsana	Khohri	Pahari
1744	–	–	–	–	–	–	–	–	17.8	–
1745	–	10.5	–	–	–	–	–	–	–	–
1746	–	6.3	–	–	–	–	–	–	–	16.32
1747	–	14.68	37.9	–	–	–	–	–	17	–
1748	–	21.9	37.1	–	–	–	–	–	–	–
1749	–	17.14	–	–	–	17.7	32	17.2	–	–

Source: Arsattas of years mentioned.

Table 2.2i Percentage of total cropped area under cotton cultivation

Year (CE)	Jalalpur	Wazirpur	Gazi ka Thana	Atela Bhabra	Piragpur	Pindayan	Mojpur	Harsana	Khohri	Pahari
1666	18.6	–	–	0.44	–	–	–	5.35	–	–
1689	–	–	–	–	–	–	–	–	–	–
1691	3.04	–	–	–	–	–	–	–	–	–
1711	5.75	–	–	7.12	–	–	–	–	–	–
1714	–	1.21	–	–	–	–	10.14	–	5	–
1716	–	5.3	–	–	–	10.16	–	–	6.5	–
1718	6.58	7.91	–	–	–	–	–	–	–	–
1720	7.74	4.41	–	–	–	8	–	3.6	–	–
1722	–	2.58	–	–	–	18	14	3.6	–	–
1727	–	–	–	12.58	–	–	–	–	–	–
1730	–	–	9.3	16.15	5.6	15.3	17	8.3	–	–
1732	–	–	8.6	–	9.1	14.98	11.48	4.6	0.5	3.22
1735	4.1	–	4.9	13.43	7.5	–	–	3.3	–	0.094
1737	10	–	10.18	8.7	6.2	10.45	–	–	–	1.04
1740	5.5	–	5.43	4.97	3.1	–	–	–	–	4.1
1741	–	–	7.5	29.62	2.6	–	–	–	4.61	–
1742	–	–	11.14	–	5.2	–	–	–	–	4.67
1743	–	–	3.75	11.18	–	–	–	–	0.3	2.62
1744	–	–	–	–	–	–	–	–	1.02	–

(Cont'd)

Table 2.2i (*Cont'd*)

Year (CE)	Jalalpur	Wazirpur	Gazi ka Thana	Atela Bhabra	Piragpur	Pindayan	Mojpur	Harsana	Khohri	Pahari
1745	–	1.93	–	–	–	–	–	–	–	0.15
1746	–	7.4	–	–	–	–	–	–	–	–
1747	–	6.6	7.37	–	–	–	–	–	1.3	–
1748	–	8.3	–	–	–	–	–	–	–	–
1749	–	4.5	10.52	–	–	8.52	6.44	2.6	–	–

Source: *Arsattas* of years mentioned.

Table 2.2j Percentage of total cropped area under sugarcane cultivation

Year (CE)	Jalalpur	Wazirpur	Gazi ka Thana	Atela Bhabra	Piragpur	Pindayan	Mojpur	Harsana	Khohri	Pahari
1666	–	–	–	–	–	–	–	–	–	–
1689	–	–	–	–	–	–	–	–	–	–
1791	–	–	–	–	–	–	–	–	–	–
1711	0.2	–	–	–	–	–	–	–	–	–
1714	–	3.54	–	–	–	–	1.1	–	–	–
1716	–	2.79	–	–	–	7.81	–	–	–	–
1718	0.6	2.12	–	–	–	–	–	–	–	–
1720	0.71	4.41	–	–	–	–	–	–	–	–
1722	–	2.58	–	0.34	–	3.11	–	0.2	–	–
1727	–	–	–	–	–	–	–	–	–	–
1730	–	–	14.63	0.16	–	3.48	2.17	0.3	–	–
1732	–	–	8.6	–	–	–	1.63	0.32	–	–
1733	–	–	–	0.18	–	3	–	0.11	–	–
1734	–	–	–	0.24	–	2	–	–	–	–
1735	–	–	7.3	–	–	–	0.55	–	0.82	1.59
1737	0.65	–	12.42	0.27	–	–	–	–	–	–
1740	0.12	–	8.02	0.24	–	–	–	–	–	–
1741	–	–	13.43	–	–	–	–	–	1.16	–
1742	–	–	5.35	–	–	–	–	–	0.2	–

(*Cont'd*)

Table 2.2j *(Cont'd)*

Year (CE)	Jalalpur	Wazirpur	Gazi ka Thana	Atela Bhabra	Piragpur	Pindayan	Mojpur	Harsana	Khohri	Pahari
1743	–	–	4.36	–	–	–	–	–	0.23	0.12
1744	–	–	–	–	–	–	–	–	–	–
1745	–	1.63	–	–	–	–	–	–	–	–
1746	–	5.94	4.24	–	–	–	–	–	–	–
1748	–	1.49	–	–	–	–	–	–	1.32	–
1749	–	2.99	6.12	0.43	–	–	–	–	–	–

Source: *Arsattas* of years mentioned.

Table 2.2k Percentage of total cropped area under indigo cultivation

Year (CE)	Jalalpur	Wazirpur	Gazi ka Thana	Atela Bhabra	Piragpur	Pindayan	Mojpur	Harsana	Khohri	Pahari
1666	–	–	–	–	–	–	–	–	–	–
1689	–	–	–	–	–	–	–	–	–	–
1691	–	–	–	–	–	–	–	–	–	–
1711	–	–	–	–	–	–	–	–	–	–
1714	–	0.26	–	–	–	–	–	–	–	–
1716	–	–	–	–	–	–	–	–	1.9	
1718	–	0.48	–	–	–	–	–	–	–	–
1720	–	1.54	–	–	–	–	–	–	–	–
1722	–	0.59	–	–	–	–	–	–	–	–
1730	–	–	–	–	–	–	–	–	–	–
1732	–	–	–	–	–	–	–	–	1.63	3.65
1735	–	–	–	–	–	–	–	–	–	–
1737	–	–	–	–	–	–	–	–	–	–
1740	–	–	–	–	–	–	–	–	–	–
1741	–	–	–	–	–	–	–	–	1.7	–
1742	–	–	–	–	–	–	–	–	–	0.2
1743	–	–	–	–	–	–	–	–	1.13	0.6
1744	–	–	–	–	–	–	–	–	0.76	–
1745	–	0.38	–	–	–	–	–	–	–	–
1746	–	1.34	–	–	–	–	–	–	–	–

(Cont'd)

Table 2.2k *(Cont'd)*

Year (CE)	Jalalpur	Wazirpur	Gazi ka Thana	Atela Bhabra	Piragpur	Pindayan	Mojpur	Harsana	Khohri	Pahari
1747	–	0.68	–	–	–	–	–	–	–	–
1748	–	1.1	–	–	–	–	–	–	–	–
1749	–	0.88	–	–	–	–	–	–	–	–
1750	–	–	–	–	–	–	–	–	–	–

Source: Arsattas of years mentioned.

Table 2.2l Percentage of total cropped area under *til* cultivation

Year (CE)	Jalalpur	Wazirpur	Gazi ka Thana	Atela Bhabra	Piragpur	Pindayan	Mojpur	Harsana	Khohri	Pahari
1666	4.21	–	–	0.29	–	–	–	0.38	–	–
1689	3.61	–	–	–	–	–	–	–	–	–
1691	1.12	–	–	–	–	–	–	–	–	–
1711	–	–	–	0.15	–	–	–	–	–	–
1714	4.52	0.12	–	–	–	–	0.48	–	0.6	–
1716	–	0.16	–	–	–	0.8	1.28	–	0.22	–
1718	0.45	2.48	–	–	–	–	–	–	–	–
1720	0.37	0.93	–	–	–	2.56	–	0.2	–	–
1722	–	1.22	–	–	–	–	4.22	1	–	–
1727	–	–	–	0.06	–	10.35	–	–	–	–
1730	–	–	0.17	0.6	0.02	3.65	1.07	4.1	–	0.38
1732	–	–	0.4	0.03	0.02	1.35	0.92	–	1.15	–
1735	2.8	–	0.02	0.3	0.03	1.09	–	0.6	–	0.84
1737	0.77	–	0.5	0.03	0.03	–	–	–	–	0.01
1740	0.87	–	0.17	0.03	0.2	–	–	–	0.76	1.13
1741	–	–	0.26	0.12	0.11	–	–	–	–	0.99
1742	–	–	0.29	0.13	0.04	–	–	–	0.2	–
1743	–	–	0.39	0.12	0.06	–	–	–	0.7	4.74
1744	–	–	–	–	–	–	–	–	–	2.72
1745	–	1.56	–	–	–	–	–	–	–	–

(Cont'd)

Table 2.21 *(Cont'd)*

Year (CE)	Jalalpur	Wazirpur	Gazi ka Thana	Atela Bhabra	Piragpur	Pindayan	Mojpur	Harsana	Khohri	Pahari
1746	–	1.95	1.01	–	–	–	–	–	–	–
1747	–	2.22	–	–	–	–	–	–	–	–
1748	–	1.11	0.45	–	–	–	–	–	–	–
1749	–	6.24	–	–	–	4.68	0.15	–	–	–

Source: Arsattas of years mentioned.

Table 2.2m Percentage of total cropped area under cultivation of other cash crops

Year (CE)	Jalalpur	Wazirpur	Gazi ka Thana	Atela Bhabra	Piragpur	Pindayan	Mojpur	Harsana	Khohri	Pahari
1666	1.75	–	–	–	–	–	–	0.5	–	–
1689	1.2	–	–	–	–	–	–	–	–	–
1691	4.64	–	–	6	–	–	–	–	–	–
1711	2.1	–	–	–	–	–	–	–	–	–
1714	–	0.24	–	–	–	–	1.5	–	3.57	–
1716	–	1.17	–	–	–	8.5	–	–	0.5	–
1718	4	2	–	–	–	–	–	–	–	–
1720	3.66	0.21	–	–	–	1.3	0.9	0.8	–	–
1722	–	1.11	–	–	–	1.2	0.8	0.8	–	–
1729	–	–	–	5.3	–	2.3	–	–	–	–
1730	–	–	2.2	–	6.8	–	–	30.7	–	8.2
1732	–	–	7.2	4	2.4	–	9.3	24.7	2.65	–
1735	2.87	–	2.9	4.57	5.2	11	5.4	32.6	–	4.2
1737	2.64	–	4.2	5.1	5	–	–	–	–	–
1740	4.15	–	1.4	5.6	7.4	–	–	–	–	11.29
1741	–	–	3.1	–	7.6	–	–	–	3.3	–
1742	–	–	–	7.3	7.2	–	–	–	–	2.36
1743	–	–	4.4	–	3.5	–	–	–	4.8	2.37
1744	–	–	–	–	8.3	–	–	–	–	5.91

(Cont'd)

Table 2.2m (*Cont'd*)

Year (CE)	Jalalpur	Wazirpur	Gazi ka Thana	Atela Bhabra	Piragpur	Pindayan	Mojpur	Harsana	Khohri	Pahari
1745	–	1.52	–	–	–	–	–	–	1.14	–
1746	–	1.25	–	–	–	–	–	–	–	–
1747	–	0.74	4	–	–	–	–	–	–	–
1748	–	0.5	5	–	–	–	–	–	–	–
1749	–	0.23	–	–	–	11.6	4.2	29.8	–	–

Source: *Arsattas* of years mentioned.

by *urad* and *moong*. Actually the cultivation of pulses was determined by the nature of the soil. The cultivation of mixed food crops such as *gojaro*, *gochani*, and *bejhari*, as well as other inferior food crops such as *kuri varti*, *ralo*, *kodon*, and *mandwa* also covered a sizeable percentage of the total cropped area, particularly in the *parganas* of Gazi ka Thana, Jalalpur, Atela Bhabra, and Mojpur.

Among cash crops, cotton was grown not only in the 10 *parganas* studied, but also in the *parganas* of Tijara *sarkar*, according to the British settlement report of Gurgaon district. Sugarcane, though grown in all the 10 *parganas* under study, was not raised in all the *parganas* of Mewat. Indigo, too, was not cultivated in all the *parganas*; the *Ain-i-Akbari* reports indigo cultivation in the *parganas* Kotla, Umara Umari, Ujina, Sakaras, Pinganwa, and Firozpur Jhirka of Tijara *sarkar*.[42]

The figures for the area under the cultivation of *kharif* and *rabi* crops in five *parganas* according to the *arsattas* (see Tables 2.3a–2.3i) show that the area under *rabi* crops was relatively quite less than that under *kharif* crops in all *parganas* except *pargana* Piragpur. This was due to various interrelated factors. The climatic conditions suitable for raising the crops of both harvests were/are different. The *kharif* crops were/are mainly rain-dependent or monsoon-oriented, while the *rabi* crops were winter-oriented and required artificial irrigation, seeds, plough, fertilizers, and bullocks—inputs that the rich peasants could afford. Therefore, it was not possible for poor peasants to grow *rabi* crops. Moreover, the intensification of *bhomia* revolts during the period, perhaps, caused a decline in the area under *rabi* crops. Notwithstanding this, as Tables 2.3d, 2.3f, and 2.4 show, the *rabi* crops were grown relatively in a larger area in *parganas* Piragpur and Atela Bhabra. Geographically, these two *parganas* were/are located in the plains where fertile land and availability of wells for irrigation supported the cultivation of *rabi* crops.

A sharp economic differentiation between the rich or privileged and ordinary peasants within the same village was reflected in disparities in the size of their landholdings, crops raised by them, and the share of produce retained by them—disparities that the *arsattas* amply bear out and Tables 2.5a–2.5d indicate.

[42] Abul-Fazl, *The Ain-i-Akbari*, vol. 2, 78, 103.

Table 2.3a Area under cultivation of *kharif* and *rabi* crops in *pargana* Pindayan

Kharif crops		*Rabi* crops	
Year (CE)	*Bighas*	Year (CE)	*Bighas*
1715	115	1715	–
1717	36	1717	92
1720	41	1717	76
1722	1,022	1722	70
1729	1,991	1729	1,034
1730	4,614	1730	1,366
1732	4,084	1732	1,216
1735	3,004	1735	2,203
1749	2,191	1749	282
Total	**17,098**		**6,339**

Source: *Arsattas* of years mentioned.

Table 2.3b Area under cultivation of *kharif* and *rabi* crops in *pargana* Mojpur

Kharif crops		*Rabi* crops	
Year (CE)	*Bighas*	Year (CE)	*Bighas*
1690	–	1690	567
1713	3,702	1713	1,395
1720	1,168	1720	07
1722	2,716	1722	482
1730	4,112	1730	2,740
1732	4,685	1732	2,738
1735	3,850	1735	3,194
1749	4,219	1749	1,106
Total	**24,452**		**12,229**

Source: *Arsattas* of years mentioned.

It can be observed from the Tables 2.5a and 2.5b that a large proportion of the area under cultivation was controlled by the richer sections of the rural society. On the contrary, ordinary peasants, who constituted the majority of the rural community, occupied a small proportion of the area under cultivation. In *pargana* Mojpur

Table 2.3c Area under cultivation of *kharif* and *rabi* crops in *pargana* Pahari

Kharif crops		*Rabi* crops	
Year (CE)	*Bighas*	Year (CE)	*Bighas*
1716	2,781	–	–
1724	24	–	–
1731	719	1731	1,143
1733	1,087	1733	300
1734	2,436	1734	2,447
1735	11,394	1735	2,157
1737	130	1737	47
1739	6,379	1739	1,197
1741	2,016	1741	703
1742	469	1742	38
1743	1,334	1743	310
1745	931	1745	1,088
1747	862	1747	75
Total	**30,562**		**9,505**

Source: *Arsattas* of years mentioned.

Table 2.3d Area under cultivation of *kharif* and *rabi* crops in *pargana* Atela Bhabra

Kharif crops		*Rabi* crops	
Year (CE)	*Bighas*	Year (CE)	*Bighas*
1664	470	1664	208
1711	802	1711	519
1712	868	1712	–
1728	2,250	1728	953
1730	2,214	1730	2,730
1731	1,839	1731	1,735
1733	1,729	1733	1,507
1734	2,126	1734	1,268
1736	1,393	1736	1,237
1737	1,449	1737	1,849
1740	1,074	1740	2,226
1741	701	1741	48
1742	567	1742	1,043
Total	**17,482**		**15,323**

Source: *Arsattas* of years mentioned.

Table 2.3e Area under cultivation of *kharif* and *rabi* crops in *pargana* Wazirpur

Kharif crops		*Rabi* crops	
Year (CE)	*Bighas*	Year (CE)	*Bighas*
1712	456	–	–
1714	3,692	1714	2,756
1716	1,305	1716	884
1717	2,417	1717	1,742
1720	2,787	1720	861
1722	3,552	1722	1,209
1725	6,269	–	–
1729	4,516	–	–
1745	5,946	1745	4,606
1746	2,433	1746	1,457
1747	4,695	1747	3,155
1748	4,203	1748	1,548
1749	5,152	1749	1,566
Total	**47,423**		**19,784**

Source: *Arsattas* of years mentioned.

Table 2.3f Area under cultivation of *kharif* and *rabi* crops in *pargana* Piragpur

Kharif crops		*Rabi* crops	
Year (CE)	*Bighas*	Year (CE)	*Bighas*
1725	156	1730	3,794
1728	2,313	1732	3,006
1730	1,752	1734	1,941
1732	2,740	1735	3,350
1734	1,558	1736	2,610
1735	2,423	1737	2,922
1736	1,732	1740	2,256
1737	1,313	1741	2,051
1740	1,523	1742	1,900
1741	750	–	–
1742	1,242	–	–
Total	**17,502**		**23,830**

Source: *Arsattas* of years mentioned.

Table 2.3g Area under cultivation of *kharif* and *rabi* crops in *pargana* Jalalpur

Kharif crops		*Rabi* crops	
Year (CE)	*Bighas*	Year (CE)	*Bighas*
1689	52	1689	31
1691	239	1689	385
1711	4,208	1709	186
1713	–	1711	1,165
1716	1,811	1713	891
1718	2,684	1718	433
1720	–	1720	725
1723	2,568	1735	374
1735	828	–	–
1737	5,990	1737	509
1739	3,268	1739	1,685
Total	**21,248**		**6,384**

Source: *Arsattas* of years mentioned.

Table 2.3h Area under cultivation of *kharif* and *rabi* crops in *pargana* Gazi ka Thana

Kharif crops		*Rabi* crops	
Year (CE)	*Bighas*	Year (CE)	*Bighas*
1730	15,359	1730	5,885
1731	8,008	1731	8,198
1734	16,304	–	–
1735	10,783	1735	6,712
1737	17,995	1737	6,859
1740	8,610	1740	3,462
1741	13,189	1741	6,880
1742	10,057	1742	6,959
1743	13,268	1743	6,797
1747	10,525	1747	4,282
1748	8,326	1748	3,251
Total	**132,424**		**59,280**

Source: *Arsattas* of years mentioned.

Table 2.3i Area under cultivation of *kharif* and *rabi* crops in *pargana* Khohri

Kharif crops		*Rabi* crops	
Year (CE)	*Bighas*	Year (CE)	*Bighas*
1664	98,746	–	–
1666	55,739	1712	9,061
1712	5,827	1713	2,637
1713	5,827	–	–
1716	13,453	1716	5,028
1727	47,792	1727	32,909
1728	11,955	–	–
1733	18,381	1733	9,357
1741	15,122	1741	8,154
1743	15,460	1743	3,256
1744	9,195	1744	12,825
1747	11,841	1747	5,460
Total	**309,338**		**88,687**

Source: *Arsattas* of years mentioned.

(Table 2.5c) during the *rabi* season the total area under cultivation was 1,263 *bighas*, out of which 1,029 *bighas* and 234 *bighas*, that is, 81.47 and 18.52 per cent, were occupied by the ordinary and rich peasants respectively. The ordinary peasants, despite being more numerous, could not compete with the relatively microscopic richer section in terms of the size of individual landholdings. Moreover, there was a vast difference in the cropping pattern adopted by the richer and the poorer strata of the peasantry. The cropping pattern on the holdings of poor peasants was dominated by food crops primarily grown to meet their subsistence requirements, whereas the richer sections devoted a large proportion of their holdings to the cultivation of cash crops and superior food crops. However, this is not to suggest that the underprivileged peasants did not cultivate cash crops. In the *kharif* season, the total area under cultivation in *pargana* Mojpur was 1,810 *bighas*, out of which 752 *bighas* and 958 *bighas* were cultivated by the ordinary and rich peasants respectively.[43] In *pargana* Pahari, in 1745,

43 *Arsatta, pargana* Mojpur, VS 1771/1714 CE.

Table 2.4 *Mal-o-jihat* from *kharif* and *rabi* crops in *pargana* Atela Bhabra, Alwar *sarkar*, *suba* Akbarabad

Year (CE)	*Mal-o-jihat*	*Kharif*	*Rabi*
1649	Rs 9,870, 5 *annas*	Rs 582, 2 *annas*	Rs 9,288, 3 *annas*
1650	Rs 15,383, 3 *annas*	Rs 8,403	Rs 6,980, 3 *annas*
1651	Rs 13,386, 8 *annas*	Rs 7,513	Rs 5,873, 8 *annas*
1652	Rs 13,784	Rs 8,801, 8 *annas*	Rs 4,982, 8 *annas*
1653	Rs 6,922	Rs 689	Rs 5,933
1654	Rs 14,470, 8 *annas*	Rs 8,841, 8 *annas*	Rs 5,629
1655	Rs 12,029, 4 *annas*	Rs 5,799, 4 *annas*	Rs 6,230
1656	Rs 10,801, 3 *annas*	Rs 5,913, 4 *annas*	Rs 4,887, 15 *annas*
1657	Rs 12,549, 8 *annas*	Rs 6,426	Rs 6,123, 8 *annas*
1658	Rs 13,943, 12 *annas*	Rs 3,086	Rs 10,857, 12 *annas*
1659	Rs 18,501	Rs 10,146	Rs 8,355
1660	Rs 16,897	Rs 7,016	Rs 9,881
1661	Rs 13,799, 8 *annas*	Rs 7,299, 8 *annas*	Rs 6,500
1662	Rs 13,151, 12 *annas*	Rs 6,214, 4 *annas*	Rs 6,937, 8 *annas*
1663	Rs 1,781, 1 *annas*	Rs 894, 11 *annas*	Rs 9,886, 6 *annas*
1700	Rs 9,493, 10 *annas*	Rs 3,695	Rs 5,798, 10 *annas*
1701	Rs 10,944, 1 paise	Rs 4,794, 9 *annas* and 3 paise	Rs 6,149, 6 *annas* and 2 paise
1702	Rs 9,741, 9 *annas* and 3 paise	Rs 3,948, 10 *annas* and 2 paise	Rs 5,792, 15 *annas* and 1 paise
1703	Rs 7,335, 2 *annas* and 2 paise	Rs 2,634, 4 *annas* and 2 paise	Rs 4,700, 14 *annas*
1704	Rs 8,478, 15 *annas*	Rs 4,118, 2 *annas*	Rs 4,358, 13 *annas*
1705	Rs 11,577, 8 *annas*	Rs 5,173, 5 *annas*	Rs 6,404, 3 *annas*
1706	Rs 16,922, 5 *annas*	Rs 7,069, 11 *annas*	Rs 9,852, 10 *annas*
1707	Rs 5,547, 6 *annas*	Rs 5,547, 6 *annas*	–
1708	Rs 7,964, 8 *annas* and 2 paise	Rs 2,982, 6 *annas*	Rs 4,982, 2 *annas* and 2 paise
1709	Rs 11,610, 6 *annas* and 2 paise	Rs 5,131, 12 *annas* and 2 paise	Rs 6,478, 10 *annas*

Source: *Taqsim pandrehsala arsatta*, *pargana* Atela Bhabra VS 1721/1664 CE; *Taqsim dehsala arsatta*, *pargana* Atela Bhabra, VS 1767/1710 CE.

Note: Total no. of villages: 17; total *reqba* (area): 61,180 *bighas*; total uncultivable area: 21,380 *bighas*; total cultivable area: 39,800 *bighas*.

Table 2.5a Percentage of area under *kharif* and *rabi* crops in *pargana* Atela Bhabra (1728 CE)

Kharif crops	Percentage of total area under gross cultivation			
	Ordinary peasants		Privileged peasants	
	Raiyat	*Mali*	*Patel*	Rajput
Cotton	21.99	–	36.78	41.18
Sugarcane	9.36	43.36	23.63	23.63
Maize	24.23	–	37.24	38.46
Kuri	32.00	–	31.80	36.18
Mandwa	34.58	–	35.00	30.32
Rabi crops				
Gajar	17.30	4.58	22.36	55.62
Kakari, baingan, onion	26.75	9.08	18.40	45.65
Cheena	29.97	–	–	70.00
Dodi	98.03	–	–	1.96

Source: *Arsatta, pargana* Atela Bhabra, VS 1785/1728 CE.

Table 2.5b Percentage of area under *kharif* and *rabi* crops in *pargana* Piragpur (1732 CE)

Kharif crops	Percentage of total area under gross cultivation			
	Ordinary peasants		Privileged peasants	
	Raiyat	Rajput	*Patel*	*Chaudhari*
Cotton	5.94	40.62	43.77	9.65
Maize	3.96	49.24	41.20	5.53
Mandwa	8.86	30.12	55.12	5.80
Kuri	7.79	36.10	48.79	7.27
Rabi crops				
Gajar	2.90	40.94	46.61	9.36
Cheena	–	72.89	27.00	–
Onion	–	84.37	15.62	–
Dodi	3.52	33.53	55.75	–

Source: *Arsatta, pargana* Piragpur, VS 1789/1732 CE.

Table 2.5c Percentage of area under *kharif* and *rabi* crops in *pargana* Mojpur (1714 CE)

Kharif crops	Percentage of total area under gross cultivation		
	Ordinary peasants	Privileged peasants	
	Raiyat	*Qanungo/Patel/Patwari*	Rajput
Kuri-varti	87.86	00.66	11.46
Kodi	0.34	12.78	86.88
Van (cotton)	28.93	54.67	16.37
Chola	92.24	7.75	–
Kaguni	77.78	22.20	–
Rabi crops			
Wheat	81.52	14.09	4.33
Barley	80.04	13.14	6.78
Gram	70.21	29.78	–
Sarson	84.36	4.42	11.20
Cheena	94.68	–	5.29

Source: *Arsatta*, *pargana* Mojpur, VS 1771/1714 CE.

Table 2.5d Percentage of area under *kharif* and *rabi* crops in *pargana* Wazirpur (1712 CE)

Kharif crops	Total area under gross cultivation	
	Ordinary peasants	Rich peasants
Ganna (sugarcane)	62.96	37.03
Kapas (cotton)	77.14	22.85
Jowar	83.20	16.79
Bajra	78.15	21.84
Moth	85.71	14.28
Til (oilseed)	75	25
Chola	100	–
Neel (indigo)	0.33	99.66
Mandwa	100	–

Source: *Arsatta*, *pargana* Wazirpur, VS 1769/1712 CE.

73.26 and 26.73 per cent of the area cultivated was controlled by the ordinary and rich peasants respectively. The area under cotton cultivation was 24 per cent of the total cropped area, out of which only 7 per cent belonged to the ordinary peasants.[44]

However, the extensive cultivation of expensive cash crops was, by and large, restricted to the holdings of the richer peasants. This was also the case with indigo cultivation. Out of 30 *bighas* devoted to indigo in a village of *pargana* Wazirpur, 29 *bighas* were cultivated by the richer peasants.[45] Despite the fact that the richer section of the peasantry was in an advantageous position vis-à-vis the small peasantry, evidence suggests that the system of agricultural production was dominated by the small peasantry. That the small peasants had meagre resources at their disposal is reflected in the pattern of distribution of plough units among individual cultivations. The unequal distribution of resources among individual peasants had repercussions on the cropping strategies followed on individual peasant holdings.

A preliminary analysis (see Table 2.6a) shows that in *pargana* Kotla the poor peasants, that is, those who had one ox each (half-a-plough), accounted for 18.6 per cent of the *asamis* (cultivators, revenue payers). Peasants who had one plough or two to three oxen (one-and-a-half plough), whom we may consider small peasants, formed the majority and together accounted for 65.31 per cent of the *asamis* (cultivators, revenue payers). Peasants who had more than two ploughs or four oxen each may be considered rich peasants. They were only 14 in number out of 2,645 *asamis*, and accounted for less than 1 per cent of the total number of *asamis*.[46] In *pargana* Pindayan (see Table 2.6b), the small peasants formed 90.72 per cent of the total number of *asamis*, while the rich peasants accounted for 7.97 per cent.[47] The picture for *pargana* Chalkaliyana (see Table 2.6c) was more or less the same, with the rich, middle, and small peasants, respectively, accounting for 6.24, 25.54, and 68.2 per cent of the total number of *asamis*.[48] It can thus be concluded that the poor peasants

44 *Arsatta, pargana* Pahari, vs 1802/1745 CE.

45 *Arsatta, pargana* Wazirpur, vs 1769/1712 CE.

46 *Yaddashti Hal Bail, pargana* Kotla, vs 1723/1666 CE.

47 *Yaddashti Hal Bail, pargana* Pindayan, vs 1786/1726 CE.

48 *Yaddashti Hal Bail, pargana* Chalkaliyana, vs 1721/1664 CE.

Table 2.6a Distribution of ploughs among individual peasants in *pargana* Kotla

Total no. of villages	=	94
Total no. of *asamis*	=	2,645
Total no. of ploughs available with these *asamis*	=	2,900

½ plough	held by	492 *asamis*	or	18.6	per cent of the total no. of *asamis*
1	"	1615	"	61.5	"
1 ½	"	101	"	3.81	"
2	"	423	"	15.99	"
3	"	14	"	0.55	"

Source: *Yaddashti Hal Bail*, *pargana* Kotla, vs 1723/1666 CE.

Table 2.6b Distribution of ploughs among individual peasants in *pargana* Pindayan

Total no. of villages	=	20
Total no. of *asamis*	=	388
Total no. of ploughs available with these *asamis*	=	386

½ plough	held by	5 *asamis*	or	1.28	per cent of the total no. of *asamis*
1	"	352	"	90.72	"
2	"	29	"	7.47	"
3.4	"	2	"	0.51	"

Source: *Yaddashti Hal Bail*, *pargana* Pindayan, vs 1783/1726 CE.

Table 2.6c Distribution of ploughs among individual peasants in *pargana* Chalkaliyana

Total no. of villages	=	100
Total no. of *asamis*	=	3,057
Total no. of plough available with these *asamis*	=	2,985 ½

½ plough	held by	781 *asamis*	or	25.54	per cent of the total *asamis*
1	"	2,073	"	67.81	"
1 ½	"	12	"	0.39	"
2	"	190	"	6.21	"
4	"	1	"	0.03	"

Source: *Yaddashti Hal Bail*, *pargana* Chalkaliyana, vs 1721/1664 CE.

having one bullock or half-a-plough and possibly very small landholdings constituted about 18–25 per cent of the total number of *asamis*. However, there are no references to peasants without any ploughs or oxen, that is, the landless and the village artisans.

The economic disparity among the cultivators had repercussions on the cultivation of different crops, as also the overall crop pattern in a particular *pargana*. The cultivation of superior crops, such as sugarcane, cotton, paddy (rice), and wheat which demanded larger investment in terms of manpower and irrigation facilities, was largely in the hands of rich cultivators who profited most out of the higher returns on these crops. In addition to the cultivation of cash crops, the rich peasants also extensively resorted to the cultivation of superior food crops. Thus, production on their holdings was generally much higher, in terms of both value of output and yield per unit of area. In contrast, the majority of *raiyati* or ordinary cultivators with meagre resources were more concerned about their subsistence. Such peasants were primarily dependent on *kharif* cultivation of millets and a few leguminous crops that were sold for fulfilling their limited cash requirements.

In order to show changes in the crop pattern, we have worked out the area under each crop for different years. The results in the case of the major cash and food crops are as follows.

The most important changes in the pattern of agricultural production in the *kharif* season was a decline in the cultivation of such cash crops as cotton, sugarcane, indigo, tobacco, hemp, and opium. Among the cash crops, cotton and sugarcane occupied an important place in the cropping pattern. *Til* (oilseed) was a quite significant crop in the region, but the area under its cultivation remained almost steady. The other cash crops, for example, hemp, opium, and tobacco, were also grown, but their cultivation was fairly restricted. The decline was more marked in the case of cotton, which was the chief cash crop. The percentage of the total cropped area under cotton cultivation declined from 10.14 to 6.44 per cent. However, the cultivation of sugarcane on the whole did not register any decline and remained fairly steady. It was not widespread, and practised only in *pargana* Gazi ka Thana where the area under it varied from 8.66 to 6.12 per cent of the total cropped area during the period of study. Rapid decline in indigo cultivation in the region during the period under study represents the most remarkable change in the crop pattern. During the 17th century, the indigo of Mewat was much in demand in the international market.[49] Its cultivation was quite widespread in the region up to the early 18th century, but declined in the course of the century. The decline seems to have been purely a local phenomenon, as there is no evidence for a corresponding decline in its cultivation in other indigo-producing regions of India.[50] In the case of food crops, the most significant change in the 17th century was a decline in the cultivation of coarse grains, such as *mandwa* and *kodon*, followed by that of pulses such as *moth*, *moong*, and *urad*. However, there was a corresponding increase in the cultivation of superior food crops, such as *bajra*, *jowar*, and paddy. *Makka* (maize) occupied an important place in the cropping pattern. However, if we take into account the overall trend in the case of maize cultivation, there is hardly any spectacular change. Inferior food crops such as *kuri-varti* were grown in all the *parganas* of the region, and their cultivation registered a marked increase. The spectacular decline in the cultivation of *moth*, which hitherto had been the most widely cultivated food crop, led to its gradual replacement by superior food crops such as *bajra*, *jowar*, *makka*, and paddy. This change seems to have been determined by the pattern of demand and improvement in irrigation facilities.

This trend is evident from the estimates made on the basis of changes in the percentage of revenue derived from each crop, and those made on the basis of the area under cultivation of different crops. The only noticeable change in the area under the cultivation of *rabi* crops was a marginal increase in the cultivation of wheat; mixed crops such as *gojaro*, *gochani*, and *bejhari*; pulses such as *arhar* (red gram) and *masoor* (lentil); and *sarson* (mustard) with a corresponding decline in the cultivation of barley. However, there was no significant change in the case of gram cultivation which remained more or less steady. Tobacco and opium were also grown as *rabi* crops, but their cultivation was fairly restricted in area. These changes are discernible in almost all the *parganas* of the region.

[49] Irfan Habib, *The Agrarian System of Mughal India 1556–1707*, 2nd rev. ed. (New Delhi: Oxford University Press, 1999), 73.

[50] Dharma Kumar and Meghnad Desai, eds, *The Cambridge Economic History of India*, vol. 2: *c.* 1757–*c.* 1970 (Cambridge: Cambridge University Press, 1982), 259, 338.

In conclusion, it may be stated that the natural and man-made factors caused immense setbacks to agricultural production in the region. However, the impact of diminishing returns from agriculture was felt differently by various segments of rural society. For the *jagirdars*, it became difficult to collect their due revenue, and they made frantic attempts to collect whatever revenue they could by resorting to arrangements such as *ijara*. The *bhomias* became more and more challenging towards the state and aggressive towards the peasantry. Not only did they endeavour to convert their temporary claims (sub-assignments) into larger *bhoms*, but also refused to pass on the collected revenue to the *jagirdars*. The *bhomias*, instead of protecting the peasants from the *jagirdars*, themselves began to oppress them with more vigour. Those superior elements (such as *patels*) who did not command control over military retainers seem to have been pushed down further. A large number of peasants who had enjoyed permanent tenures (*paltis*) earlier were reduced to being wandering peasants (*pahis*). Thus, while the uncertainties of revenue collection caused anxiety to the *jagirdars*, the unending problem of surviving at the bare subsistence level beset the life of the bulk of peasantry. The only beneficiaries of this agrarian turmoil were the *bhomias* and the *bohras* (moneylenders). The former caused the weakening of the state control in the area, and the latter further strengthened their grip on the peasantry.

3 SOCIAL FORMATION OF MEOS

FROM TRIBE TO CASTE

INDO-PERSIAN CHRONICLES AND MEO ORAL traditions inform us that before their peasantization, the Meos, settled in the Kala Pahad and other hills of the Aravali range, ravines, and dense forests in the Mewat region, belonged to various tribal groups and were engaged in cattle-lifting, raids, and robberies on traders and travellers, thereby becoming a great source of trouble to the people of Delhi and its neighbourhood. On account of their depredatory activities, they were commonly spoken of as 'Meo', the word being derived from 'mewas' which means a hiding place for robbers. The Aravali hills were thus home to a number of tribal communities who had to struggle a lot to eke out their living. But their geographical and social isolation enabled them to lead a life of relatively greater degree of social and political freedom.

I

Abdul Aziz has identified 12 rural sites on the high hills which were claimed by the Meo *pals* as the sites of their original settlements. Although all the 12 sites of the Meo *pals* now stand deserted and ruined,[1] what is more remarkable is a trend of continuity of settlements between the old and the new sites and the current existence of all the 12 settlements in the plains. The abandonment of the original sites in the hills and the subsequent occupation of new sites in the plains by the Meo *pals* indicate a massive migration of the Meo population from hills to plains. This is attested by the Jagga records and some Meo oral traditions.

The Jagga records[2] inform that the ancestors of the Deharwal Meos lived in the Kala Pahad and were known as 'Naths' or snake charmers. Owing to this perceived common ancestry, they considered (and still consider) the Naths as their kin. The ancestral villages of the Deharwal Meos were at Meoli (near Nuh) colonized by Mewa Singh, the head of 52 *khorei* (settlements) in the Kala Pahad. The name 'Dehrawal' was derived from Dehar which comprised the low-lying area near the Kotla Lake in the Nuh region. Another Meo group hailing from Shahbad (Tijara *sarkar*) had Sapen (snake charmer) as its *gotra*, identical to that of the Naths.

The folk tradition of the Landawat Meos—also known as Baghoria Meos after Baghore, the ancestral village of their *pal*—explains the circumstances in which they migrated from the Kala Pahad to the plains near Ramgarh *tehsil* in Alwar district. In course of their peasantization, they had to face a lot of difficulties in making the plains arable because the whole area was covered by thorny bushes and thick forests.

The Jagga records also locate the ancestral settlements of five *Jadonvamshi* Meo *pals*, namely Chhiraklot, Pundlot, Daimrot, Duhlot, and Nai, in the Kala Pahad region. Their main occupations were cattle rearing, cattle lifting, raids, and robberies. Folklore also considers these five Meo *pals* to be brethren or forming a fraternity; even today these *pals* prohibit intermarriage on account of their supposed kinship. According to a popular story of the origin of these *pals*, a local

[1] Abdul Aziz, 'Measurement of Agricultural Productivity: A Case Study of Mewat', unpublished PhD thesis, North Eastern Hill University, Shillong, 1981, 10–34.

[2] Jagga records, *pothi* no. 1, in personal possession of Jagdish, son of Shri Ghasi Ram Jagga, village Khuteta Kalan, *tehsil* Ramgarh, district Alwar, Rajasthan.

king, upon receiving numerous complaints against the robberies committed by these *pals*, sent his army to capture the leaders of these five 'rogue' groups. However, all the five escaped from the clutches of the army, in the guise of a juggler, a snake charmer, a drummer, a basket weaver, and a grass-cutter. Subsequently, they settled in the plains and took to farming. The juggler settled in the Lachhmangarh region of Alwar and founded a village called Kajhota which later came to be known as the ancestral village of the Daimrot *pal*. The snake charmer took to agriculture in the vicinity of Alwar and founded a village called Nimly which became the ancestral village of the Pundlot *pal*. The third Meo leader settled near Firozpur Jhirka and established the Chhiraklot *pal*. The fourth leader settled in the Ramgarh region of Alwar and became the founder of the Nai *pal*. The fifth one settled in the region between Nagar (Bharatpur) and Firozpur Jhirka and became the founder of the Duhlot *pal*.

The Jagga records indicate the peasantization of Meos between late 14th and early 16th centuries when the region was ruled by the Khanzadas.[3] During this period, many new Meo villages were established in the plains between Nuh–Firozpur Jhirka and Tijara regions. These new villages were in the vicinity of Kala Pahad. Geographically, the Meo villages fall into three divisions: (a) the area adjoining Kala Pahad comprising Nuh, Ferozpur Jhirka, Taoru, Punahana, Tijara, and Ramgarh; (b) Kishangarh, Lachhmangarh, and Rajgarh; and (c) Alwar, Kama, Deeg, and Pahari.

That their migration from hills to plains within Mewat continued up to late medieval period is evinced by the dispersal of members of the same *pal* in different areas. For instance, the Daimrot *pal* consists of 160 villages, divided into three clusters. Of these, the biggest cluster, consisting of 108 villages, was settled in Lachhmangarh *tehsil* (Alwar district); the second cluster of 40 villages, in the area between Firozpur Jhirka and Kama (Bharatpur district); and the third cluster of 12 villages, in the area near Punahana (Firozpur Jhirka *tehsil* of Gurgaon district). All these clusters had their own *chaudharis*. The Nai *pal*, too, underwent a similar process of dispersal. Originally settled between Ramgarh and Alwar, the *pal* split up into two clusters. The biggest one, consisting of 50 villages, settled to the west of

[3] Jagga records, *pothi* no. 1.

Ramgarh town, while the second cluster of 10 villages settled near Kama town (Bharatpur district). Though belonging to the same *pal*, they were separated by a distance of about 50 kilometres and had their own *chaudharis*. This phenomenon of villages of the same Meo *pal* settling down in different areas indicates that as the cultivable land might have become insufficient to support the rising population of a *pal*, some families of the *pal* migrated to plains in Mewat where they could find land sufficient for settlement and suitable for cultivation.

All Meo *pal*s underwent the concurrent processes of emigration, relocation, and peasantization. This is also implicit in a major shift in the way the Meos were described in the Indo-Persian court chronicles. The accounts of Meo raids and robberies in the Indo-Persian chroniclers of the early Sultanate period, such as those of Minhaj Siraj and Barani, are not found in the works of this genre from the late Sultanate period. After the 15th century, the Indo-Persian court chronicles, however, mention the non-payment of land revenue (*kharaj*) by the Meos, indicating that they had already become a settled agrarian peasant community by then. Their conflicts with the state on the issue of land revenue further intensified during the Mughal period.

Now the question that rises is: Under what circumstances the Meos were forced to migrate from the Aravali hills to the plains, and when and how did they transform themselves from a tribal to a peasant community? Going by the early Indo-Persian court chronicles, they might well have posed a serious law and order problem in the early days of the Delhi Sultanate, threatening the smooth conduct of trade and flow of commercial traffic through the Mewat region. However, a combination of several factors contributed to their peasantization, especially in the post-Tughlaq period. First, the rigorous military campaigns by the sultans of Delhi against them must have forced them to give up their 'lawless' activities. Second, the increasing Meo population in the Aravali hills must have caused a scarcity of resources. The massive clearing of forests in Mewat carried out by Balban must be viewed from this perspective. Barani reports that immediately after ascending the throne of Delhi, Balban tried to contain the Mewati menace. He 'employed himself in harrying the jungles and routing out the Mewatis'; he 'built a fort at Gopal-gir, and established several posts in the vicinity of the city, which he placed in the charge of Afghans, with assignments of land [for their maintenance]'.[4] Large-scale deforestation drive, construction of forts, appointment of Afghan soldiers, and introduction of a system of land assignments for their maintenance—all were accompanied by the attempts to create conditions conducive for the introduction of agriculture in Mewat. The first major initiative in this regard was the conversion of forest land into agricultural land.

However, more than the aforementioned factors, it was the formation of the state of Khanzadas (1390–1527), who had carved out a small principality at Kotla in the vicinity of Tijara in Mewat—a development that socio-economically transformed the Meo population.[5] The Khanzadas, who were Jadon Rajputs prior to their conversion to Islam, exercised considerable pressure on the Meos to abandon their predatory activities and take up cultivation in order to strengthen the economic base of the state through an assured means of state income from land revenue. The Khanzadas had the plains of Mewat brought under cultivation and seem to have pressurized the tribal communities living in the Aravali hills to take up agriculture. Not only is this borne out by the aforementioned folktale of the five *pals* who were forced to relocate to the plains and take up cultivation, but the Jagga records, too, reveal that in the early 15th century, five *pal* villages were founded in the *parganas* of Nuh, Firozpur-Jhirka, Ramgarh (Khilohra), and Lachhmangarh.[6] Significantly, the Tijara region where these five *pals* had settled was the epicentre of the Khanzada state in its early days. Being under tremendous state pressure to abandon their previous plundering activities, the Meos were hardly left with any alternative except shifting to agriculture. This is evident from one instance of Khanzada ruler Ahmad Khan Mewati sending his soldiers to arrest the Meos of Sonkh village on account of their non-payment of land revenue.[7] The early 16th-century historical ballad 'Hasan Khan ki Katha' mentions 12 Meo *pals* serving in the army of Hasan Khan

4 Barani, 'Tarikh-i-Firozshahi', in *History of India as Told by Its Own Historians*, vol. 3, 103–4.

5 See Chapter 1.

6 This region was situated in the vicinity of Kala Pahad.

7 *Bandhak* no. 12, *granthank* no. 13, Non-archival Records of Alwar State, Rajasthan State Archives, Bikaner.

Mewati,[8] who had fought against Babur in the Battle of Khanwa. This shows that by this time the Meos had not only become peasants but also turned into soldiers.

In the *Ain-i-Akbari*, Abul-Fazl mentions the zamindari rights of the Meos over many *parganas* of Mewat during Akbar's reign. In Tijara *sarkar*, out of a total of 18 *parganas*, the Meos exclusively held zamindari rights over 14 *parganas* and shared their zamindari rights over another four *parganas* with other castes like Khanzadas and Thathars.[9] In Alwar *sarkar*, out of a total of 43 *parganas*, they exclusively controlled five *parganas* and shared zamindari rights over another seven *parganas* with other castes such as Khanzadas, Jats, and Gujjars. The *Ain-i-Akbari*, however, does not mention the existence of any Meo zamindari in the rest 31 *parganas* of Alwar *sarkar*.[10] In Sahar *sarkar*, they did not have any *pargana* exclusively under their zamindari, but shared their zamindari rights over four out of seven *parganas* with other castes such as Jats, Thathars, and Gujjars.[11] That in the rest three *parganas* they did not have any zamindari rights at all shows that the process of peasantization of the Pahat Meos settled there remained slow during Akbar's reign. In Rewari *sarkar*, the two *parganas*, namely Taoru and Sohana, were part of Mewat, but had no Meo zamindari during Akbar's reign.[12] It may therefore be inferred that the peasantization of Meos in these *parganas* was not widespread enough to give rise to Meo zamindaris.

From the statistics of Meo zamindaris in Mewat, it may be concluded that the administrative integration of Mewat into the Mughal empire during Akbar's reign contributed significantly to the process of Meo peasantization. This process continued in the centuries following Akbar's reign, and by the second half of the 19th century, we come across a large number of Meo peasant households in the Alwar region. According to the census of 1872, out of the total 180,225

8 Narsingh Meo, 'Hasan Khan ki Katha', *Shodh Patrika*, vol. 4 (October–December) (Udaipur: Rajasthan Vidyapeeth, 1970), 53–62.

9 Abul-Fazl, *The Ain-i-Akbari*, vol. 2, 203–4.

10 Abul-Fazl, *The Ain-i-Akbari*, vol. 2, 202–3.

11 Abul-Fazl, *The Ain-i-Akbari*, vol. 2, 206.

12 Abul-Fazl, *The Ain-i-Akbari*, vol. 2, 298.

households in the Alwar state, the population of Meo peasant households was 94,546, accounting for more than half the population of the region[13]—a stark contrast to the situation during Akbar's reign, wherein the Meos did not have zamindaris in 31 out of 43 *parganas* of Alwar *sarkar*. We may, therefore, assume that the process of Meo peasantization in this *sarkar* intensified during the period between Akbar's death and the mid-19th century. This process was characterized by a prolonged struggle with nature whereby the Meos cleared the dense forests to render land arable and adopted plough technology for cultivation. Similarly, the Pahat Meos had come to occupy larger number of villages than any other caste in the *parganas* of Pahari, Kama, Nagar, and Kho-mujahid of Sahar *sarkar* by the second half of the 19th century.[14] A report of 1840s shows that the Meos held 47 out of 55 villages in *pargana* Taoru; and 47 out of 169 villages in *pargana* Sohana.[15] This indicates that the process of Meo peasantization in these *parganas* had gathered momentum in the period after Akbar's death. The following observation of the report's author and the first British Collector of Gurgaon district, A. Fraser, testifies to the growing reputation of the Meos as a peasant community:

> The Meos have been considered to be remarkable for their lawless and thieving propensities; but in these respects they are now less conspicuous than either Rangurs or Goojurs. I have not seen more beautiful cultivation in India than I have observed in Firozepoor, a purgunah exclusively Meo; and their attachment to the soil, a feeling beyond all others strong in India is in this race stronger than in most.[16]

Thus, the first phase of the process of Meo peasantization was more marked in Tijara *sarkar*, the core area of the Khanzada chiefdom. Later, the Meos settled in Alwar, Sahar, and Rewari *sarkars*. Thus, gradually the Meos were transformed from a tribal to a peasant community, organized through the *pal* system and other institutions

[13] P. W. Powlett, *Gazetteer of Ulwur* (London: Trubner & Co., 1878), 37.

[14] Cunningham, *Report of a Tour in Eastern Rajputana in 1882–83*, 24.

[15] A. Fraser, *Statistical Report of Zillah Gurgaon* (Lahore: n.p., 1846), Appendix C, p. xxi; Appendix P, p. cxxi.

[16] Fraser, *Statistical Report of Zillah Gurgaon*, 15.

of settled agrarian society. The Jagga caste played an important role in restructuring the Meo identity on the basis of Hindu *gotra* system which brought about significant changes in their social life. The names of the founders of Meo villages and the years of their establishment are mentioned in the Jagga records. These records indicate that the process of peasantization among the Meos was facilitated by the pre-existing *pal* system, since tribes belonging to a particular *pal* tended to occupy particular areas and establish villages there. For example, the ancestral villages, Kajhota and Doha, of the Daimrot and Duhlot *pals* were founded in 1423. Similarly, Neekach and Nimaly, the ancestral villages of the Nai, Chhiraklot, and Pundlot *pals*, were established in 1428 and 1458 respectively. According to the Jagga records, their *gotras*[17] were derived from the names of their chiefs who had founded their ancestral villages. For example, the name 'Chhiraklot' of a Meo *pal* and *gotra* is derived from that of its chief Chhirakan. Similarly, the Duhlot *pal* traces its name from that of its chief. Several *gotra* names, too, originated from the names of various chiefs, such as Duhal from Duhlot, Mangria from Mangraj, Besar from Besar Singh, Matiavat from Matia Singh, and Sugdhavat from Sughadh Singh. In Sahar *sarkar*, the *gotra* name of the Meos of Sakatpur, Khangavali, Baghola, and Meerpur villages is Bahmanavat. According to the Jagga records, the Meos of these villages were previously Brahmins, who, due to social insecurity, joined the Pahat *pal* and became part of the Meo community. It is significant that each Meo family has some *gotra* name or the other, but many of them were not originally part of the *pal* system. This suggests that the Meo social structure also extended beyond the confines of the *pal* system.

II

The terms *raiyati* or *asami* were synonymous and covered all categories of cultivators paying land revenue to the state.[18] There have

[17] According to the Jagga records, the Meos are divided into about 80 *gotras*, while the British settlement reports mention 52 *gotras* (e.g., Fraser, *Statistical Report of Zillah Gurgaon*, 29–30; Powlett, *Gazetteer of Ulwur*, 37–8).

[18] *Yaddashati Hal Bail, pargana* Chalkaliyana, VS 1722/1665 CE; *pargana* Kotla, VS 1723/1666 CE; *pargana* Pindayan, VS 1783/1726 CE; *Arsatta, pargana* Atela Bhabra, VS 1785/1728 CE; *Dastur-al-amal, pargana* Khohri, VS 1723/1666 CE.

been major studies on various regions of medieval India;[19] of these a few are on agrarian economy and rural society of medieval eastern Rajasthan,[20] of which Mewat was a part. The medieval records indicate that the peasantry of Mewat was economically differentiated and socially stratified.[21] The position of a peasant was determined by his economic strength (size of landholding and income), social status (rank in rural caste hierarchy), and official position in the land revenue administration. The peasants belonging to upper castes, that is, Brahmins, Rajputs, *mahajans*, and other members of the rural aristocracy (*patels*, *patwaris*, *qanungos*, and *chaudharis*), were designated as *khudkashta* peasants.[22] In Mewat, the *khudkashta* peasants were also called *gharuhallas*, that is, those who possessed their own ploughs, bullocks, seeds, and other agricultural implements;[23] and *riyayatis*, that is, peasants who had their personal holdings assessed on concessional rates. They had to pay land revenue to the Mughal state at the rate of 25–33 per cent of their gross produce.[24]

The size of the landholdings of a *khudkashta* determined whether he required hired labour or not.[25] Those *khudkashtas* who held one

[19] A. R. Kulkarni, 'The Indian Village with Special Reference to Medieval Deccan (Maratha Country)', General Presidential Address, *Proceedings of the Indian History Congress*, 52nd session (New Delhi, 1992); Indu Banga, *Agrarian System of the Sikhs: Late Eighteenth and Early Nineteenth Century* (New Delhi: Manohar, 1978); H. Fukuzawa, *The Medieval Deccan: Peasants, Social Systems and States, Sixteenth to Eighteenth Centuries* (New Delhi: Oxford University Press, 1991); Chetan Singh, *Region and Empire: Panjab in the Seventeenth Century* (New Delhi: Oxford University Press, 1991).

[20] Satish Chandra, *Medieval India: Society, the Jagirdari Crisis and the Village* (New Delhi: Macmillan, 1982); S. P. Gupta, *The Agrarian System of Eastern Rajasthan (c. 1650–1750)* (New Delhi: Manohar, 1986); Dilbagh Singh, *The State, Landlords and Peasants: Rajasthan in the 18th Century* (New Delhi: Manohar, 1990).

[21] *Dastur-al-amal, pargana* Khohri, VS 1723/1666 CE; *Arsatta, pargana* Piragpur, VS 1789/1732 CE; *pargana* Mojpur, VS 1771/1714 CE.

[22] *Arsatta, pargana* Mojpur, VS 1771/1714 CE; *pargana* Piragpur, VS 1789/1732 CE.

[23] *Yaddashti Hal Bail, pargana* Kotla, VS 1723/1766 CE; *pargana* Pindayan, VS 1783/1726 CE; *pargana* Chalkaliyana, VS 1722/1665 CE.

[24] *Dastur-al-amal, pargana* Atela Bhabra, VS 1767/1710 CE; *pargana* Mojpur, VS 1770/1713 CE; *pargana* Khohri, VS 1723/1666 CE.

[25] *Yaddashti Hal Bail, pargana* Chalkaliyana, VS 1722/1665 CE.

plough or two bullocks used to cultivate their fields with the help of family labour, supplemented by hired labour at the time of harvesting or sowing.[26] But the owners of large family holdings depended on regular hired labour. They also leased out their livestock and equipments that yielded substantial additional income. For example, in *pargana* Chalkaliyana, Begraj and Narwar of Kakrauli Mota village, and Lakhman of Phogat Dhani village held 21½, 8½, and 4 ploughs, respectively, in their possession.[27] This implies that they possessed landholdings that could not be cultivated with the help of family labour alone. On the other hand, 10 Brahmin *asamis* of Dhareru village in the same *pargana* held two ploughs each, and used to cultivate their fields with the help of family labour, resorting to hired labour at the time of harvesting and sowing.[28] Similarly, 12 *bania asamis* of Sanwar village and 10 Brahmin *asamis* of Kadma village in *pargana* Chalkaliyana held one plough each, and always used family labour in cultivation.[29] However, regardless of whether the labour was familial or hired, an essential aspect of the region's agriculture was that the responsibility of providing agricultural implements rested with the *khudkashta* peasants.

The *khudkashta* peasants were expected by the state to improve and extend cultivation in view of their superior land rights and relatively better economic conditions. The position of a *khudkashta* in the rural society was determined by his official status in the rural administration and the number of ploughs at his disposal. If he had an official status of *patwari*, *qanungo*, and *chaudhari*, he always enjoyed an advantageous position in terms of the payment of land revenue and other cesses, in comparison to the other *khudkashta* peasants belonging to higher castes.[30] He had to pay nominal land revenue on his personal holdings and was exempted from the payment of *malba* (common financial pool of the village) and other cesses.[31] Other *khudkashtas* who

[26] *Yaddashti Hal Bail*, *pargana* Chalkaliyana, VS 1722/1665 CE.

[27] *Yaddashti Hal Bail*, *pargana* Chalkaliyana, VS 1722/1665 CE.

[28] *Yaddashti Hal Bail*, *pargana* Chalkaliyana, VS 1722/1665 CE.

[29] *Yaddashti Hal Bail*, *pargana* Chalkaliyana, VS 1722/1665 CE.

[30] *Dastur-al-amal*, *pargana* Piragpur, VS 1789/1732 CE; *pargana* Mojpur, VS 1770/1713 CE; *pargana* Khohri, VS 1723/1666 CE.

[31] *Chithi* to the *amil*, *pargana* Piragpur, Bhadva Sudi 2, VS 1800/1743 CE.

merely had a high-caste status had to pay their land revenue and other cesses at customary rates.[32] Thus, land could be held by different kinds of *khudkashtas* on different terms and conditions. However, both the *riyayati* and non-*riyayati* sections of the *khudkashta* peasantry were characterized by: (a) the ownership of land that they cultivated; and (b) the use of personal ploughs, bullocks, seeds, and other implements. In normal conditions, the *khudkashta* peasants could not expand their landholding at the cost of *raiyati* peasants. For instance, in 1716, Jat Chaudhary had cultivated the common land of *qasba* Pahari. The matter was taken up by the *amil* who took control of the standing crop on that land and had it harvested by the hired labourers, thereby producing 60 *maunds* of grain.[33] However, in times of drought, there were many incidents of the lands of *palti* peasants being occupied by the *khudkashtas*. For instance, the Meo peasants of six villages in *pargana* Khohri complained to the *diwan* of Amber that during drought they had left their villages in search of livelihood, but upon their return found their lands occupied by the high-caste Rajputs.[34] This suggests that the state was not able to prevent the *khudkashta* peasants from expanding their landholdings at the cost of small peasants. In fact, whenever some peasants abandoned their fields and villages due to the high-handedness of the *jagirdars* or *ijaradars*, the *khudkashtas* tended to convert the abandoned land into their *gharujot* (personal holding). Nevertheless, the *amils* used to issue injunctions from time to time to the *khudkashtas* against occupying the lands of those *palti* peasants who had abandoned them.[35] Such restrictions on the expansion of the *khudkashta* landholdings seem to have been motivated by the fear that it would result in the loss of revenue.

The second category of peasants was known as *gaveti* or *palti* who formed the single largest stratum, as also the majority, of the peasantry and bore almost the entire burden of revenue. Irrespective of their residential status and ownership of land, they were not termed

[32] *Dastur-al-amal, pargana* Khohri, vs 1723/1666 CE; *pargana* Mojpur, vs 1770/1713 CE.

[33] *Arsatta, pargana* Pahari, vs 1773/1716 CE.

[34] *Chithi* to the *amil, pargana* Khohri, vs 1784/1727 CE.

[35] *Chithi* to the *amil, pargana* Pahari, Fagun Vadi 10, vs 1784/1727 CE; *pargana* Piragpur, Posh Vadi 1, vs 1791/1734 CE; Kartik Vadi 4, vs 1782/1725 CE; Chait Sudi 6, vs 1793/1736 CE.

as *khudkashta*. Most of them belonged to the intermediate or middle castes, namely Jats, Meos, Gujjars, Ahirs, Meenas, and Malis.[36] They were non-privileged members of the peasant community and were inferior in social status to the *khudkashta/riyayati* peasants.[37] They had to pay land revenue at the rate of 40–50 per cent of their gross produce—much higher than that charged from the *khudkashtas*—as well as several other cesses.[38] Majority of the *paltis* had to depend on *taqavi* (agricultural loan) advanced by the *mahajans* and zamindars. In many Rajasthani documents, we find them borrowing money from the *mahajans* to purchase seeds, ploughs, bullocks, and so on.[39] For instance, in 1729, the *paltis* belonging to 10 villages of *pargana* Pahari took loan from the *mahajans*, but, due to their miserable economic conditions, could not repay it according to the terms set by the *mahajans*. Yet, the *amil* forced them to repay the loan amount along with the land revenue.[40] In 1729, peasants belonging to an unspecified village of *pargana* Pahari took loan from the *mahajans*, but, as they could not return the amount on time, the entire agricultural produce of the village was seized by the *amil* to recover the loaned amount.[41] At the same time, in 1730, we find that peasants belonging to 18 villages of *pargana* Mandawar returned the loan amount well before time.[42] The *mahajans* used to extend loans to the *paltis* at high rates of interest.[43] For instance, the peasants belonging to a village of *pargana* Pahari borrowed money of 1,221 rupees from the *mahajan* to purchase seeds and bullocks. At the harvest time, they returned the principal with interest amounting to of 235 rupees and 12 *annas*.[44] The *mahajans* used to extend loan to the needy *paltis* only when either the *amil* or the zamindar of the village

36 See *hasil farohi* section in the *arsattas*.

37 *Dastur-al-amal*, *pargana* Piragpur, VS 1789/1732 CE; *pargana* Mojpur, VS 1770/1713 CE.

38 *Dastur-al-amal*, *pargana* Khohri, AH 1049/1639–40 CE; *pargana* Mojpur, VS 1770/1713 CE; *pargana* Sonkhar-Sonkhari, VS 1773/1716 CE.

39 *Arsatta*, *pargana* Pahari, VS 1788/1731 CE; *Arzdasht*, Bhadva Sudi 6, VS 1741/1684 CE.

40 *Arsatta*, *pargana* Pahari, VS 1786/1729 CE.

41 *Arsatta*, *pargana* Pahari, VS 1786/1729 CE.

42 *Arsatta*, *pargana* Mandawar, VS 1787/1730 CE.

43 *Arsatta*, *pargana* Pahari, VS 1786/1729 CE; *pargana* Khohri, VS 1773/1716 CE.

44 *Arsatta*, *pargana* Pahari, VS 1786/1729 CE.

submitted his undertaking promising repayment by the *paltis*. There are some instances of Meos peasants belonging to the villages of *pargana* Khohri being denied loan by the *mahajans* due to the absence of any undertaking in their favour from the *amil*.[45] In the years of drought or famine, the economic conditions of the *paltis* became more miserable, and sometimes, unable to bear the situation, they had to leave their villages and migrate elsewhere. It is borne out by the evidence that a large number of *paltis* became extremely impoverished due to the cumulative effect of natural and man-made calamities.

The third category of peasants was known as *pahi*. These were mainly depressed peasants who wandered from village to village and *pargana* to *pargana* in search of better livelihood opportunities. They usually cultivated the arable wastelands or the lands abandoned by the *paltis* in the neighbouring villages without becoming the residents of these villages or the proprietors of lands they cultivated. They tilled such lands as tenants and had no right to sell or mortgage them. They could keep the lands under their tillage as long as they wished, on the condition of paying land revenue regularly. In normal conditions, such *pahis* were required to pay land revenue at customary rates.[46] It is evident from the *dastur-ul-amals* that in depopulated or newly settled villages, the *pahis* paid their land revenue at lower rates than did the *paltis*.[47] The *pahis* were granted *patta* (lease agreement) for the cultivation of *banjar* (virgin land); the *patta* fixed the land revenue demand at a concessional rate of 33 per cent of the gross produce, this concession being extended for 2–3 years.[48]

Those *pahis* who had their own ploughs and bullocks could bargain with the *amil* or other land revenue officials and get favourable terms and conditions for cultivation.[49] Those who came from other *parganas*

45 *Chithi* to the *amil*, *pargana* Khohri, Mah Vadi 5, VS 1784/1727 CE.

46 Dilbagh Singh, 'Caste and Structure of Village Society in Eastern Rajasthan during the Eighteenth Century', *Indian History Review* 2 (1976): 299–311.

47 *Chithi* to the *amil*, *pargana* Khohri, Asadh Vadi 9, VS 1781/1724 CE; Asadh Vadi 11, VS 1781/1724 CE.

48 Singh, 'Caste and Structure of the Village Society'.

49 *Arzdasht*, *pargana* Pahari, Bhadva Sudi 6, VS 1741/1684 CE. On account of their possession of ploughs and bullocks, the Ahir *pahi* peasants were given concessions in the payment of land revenue on the lands they cultivated in *pargana* Pahari.

and far-off villages were known as *pahi gaharla pargana*.[50] Such *pahis* were essentially migratory cultivators who were permitted to settle with their families and construct their hutments or *chappars* in the village.[51] They had their own ploughs and bullocks.[52] As a rule, they were offered attractive terms and conditions on the consideration that they had to leave their native villages. In due course of time, such *pahis* became the permanent residents of the villages they had settled in, and acquired the status of *palti*, thereby becoming an integral part of the village community.[53] For instance, three *pahis* named Masto, Shauma, and Harkishan who had come from *pargana* Narnol and settled in Sanwar village of *pargana* Chalkaliyana acquired the status of *palti*.[54] Similarly, Ram Singh of Biran village, Bhimo Jat of Pali village, Talo of Bhatol village, and Dala and Shivebla of Basaiyra village of the *parganas* Tosham, Kanore, Hansi, and Damra, respectively, had elevated their status from *pahi* to *palti* in Sanwar village.[55] Six *pahi* peasants who had come from different *parganas* acquired the status of *palti* in Dhareru village of *pargana* Chalkaliyana. Manbhar and Prama from Saamar village of *pargana* Rohtak also raised their status from *pahi* to *palti* in Ramsingh pura of *pargana* Chalkaliyana.[56] Twelve Jat peasants who had come from Shekhawati in *pargana* Churu (Rajasthan) acquired the status of *palti* in Mithathal village of *pargana* Chalkaliyana.[57] It appears from the Rajasthani documents that the percentage of *pahis* in the rural community varied across villages and *parganas*. For instance, in *pargana* Pindayan, the *pahi* peasants constituted 19.7 per cent of the peasant community.[58] In Uchhari village of *pargana* Pindayan, out of a total of

[50] *Dastur-al-amal*, *pargana* Khohri, vs 1723/1666 CE.

[51] *Arsatta*, *pargana* Pahari, vs 1791/1734 CE; *Arzdasht*, *pargana* Pahari, Bhadva Sudi 6, vs 1741/1684 CE.

[52] *Yaddashti Hal Bail*, *pargana* Chalkaliyana, vs 1722/1665 CE; *pargana* Pindayan, vs 1783/1726 CE.

[53] *Arsatta*, *pargana* Pahari, vs 1790/1733 CE; *Yaddashti Hal Bail*, *pargana* Chalkaliyana, vs 1722/1665 CE.

[54] *Yaddashti Hal Bail*, *pargana* Chalkaliyana, vs 1722/1665 CE.

[55] *Yaddashti Hal Bail*, *pargana* Chalkaliyana, vs 1722/1665 CE.

[56] *Yaddashti Hal Bail*, *pargana* Chalkaliyana, vs 1722/1665 CE.

[57] *Yaddashti Hal Bail*, *pargana* Chalkaliyana, vs 1722/1665 CE.

[58] *Yaddashti Hal bail*, *pargana* Pindayan, vs 1783/1726 CE.

29 ploughs, 11 ploughs belonged to the *pahis*, whereas in Gharatwari, Kapaho, Toda Khurd, and Jai Singhpura villages of the same *pargana*, the presence of *pahi* is not attested.[59]

In Mewat, the percentage of *pahis* increased from late 17th to early 18th centuries, a period during which massive agrarian disturbances were taking place. This is evident from an *arzdasht* wherein the *amil* of the Amber state wrote to his chief (*raja*) that only 14 villages out of 204 villages in *pargana* Pahari were settled before the *pargana* was included in Amber's *tankhwah jagir*, but now 100 villages were more colonized with the help of Ahir *pahis*.[60] Similar conditions prevailed in *pargana* Khohri where attempts were made to resettle a large number of villages deserted in the wake of agrarian disturbances caused by the Jats and Meos. The *amil*'s concern for the rehabilitation of such deserted villages is borne out by the Rajasthani documents wherein he repeatedly mentions his efforts to rehabilitate deserted villages with the help of *pahi* peasants. For instance, in 1664, 32 deserted villages of *pargana* Khohri were rehabilitated by the *pahi* caste peasants.[61]

Finally, at the bottom of the hierarchy were the *kamins* or low-caste landless agricultural workers who sold their labour for wages. This vast body of landless rural poor fulfilled the labour requirements of the entire land-owning peasantry. Their labour was not much in demand throughout the year, but increased hugely at the time of sowing and harvesting. They were prevented from acquiring any land for full-time cultivation by the dominant landholding castes who needed their labour round the year, particularly in the peak season. This was perhaps the basic reason for not allowing them to own land even when favourable conditions of land–man ratio existed. Here, it is significant to note that the Mughal state aimed 'to generate larger revenues from the village and lower the wage cost in the cities',[62] without disturbing the pre-existing caste inequities.

59 *Yaddashti Hal bail*, *pargana* Pindayan, VS 1783/1726 CE.

60 *Arzdasht*, Fagun Sudi 12, VS 1746/1689 CE.

61 *Arshatta*, *pargana* Khohri, VS 1721/1664 CE.

62 Irfan Habib, 'Caste System in Indian History', in *Essays in Indian History: Towards a Marxist Perception*, ed. Irfan Habib (London: Anthem Press, 2002), 172–3.

Nevertheless, the *kamins* were indispensable for agricultural production and even for normal functioning of the rural society, as they provided perennial cheap labour to the privileged section of the rural society, that is, *khudkashtas/gharuhallas*, as also part-time or seasonal labour to others at the crucial time of sowing and harvesting.[63] In return, they received a fixed share of the produce in accordance with the customary practices. Thus, low-caste *chamars* (cobblers) and *dhanuks* (weavers), while pursuing their traditional hereditary occupations, also worked as *halis* (ploughmen) on the lands owned by the high-caste peasants. In many cases, the *chamars*, along with the other artisanal castes, even had ploughs and bullocks. For instance, four *chamar asamis* had one plough each in Bamla, Kadma, and Bijana villages of *pargana* Chalkaliyana respectively.[64] In Bhahu, Golari, and Mohammadpur villages of the same *pargana*, *chamars* possessed half-a-plough each.[65] Although the *chamars* appeared as cultivators in a few cases, in majority of cases they were landless labourers working for the *khudkashta* peasants.

The unequal distribution of resources among these different categories of peasants, the ability of the socio-economically dominant sections to accumulate reserve capital, and the pattern of its investment had a far-reaching impact on the degree of peasant stratification. The pre-existing inequalities in the rural society became aggravated with the passage of time, tilting the balance of social and economic power more and more in favour of the richer sections despite the abundance of land.

III

The Khanzadas were the first Muslim ruling group to play an important role in the social, cultural, and economic history of the region. The social history of the Khanzadas begins during the later part of the reign of Firozshah Tughlaq. After the death of the Firozshah Tughlaq, the Khanzadas formed a chiefdom in the vicinity of Tijara and emerged

63 Irfan Habib, *The Agrarian System of Mughal India 1550–1707*, 2nd rev. ed. (New Delhi: Oxford University Press, 1999), 123–60.

64 *Yaddashti Hal Bail, pargana* Chalkaliyana, vs 1722/1665 CE.

65 *Yaddashti Hal Bail, pargana* Chalkaliyana, vs 1722/1665 CE.

as a ruling class in the region. In the early days of their rule, Indori, Kotla, and Tijara used to be their capitals; later, they extended their territory up to the Alwar town which became their capital. The local tradition of the Khanzadas testify to their claim over a vast territory in the Mewat region: they declare that they held 1,484 *kheras* (towns and villages) under their jurisdiction in the early 16th century.[66]

The Khanzadas were divided into two social categories, namely the Khanzadas of Mewat and the Khanzadas. The Khanzadas of Mewat were Jadon Rajputs who had converted to Islam.[67] The Khanzada chiefs from Bahadur Nahar to Hasan Khan belonged to this category. The second category constituted mainly of the former Firozi slaves.[68] As discussed in Chapter 1, according to the *Tarikh-i-Mubarakshahi*, after Firozshah Tughlaq's death, a large number of former Firozi slaves, opposed to the new sultan, Muhammad Shah, were forced to leave Delhi and sought refuge with Bahadur Nahar at Kotla, his fortress in Mewat. These Firozi slaves, with their vast knowledge and experience in land revenue and military administration, were absorbed in the administrative structure of the infant Khanzada chiefdom and, in turn, must have played a very important role in its consolidation. The key politico-administrative role of the Firozi slaves in the Khanzada chiefdom is attested by a traditional account of their ceremonial role of putting *tilak* (auspicious mark) on the forehead of every new Khanzada chief—a role also performed by the Jats in Bikaner and the Meenas in Amber for the chiefs of these states.[69] Though a ceremonial practice, it reminded them that the state acknowledged their cooperation and contribution in state formation and administrative functioning. On the socio-religious position of the Khanzadas, P. W. Powlett writes:

> [I]n social rank they are far above the Meos, and though probably of more recent Hindú extraction, they are better Musalmáns. They observe no Hindú festivals, and will not acknowledge that they pay any respect to Hindu shrines. But Brahmins take part in their marriage contracts, and they observe some Hindu marriage ceremonies. Though generally as poor

66 Powlett, *Gazetteer of Ulwur*, 7.

67 Abul-Fazl, *The Ain-i-Akbari*, vol. 2, 202–4.

68 According to Abul-Fazl, *The Ain-i-Akbari*, vol. 1, 354, the Khanzadas of Mewat belonged to Juhiya Rajput clan.

69 Powlett, *Gazetteer of Ulwur*, 134–5.

and ignorant as the Meos, they, unlike the latter, say their prayers, and do not let their women work in the fields.[70]

On the origin of the Khanzadas, Fraser writes: 'They represent them as being descended from the Jadoon [Jadon] Rajputs. One account ... represents the Khanzadas as descended from a Dhanuk (low caste) named Beejbul converted to Mahomedanism as before with the title of Khan, and hence Khanzadas.'[71] The author of *Arzang-i-Tijara* adds that, during marriages, they paid their respect to and worshipped Bejal, their ancestor.[72] It thus appears that one Bejal or Bejbul must have the ancestor of some Khanzada families who might have embraced Islam during the reign of Firozshah Tughlaq. Whatever and however disparate may have been their actual origins, the Khanzadas had forged their social identity as the local elite of Mewat by the end of the 16th century, as testified by their zamindari rights in many *parganas* of the region.[73]

The Khanzadas were the first Muslims to introduce Islamic culture in Mewat. The archeological survey of the region by Alexander Cunningham shows that they had constructed many mosques in the towns and villages of the region. For instance, Bahadur Nahar built a fine stone mosque at Kotla in 1399 during the reign of Muhammad Shah;[74] Hasan Khan Mewati, in Tijara in the early 16th century;[75] and Jalal Khan Khanzada at Indori.[76] Similarly, mosques were constructed in other towns such as Shahbad, Bhindusi, Nimali, Sarheta, Mandha, Masit Palah, Jewano, Sohna, Bhondsi, Pinangwan, and Malab during the early 16th century.[77] The Non-archival Records of the Alwar State,

70 Powlett, *Gazetteer of Ulwur*, 40.

71 Fraser, *Statistical Report of Zillah Gurgaon*, 14n.

72 Sheikh Muhammad Makhdum, *Arzang-i-Tijara* (Urdu) (Agra: Agra Akhbar), H. 1290/ 1873 CE, trans. (Hindi) Anil Joshi (Alwar, 1989), 6.

73 Abul-Fazl, *The Ain-i-Akbari*, vol. 2, 202–4.

74 Cuningham, *Report of a Tour in Eastern Rajputana in 1882–83*, 16. The date of construction of the mosque is written at the entrance gateway of the mosque at Kotla. In the court of the mosque there is a fine tomb, which is said to be that of Bahadur Nahar himself.

75 Cuningham, *Report of a Tour in Eastern Rajputana in 1882–83*, 117.

76 Cuningham, *Report of a Tour in Eastern Rajputana in 1882–83*, 134.

77 Cuningham, *Report of a Tour in Eastern Rajputana in 1882–83*, 118, 119, 127, 135–7.

too, mention that 41 mosques were constructed by the Khanzadas in the villages and towns of Alwar *sarkar*.[78] The large number of mosques also reflects the size of the Muslim population in the region.

Another important agent of defusing Islamic culture in the Mewat region were the *qazis* appointed by the Khanzadas to maintain the Islamic law (Sharia) among the Muslim population and settle local disputes (criminal and civil) between the Muslims (Khanzadas) and the non-Muslims (mainly the Meos). The Islamic laws, during the period of the Khanzada rule, must have also influenced the social life of the Meos who came from a tribal background. This is corroborated by Powlett who writes:

> The Meos are now all Musalmans in name; but their village deities ... are the same as those of Hindú Zamindars. They keep, too, several Hindú festivals. Thus the Holi is with Meos a season of rough play, and is considered as important as festivals as the *Muharram*, *Id*, and *Shabíbarát*; and they likewise observe the *Janam ashtmí*, *Dasehra* and *Diwálí*. They often keep Brahmin priests to write the *pílí chithí*, or note fixing the date of marriage.[79]

Cunningham adds that the Meos worshipped Sayyid Salar Masud with great respect, and the banner of Salar Masud was held in every Meo village at *Shab-i-barat*.[80]

After the decline of the Mughal empire, the socio-economic and political position of the Khanzadas declined drastically. The author of *Arzang-i-Tijara* says that due to fear of the Meos, many Khanzada families migrated eastward and took to trade in the Gangetic cities, while some joined the military service of the Rajput Narukas of Alwar and the British.[81] But the Khanzadas who had been living in the villages of Mewat as *khudkashta* peasants or zamindars were oppressed by the Meos. The Non-archival Records of Alwar State highlight that many Khanzada villages were forcibly evacuated by the Meos. These villages were Gadhola, Alawalpur, Amli Sahabad, Babuhera, Khizarpur, Muradbas, Bharkol, Hasanpur Bara, Dhoj, Shalahera, Kaliabad, Palaria, Hadia, Mohammadabas, Ghatawasan, Kherli Kalan, Ghata,

78 *Bandhak* no.3, *granthank* no. 66.

79 Powlett, *Gazetteer of Ulwur*, 38.

80 Cunningham, *Report of a Tour in Eastern Rajputana in 1882–83*, 23.

81 Makhdum, *Arzang-i-Tijara*, 5.

Shamshabad, Pinangwan, Shahebpur, Fakharpur Khohri, Bazidpur, Bagada Pahari, Naharpur, Fatehpur, and Bahadurpur.[82] Most of these were occupied by the Dahangal and Baghoria Meo *pals*.[83] The main reasons for the Meo occupation of the Khanzada-owned lands were high soil fertility and availability of sweet groundwater for irrigation. Commenting on the decline in the Khanzadas' power and wealth and speculating on their fate, Fraser writes:

> The Khanzadas, some centuries ago, did, beyond doubt, possess extensive property in this district [Gurgaon] and the ruins and tombs in the vicinity of Sohna (also in other places) forcefully attest their past importance. The power of Khanzadas is popularly stated to have waned about three centuries ago, when they were supplanted by the Meos. What has become of them? Have they gradually merged into the conquering class? Have they been destroyed in the struggle for property occurring under weak government.[84]

Powlett, however, reveals their reduced social status in the late 19th century: 'There are twenty-six Khanzada villages in the state [Alwar], in most of which the proprietors themselves work in the fields and follow the plough.'[85] Another settlement officer, F. C. Channing, too, mentions:

> In Alwar ... the Khanzadas have fallen from their ancient rank, and now possess but few settlements. I have a suspicion that they are more intimately connected than they acknowledge with the Meos whom they seem to me to resemble in personal appearance. They do not ordinarily intermarry with Meos, but the Meo inhabitants of Ghatwásan, Poul, Nasírbas, Kherli Khurd and Muhammadabas in the Firozpur Tahsíl profess to have been formerly Khanzádas, and to have become Meos by intermarriage.[86]

Thus, as per Channing's testimony, the Khanzadas of these villages apparently merged their social identity with the Meos.

[82] *Bandhak* no. 3, *granthank* no. 81; *bandhak* no. 4, *granthank* no. 43; *bandhak* no. 5, *granthank* no. 89; *bandhak* no. 12, *granthank* no. 10, 89; *bandhak* no. 66, *granthank* no. 3, 7; *bandhak* no. 67, *granthank* no. 4, 6; *bandhak* no. 68, *granthank* no. 4, 5; *bandhak* no. 71, *granthank* no. 6, 7, 12.

[83] *Bandhak* no. 3, *granthank* no. 81; Makhdum, *Arzang-i-Tijara*, 22–5.

[84] Fraser, *Statistical Report of Zillah Gurgaon*, 14.

[85] Powlett, *Gazetteer of Ulwur*, 40.

[86] F. C. Channing, *Land Revenue Settlement of the Gurgaon District*, 30.

Thus, the Khanzadas who had been absorbed in the land revenue administration and nobility by the Mughal state suffered a sharp decline in their socio-economic status after the decline of the Mughal state. And the Meos, who asserted their social identity more aggressively in the Mewat region, occupied the more fertile lands and the villages of the Khanzadas.

IV

The territory of Mewat has been subdivided into 13 Meo *pals*; 12 of these are referred to as *pals* and one, namely the Pahat Meo *pal*, as *palakra*. The word *palakra* has the same meaning as *pal*, except that it signifies smallness of size and inferior status. Nevertheless, in practice, all of them are equal in status. When and why the Pahat Meo *pal* came to be called *palakra* is not known. There is a popular traditional perception among the Meos that during Akbar's reign when all the Meo *pals* had distributed land among themselves amicably, the representatives of the Pahat clan arrived late and were therefore contemptuously called *palakra*, not *pal*. But it seems that the name owes to certain historical circumstances. The Pahat Meos, located in the Kama-Pahari and Deeg *parganas* of Mathura-Bharatpur which was part of the Braj region, were culturally different from the other Meo *pals*. This is indicated by the stories of 'Dariya Khan Meo and Shashi Badani Meeni' and 'Panch Pahad ki Ladai', popular among them. The love story of 'Dariya Khan Meo and Shashi Badani Meeni' centres on the conflict between the Pahat Meos and the Meenas that ensued over Dariya Khan Meo's refusal to eat meat at his Meena bride's house, indicating the differences in the food habits between the two communities.[87] The story 'Panch Pahad ki Ladai' narrates the conflict between the Pahat Meos and Mughal state: it was essentially an agrarian revolt of the Pahat Meos of Kama-Pahari and Deeg *parganas* and the Jats of the Braj region against the Mughal state during the reign of Shahjahan (1650). The emperor entrusted Amber Raja and his son Kirat Singh with the responsibility to crush the rebels. Upon their success, both were rewarded by the emperor with a rise in their *mansabs*. Both Persian and Rajasthani sources reveal that the agrarian revolt of the Pahat

[87] Cunningham, *Report of a Tour in Eastern Rajputana in 1882–83*, 3–4.

Meos was not different in nature from that of the Jats of Braj later during Aurangzeb's reign, while the Rajasthani sources highlight the solidarity between the Pahat Meos and the Jats during these revolts.[88] Therefore, culturally, the Pahat Meos found themselves closer to the Jats than to other Meo *pals*, and their cultural differences from the other Meos probably led them to forge a distinct social identity that is also confirmed by the Rajasthani sources.[89] Therefore, the Pahat Meos came to be addressed as *palakra* rather than *pal* by other Meo *pals* despite the fact that former possessed a large area under cultivation and enjoyed a favourable socio-economic position in the Mewat region. In this context, it should also be noted that the Pahat Meos have always refuted the allegation that their representatives were latecomers to the Meo *pal* assembly during Akbar's reign and have maintained that the question of their late appearance at the assembly did not arise because Akbar had given them a respectable position. This is reflected in a popular folk saying:

पंच पहाड की राजाहि और पूरो तेरा दल।
आधे अखबर बादशाह, आधे पहाट् टोडरमल।।

[In the kingdom of the five hills, with its force complete, one half belongs to emperor Akbar and the other half to Todar Mal.][90]

This statement was supposedly made before Akbar by Todar Mal, the zamindar of Pahat Meos, when the former once sent for Todar

[88] S. Nural Hasan, 'Further Light on Zamindars under the Mughals: A Case Study of (Mirza) Raja Jai Singh under Shahjahan', *Proceedings Indian History Congress*, 39th session (Hyderabad, 1978), 497–502; Inayat Khan, *The Shahjahannama*, trans. A. R. Fuller, ed. and comp. by W. E. Begley and Z. A. Desai (New Delhi: Oxford University Press, 1990), 448–9; Khan and Hayy, *The Maathir-ul-Umara*, vol. 1, 813; *Arzdasht*, Sawan Sudi 6, VS 1750/1693 CE; Asadh Vadi 15, VS 1766/1709 CE; Kartik Vadi 4, VS 1766/1709 CE; *Chithi* to the *amil, pargana* Pahari, VS 1784/1727 CE; VS 1781/1724 CE; *Arsatta, pargana* Pahari, VS 1788/1731 CE; Bhardwaj, 'Socio-economic Conditions in the Mewat Region, c. 1650–1750', 245–54.

[89] *Arzdasht*, Mah Vadi 9, VS 1774/1717 CE; *Chithi* to the *amil, pargana* Pahari, VS 1784/1727 CE.

[90] This Todar Mal was the chief of the Pahat Meos and should not be confused with Raja Todar Mal, Akbar's revenue minister (Cunningham, *Report of a Tour in Eastern Rajputana in 1882–83*, 26).

Mal and demanded to know why he considered himself equal to the Mughal emperor. By this statement, Todar Mal conveyed to Akbar that just as the latter was the emperor of the Mughal state, so was he (Todar Mal) the king (zamindar) of his region; and hence one half of the produce belonged to him and the other half to the emperor. The folklore further has it that Akbar was so pleased with his reply that he gave Todar Mal a *jagir* with the rank of *mansabdar*.[91] The folklore perhaps sought to convey the message to other Meo *pals* that the Pahat Meos were in no way inferior to them and also legitimize the Pahat Meo chief's claim over half of the area's produce in the face of the Mughal attempt to bring the area under their land revenue system. Therefore, it is not likely that the Pahat Meos were called *palakra* on account of their late arrival for the allotment of land among the Meo *pals* by the emperor. Rather, their separate cultural identity allowed little interaction with other Meo *pals*, which provoked the latter to coin the disparaging name *palakra* for them.

It may be pointed out that the popular folk tradition of the Pahat Meos arriving late for receiving land from the emperor appears to be the invention of bards (*mirasis*) during the late 18th and early 19th centuries. It was at this time that the *pal* polity of the Meos assumed a concrete shape, and the *chaudhari* or chief of each *pal* began to glorify his own *pal* and demonstrate his socio-economic and political power through songs and legends composed by his own bards.[92] It also became the moral duty of the bards to sing songs or narrate legends in praise of their respective *pals* and *chaudharis*. It seems that the *chaudharis* of the Meo *pals* adopted the Rajput practice of patronizing bardic oral histories of their clans. It may be noted that this tradition

91 Cunningham, *Report of a Tour in Eastern Rajputana in 1882–83*, 25–6.

92 Each *pal* had its own group of bards whose task was to prepare the oral history of the *pal* in the form of legends. Most of these legends happen to glorify and attribute several acts of valour to one or the other *pal*. A bard's success depended on how evocatively he managed to sing or narrate the legends and how large an audience he managed to move; he, in turn, received gifts from the *pal chaudharis*. For example, in 1882, when Mirab Khan (*chaudhari* of the Garwal Meos) died at Reoli village near Firozpur-Jhirka, the bard was rewarded with one camel and one gold *mohur*, besides clothing and other items, by the sons of the late *chaudhari* for his narration of the legend at the funeral feast on the 40th day after the *chaudhari*'s death.

of bardic legends and songs started first in the domain of the Pahat Meos due to the influence of the Jats of Bharatpur. This is evident from the fact that the terms used by the bards of the Pahat Meo *pal* to address their *chaudharis*, such as *rao, raja, mal, sardar,* and *thakur*, were the same as those used to address the 18th- and 19th-centuy Jat chiefs of Bharatpur, namely Rao Churaman, Rao Badan Singh, Thakur Badan Singh, Raja Mohkam Singh, Raja Surajmal, and so on. Thus, folktales of the Pahat Meos, such as 'Panch Pahad ki Ladai' and 'Dariya Khan Meo and Shashi Badani Meeni', are apparently bardic compositions of late 18th or early 19th centuries. Significantly, the early 16th-century ballad 'Hasan Khan ki Katha' omits the Pahat Meos from the list of 12 Meo *pals* whose *chaudharis* were invited by the Khanzada chief Hasan Khan Mewati to his court before the Battle of Khanwa against Babur.[93] This further supports the possibility that the Pahat Meos became part of the pan-Meo community only after the 18th century.

The 13 Meo *pals* into which most Meos were divided were clustered into four groups, each of which claimed descent from a Rajput clan or caste group and carried its name. The Rajput clans, in turn, belonged to two chief *puranic* lineages (*vamshas*), namely *chandravamsha* and *suryavamsha*. One group of five *pals*, namely Chhiraklot, Duhlot, Daimrot, Nai, and Pundlot, was linked with the Jadon Rajputs, while another group of five, namely Balot, Dairwal, Kalesa, Landawat, and Rajawat, with the Tanwar Rajputs; both the Jadons and the Tanwars were regarded as *chandravamshis*. A third group of two *pals* was linked with the Kachhwaha Rajputs and the fourth group, consisting only of the Pahat Meos, with the Chauhan Rajputs; both the Kachhwahas and the Chauhans were regarded as *suryavamshis*.[94] It seems that the Meos forged this new social identity based on their claim to descent from Rajput clans only after their peasantization. Their peasantization, however, did not occur simultaneously but in different periods of time during which they were divided into various groups. In the initial stages, *pals* were tribal social units each of which had its independent

93 Meo, 'Hasan Khan ki Katha'.

94 A large number of Meos were not associated with any *pal*; they were/are just called *nepalia* (without *pal*).

identity, its head being regarded as the *chaudhari* of the *pal*. The Jaggas aided in the transformation of their tribal identity into a new prestigious identity by preparing their genealogical records. The state, too, might have contributed to this process. Each *pal* was located in a fixed territory and the *pal* system enabled them to develop strong social bonds because they considered their kinsmen as the progeny of a common ancestor.

However, the Meos were not an exception in this regard, as the identity of the Meenas was also transformed through their association with the Rajputs. Eastern Rajasthan, controlled by the Rajputs, was a fertile agricultural zone, large parts of which were cultivated by the Meos and the Meenas. During the pre-Sultanate period, the Badgujars and the Jadon Rajputs (Surasenas) ruled this region which, after the reign of Firozshah Tughlaq and till the reign of Akbar, came under the rule of the Khanzadas. With the Khanzadas being originally Jadon Rajput converts to Islam, it is also possible that the Jaggas, with help of the Khanzada political elite, linked the five Meo *pal*s with the Jadon Rajputs in order to provide legitimacy to or strengthen the social base of the new Khanzada state. This region became part of the *tankhwah jagir*s of the Kachhwahas and other imperial *mansabdar*s in the hey-day of the Mughal rule, and witnessed, in the late 18th century, the emergence of the state of Alwar under Naruka (Kachhwaha) Rajputs with a substantial Meo population. Again, the Rajputization of the Meos and Meenas, that is, accounts of their mythical origin from the Rajputs, served to buttress the expansion of the Rajput state.

The myth of Rajput origin and adoption of Hindu *gotra*s helped the Meos construct a new and more prestigious social identity in the Mughal period. This new identity was not restricted to adopting Hindu *gotras* alone, but also encompassed the observance of Hindu festivals, traditions, and rituals, and giving Brahmins an important role in their social and cultural life, particularly in marriage and birth ceremonies. It is to be noted that in pre-colonial times, like the Meos, several tribes in other parts of India which had undergone the process of peasantization tried to exploit myths of Rajput origin and embrace Hindu customs and traditions in order to forge new social identities. Among these, some tribes were even able to assume the status of Rajputs by developing state systems, although many others failed to do so.[95] It may be observed here that the unsuccessful claims of the Meos to Rajput status was the outcome of their inability to ultimately carve out a state for themselves. Similar is the case of the Meenas who made a transition from tribalism to agriculture but failed to create a state.[96]

It is necessary here to interrogate some significant points raised about the Meo *pal* system by Shail Mayaram. She argues that the Meo *pal* polity was traditionally autonomous and hostile to monopolistic sovereignty; favoured decentralization of power; and retained its pristine character without undergoing any change over a long period of time. In her words, 'Contrasted with the imperial [Mughal] system is the Meo Pal, which is the territorial unit of the relatively autonomous self-governing community.' Thus, given this inherently autonomous nature of the Meo *pal* polity, confrontation with powerful Mughal and Rajput states was inevitable.[97] It would be interesting to examine Mayaram's assumptions in the light of historical developments. *Pal* can be defined as a social unit characterized by a strong feeling of brotherhood on account of all its members claiming descent from a common ancestor, even though it literally means that only a group of tribes originated from a common ancestor. Like the Meos, the Meenas and Bhils are also divided into *pals*. In a tribal society, the position of the *pal chaudhari* was like that of a tribal chief who would consult the important members (*thama*) of his *pal* before delivering judgements or taking decisions. His main duty was to organize raids with the help of other members of the tribe and protect the tribe from external aggression. The *pal* system of the Meos underwent unprecedented changes in the wake of their peasantization. As the Meo tribes got transformed into a cultivating class, the power of the *pal chaudhari*

95 Surjit Sinha, 'State Formation and Rajput Myth in Tribal Central India', in *Man in India* 42, no. 1 (April–June 1962): 35–80.

96 S. H. M. Rizvi, *Mina: The Ruling Tribe of Rajasthan: Socio-Biological Appraisal* (New Delhi: B. R. Publishing Corporation, 1987); Saraswat Rawat, *Mina Ithihas* (Hindi) (Jaipur: Jhunthlal Nandala, vs 2025); Nandini Sinha, 'Reconstructing Identity and Situating Themselves in History: A Premilinary Note on the Meenas of Jaipur Locality', *Indian Historical Review* 27, no. 1 (2000): 29–43.

97 Shail Mayaram, *Against History, Against State: Counterperspectives from the Margins* (New Delhi: Permanent Black, 2004), 120.

diminished and the nature of his authority changed. Now, the *chaudhari* could no longer rely on raids to support his family and clan, but rather had to depend on the rains and the loans from moneylenders for raising desirable crops. In the event of non-payment of revenue, the helpless *chaudhari* could neither protect the defaulting peasants from the lashes of revenue authorities nor himself pay their share of revenue.

This diminution in the position and role of the *chaudhari* also meant a prolonged struggle for survival for the individual peasant. In the event of crop failure or famine, it was no longer possible for the peasant to conduct raids as before; he was forced to abandon his village and take up agricultural work elsewhere as a *pahi*. The Mughal administrative control was relatively stronger in Mewat due to its strategic location between the two centres of Mughal power, Delhi and Agra, and probably acted as a check on Meo depredations. The Persian and Rajasthani records of the Mughal times, too, no longer refer to the Meos as raiders or robbers, indicating that they had, by and large, abandoned their earlier predatory activities. (The description of Meos as 'raiders' or 'robbers' is found in the earlier writings of Minhaj Siraj and Barani during the Sultanate period, or in the later colonial British records that, in turn, drew upon Siraj and Barani's writings.) However, the Rajasthani sources do describe them as *mufsid* (rebel)—a term largely used for the Rajputs (Narukas and Chauhans), frequently for the Jats and the Meos, and generally for all those peasants and zamindars who defaulted in revenue payment or defied state orders. With their transformation into a settled peasant community, not only did their subsistence base and the character of their clan leadership undergo a major change, their social-cultural life, too, witnessed a certain degree of 'Hinduization', as discussed earlier. Nevertheless, they emerged as a dominant community in the region.

Now, in the context of this change in the role of the *pal chaudharis* with the peasantization of Meos and the integration of Mewat with the Mughal administration, it is pertinent to examine the extent of the role of the chaudharis in the *pal* system in resolving the disputes of Meo peasants during the Mughal period. Did these *chaudharis* exercise independent decisions like a sovereign in the settlement of mutual conflicts of Meo peasants as has been suggested by Mayaram?

The *hasil farohi* (tax on crime) column of the *arsattas* mentions the details of different kinds of disputes and criminal cases over land, crops, and women involving the cultivators, including the names, the native villages, and the caste status of the accused, as also the penalties in the form of fines (in rupees and *takas*) imposed by the *amil* or the *faujdar* in accordance with the nature of offence. For instance, Manna Meo of village Pahari in *pargana* Pindayan lodged a complaint at the *sarkar* (*darbar* of the *amil*) against the misconduct of Tara Meora who had fixed his daughter's engagement with the son of Manna Meo, but married her off to another boy. The case was investigated by the *patel* of the village, and Tara Meora was found guilty and penalized. This kind of problem was considered a serious matter in the Meo society, and communitarian pressure was exerted on the person who broke off an engagement. But the *pal chaudhari* is not found to have played any role in the settlement of this matter.[98] In another case, Penna Meo of village Nainapur in *pargana* Harsana lodged a complaint at the office of *amil* against Govinda Meo, who had run off with his wife (*lugai*). The probe found Govinda guilty, and the *amil* imposed upon him a fine of 11 rupees. Such cases happened to be common in the Meo community, but, again, we find that the *chaudhari* did not play any role in the conflict resolution.[99] Cases of fights among the Meos and punishments meted out therein, too, have been reported in the *arsattas*. For instance, about 28 cases of clash among the Meos of *pargana* Khohri are reported to have taken place, wherein the *amil* imposed a fine of 28 rupees on the guilty for unlawful activities. No involvement of the *pal chaudharis*, however, is noticed in these cases.[100]

Stealing of crop, grain, or cattle was also a common crime among the Meos. If caught or proven guilty, the thief was definitely punished by the state. Such was the case of Jenna Meo of village Mirhu in *pargana* Pahari who was caught red-handed while stealing grain from the house of a fellow Meo peasant of his own village. An enquiry led to his conviction, and he was arrested and imprisoned by the *amil*. When the personnel of the *amil* searched Jenna's house, nothing was found because he had already sold the stolen grain. Therefore, the personnel

98 *Arsatta, pargana* Pindayan, vs 1777/1720 CE.

99 *Arsatta, pargana* Harsana, vs 1787/1730 CE.

100 *Arsatta, pargana* Khohri, vs 1773/1716 CE.

took away two bullocks found in his house and sold them at the rate of 12 rupees.[101] Similarly, Kuka Meo of village Khedali Nai in *pargana* Mandawar had stolen the share (gram) of his Meena partner. Having proved his crime, the state imposed on him a penalty of 5 rupees.[102] In another case, a Meo peasant of Khoh village in *pargana* Pahari had occupied the fields of another peasant adjacent to his own. With the help of the *qanungo*, the *amil* got the fields of the land-grabber measured by the *patwari*, and the seized land was returned to the complainant.[103]

Mayaram's argument that the *pal chaudhari* played the role of a sovereign chief in settling internal disputes among the Meos of his *pal* may also be questioned in the light of the flexibility in the marriage norms of the Meos over which the *chaudhari* had little control during the Mughal period. According to the *gharecha* or *gharijna* custom, a Meo man could marry a woman of any caste, and children born of her would enjoy equal rights to property inheritance. The Shah Chaukha cult, popular in Mewat, facilitated this practice. Meo men who desired to marry would gather in the fair of Shah Chaukha, and a woman brought home by a Meo as his wife would be taken to the shrine of Shah Chaukha for his blessings. The *gharecha* column in the *arsattas* informs us of cases wherein Meo men married women of other castes and paid *hasil gharecha* (tax on remarriage) to the state. For instance, Bhajru Meo of *qasba* Jalalpur married Cheta Gujjar's wife and paid *hasil gharecha*.[104] So did Nooro Meo of *pargana* Mojpur who married Uda Meena's wife,[105] and Dalo Meo of village Bhadpura in *pargana* Mandawar who married Dayaram Meena's wife.[106] Further, by the same custom, a Meo man, in the event of his younger or elder brother's death, could treat the widow of the deceased as his wife. In Mughal India, the custom was not exclusive to the Meos, but prevalent among some middle castes, such as Jats, Ahirs, Gujjars, and Malis, as well. The *arsattas* also refer to the frequent sale and purchase of

101 *Arsatta, pargana* Pahari, VS 1788/1731 CE.

102 *Arsatta, pargana* Mandawar, VS 1787/1730 CE.

103 *Arsatta, pargana* Pahari, VS 1807/1750 CE.

104 *Arsatta, pargana* Jalalpur, VS 1784/1727 CE.

105 *Arsatta, pargana* Mojpur, VS 1789/1732 CE.

106 *Arsatta, pargana* Mandawar, VS 1781/1724 CE.

married women. We come across several instances of women married twice, that is, a married woman sold off by her husband to another. This shows that in medieval peasant society women were treated as chattel, their chief function being bearing children and sharing the burden of farming.

On the grounds of similarities in the tribal identity of the Meos and Meenas, the British administrators-cum-ethnographers considered them as belonging to the same 'race'. As a further evidence for this, they cited the folk love story of 'Dariya Khan Meo and Shashi Badani Meeni' to argue that marriage relationships once existed between the two communities but later broke off. According to the story, set in Akbar's reign, Todar Mal Pahat, the zamindar of Ajangarh, and Rao Bada Meena, respectively the fathers of Dariya Khan Meo and Shashi Badani, were close friends and arranged the marriage of their children. However, during the marriage, a clash between the Meos and Meenas took place at the bride's house when the Meenas tried to compel the vegetarian Meos to eat non-vegetarian food. The ensuing estrangement of relationship thus led to a prohibition of intermarriage.[107] But Rajasthani records contain several instances of intermarriage between the Meos and Meenas and thus do not corroborate the inference from this story that marriage relations between the two came to an end following this friction. Therefore, the story proves neither of the two arguments—that the Meos and Meenas once belonged to one 'race' and thus had matrimonial relations, and that these relations were terminated after a single decisive conflict. Apparently, this story was popularized by the region's bards (*mirasis*) because it was associated with two important zamindars and involved a large number of Meos and Meenas. That the Meos and the Meenas did not belong to the same 'racial' stock is also evident from several 17th- and 18th-century documentary references to *hasil gharecha* paid by the Meos for entering into marriage ties with not only the Meenas but also other castes, such as Jats, Ahirs, Gujjars, Telis, and Bhats.

107 Powlett, *Gazetteer of Ulwur*, 38; Channing, *Land Revenue Settlement of the Gurgaon District*, 29; D. Ibbetson, *Panjab Castes: Being a Reprint of the Chapter on "The Races, Castes and Tribes of the People" in the Report on the Census of the Panjab Published in 1883* (Lahore: Superintendent, Government Printing, 1916), 179; Cunningham, *Report of a Tour in Eastern Rajputana in 1882–83*, 27.

From the foregoing discussion of the Meo peasant society, we can safely argue that the *pal chaudharis* did not play any significant role in the resolution of disputes pertaining to engagements, marriages, and thefts of grain and cattle, at least during the Mughal period. Rather, these conflicts were resolved by the *amils* on behalf of the state. In other words, in order to solve their disputes and problems, the Meo peasants approached the state instead of their *pal chaudharis*. At the same time, it is feasible that Akbar obtained the services of the *pal chaudharis* by accommodating them in the Mughal revenue administration. Therefore, the position of the *chaudharis* turned out to be more like zamindars, their main responsibility being collection of revenue from the cultivators. After the fall of the Mughal empire, large parts of Mewat was absorbed into the Alwar state, while the territory of the Pahat Meos was incorporated into the Bharatpur state of the Jats. In both these states, the burden of land revenue on the Meos was increased to the point of driving them to rebellion. The *pal chaudharis* reaped the benefits of this contentious situation because after the decline of the Mughal state they had not been incorporated into the state structure by the rulers of states in which their territories had been absorbed. Hence, the *pal chaudharis* began to organize their own *pal* communities and, possibly, might have attained the sovereign position in the post-18th-century period.

Yet another important and related argument of Mayaram is that the Meos were perpetually and uncompromisingly against the state, whether Mughal or Rajput. This argument ignores multiple forms of negotiations and interactions between the Meo peasants and the state. Resistance, defiance, and rebellion constituted only one of these forms, the other important form being supplication before the dominant power to get concessions and relief. Petitioning was thus an important 'weapon of the weak' in the hands of the Meo peasants,[108] as will be discussed in the next chapter.

As we have observed, the Meo *pal* polity and Meo autonomy were non-existent during the Mughal period. This is because the land revenue and *jagirdari* systems of the Mughals transformed each village of Mewat into an administrative-cum-revenue-paying unit and placed

[108] James C. Scott, *Weapons of the Weak: Everyday Forms of Peasant Resistance* (New Delhi: Oxford University Press, 1990).

all of them under larger units, namely *parganas*. In tying the peasant society with such units, the Mughal state hardly conceded any space for their autonomy. Further, even after the decline of the Mughals, the Meos could not establish their independent state because in a large portion of Mewat (Alwar *sarkar* with 43 *parganas*), the Naruka Rajputs had established their zamindaris leading to the foundation of the Alwar state (1784). The Jats, too, set up their zamindaris in the *parganas* Kama Pahari and Khohri, thus leading to the formation of the Bharatpur state. Therefore, in such circumstances, the Meos got sandwiched in the power struggle among various competing groups of Rajputs and Jats and could not establish their own state.

V

The process of peasantization laid the foundation for many changes in the socio-cultural life of the Meos from the 16th to 18th centuries. During the late 16th century, one section of Meos had even joined the Mughal administrative service and, due to their regular interaction with the Mughal state, had begun to adopt Islamic practices and way of life.

In the *Ain-i-Akbari*, the Meos are broadly divided into two categories: (a) the agriculturists (peasants and primary zamindars) and (b) the Meoras and *khidmatiyyas* (post-carriers, spies, and palace guards). It is the Meoras and the *khidmatiyyas* who played an important role in the diffusion of Islamic culture among the Meos of Mewat during the Mughal period. The Persian and Rajasthani sources reveal that they were an integral part of Mughal postal and espionage system until the decline of the empire. About them, Abul-Fazl writes:

> They are the native of the Mewat and are famous as runners. They bring from great distances with zeal anything that may be required. They are excellent spies, and well perform the most intricate duties. They are likewise always ready to carry out orders. The caste which they belonged to was notorious for highway robbery and theft; former rulers were not able to keep them in check. The effective orders of His Majesty have led them to honesty; they are now famous for their trustworthiness.[109]

[109] Abul-Fazl mentions that 1,000 Meoras were employed as *dak*-carriers by Akbar (*The Ain-i-Akbari*, vol. 1, 262).

Muhammad Arif Qandhari, the author of *Tarikh-i-Akbari*, adds:

> Emperor Akbar employed four thousand foot-runners (Dak-carriers). They are experts in espionage also; they are on his majesty's service day and night so that news and reports reach everyday from all sides of the world. This class of men run as fast as lion, so that within ten days news comes from Bengal which is at a distance of seven hundred *kurohs* (*kos*) from Agra. His majesty gets all information of good or bad and profit or loss.[110]

Irfan Habib, in his analysis of the organization of Mughal postal communication system, has pointed out that it was not possible for a single Meora who could have run at a speed of 70 *kurohs* (about 158 miles) a day and night to reach his destination. Therefore, it must imply a relay system.[111] Indicating the existence of a relay system, Qandhari also states that Akbar established *dak chowkis* (postal stations) at every 5 *kurohs* (about 11 miles) and at each *chowki* two horses were kept besides the Meora foot-runners.[112] It thus appears that Akbar enrolled strongly built young Meos into the Mughal postal system who could run fast and survive in hostile weather and terrain. In doing so, Akbar not only developed the postal system as an important institutional mechanism for ensuring the security and consolidation of the Mughal empire, but also successfully transformed the Meo youth into loyal and faithful servants of the Mughal state. The following incident serves as an evidence of this new relationship that Akbar established with the Meos. In 1567, when Akbar came to know that Ali Quli Khan and his brother Bahadur Khan, nobles of the Turani faction of Mughal nobility, had rebelled, he organized a military campaign against them. Upon reaching Manikpur, he sent Hatwa Meora to find out the exact position of the rebels. According to Abul-Fazl, Hatwa Meora, a swift and intelligent courier, brought the much-needed news within 24 hours that the rebel nobles had constructed a bridge over Ganga near Singraur (modern Nawabganj) and crossed the river. When Akbar heard about this development, he

110 Muhammad Arif Qandhari, *Tarikh-i-Akbari*, trans. Tasneem Ahmad (Delhi: Pragati Publications, 1993), 62. He says that Akbar employed 4,000 Meos in the *dak* system.

111 Irfan Habib, 'Postal Communication in Mughal India', *Proceedings of the Indian History Congress*, 46th session (Amritsar, 1985), 236–52.

112 Qandhari, *Tarikh-i-Akbari*, 62.

immediately proceeded to take action against them. Abul-Fazl further adds that Hatwa Meora was loyal to Akbar and always accompanied him.[113] Channing, too, mentions that Akbar trusted the Meoras so much that he kept them as his bodyguards.[114]

Abul-Fazl observes that Akbar also posted Meo infantrymen called *khidmatiyyas* outside the palace to watch, guard, and see to it that his orders were carried out.[115] It seems that Akbar had understood the problems created by the isolation of the Meos who had been disparaged as troublemakers in the earlier centuries. He thus not only administratively and politically integrated the Mewat region into the Mughal state, but also brought about the social assimilation of the Meos. Once Akbar had developed the Mughal postal service with the help of the Meoras, the other Mughal emperors followed the same policy. For instance, chronicler Khafi Khan also points out that the Meoras were mainly *dak*-carriers during Aurangzeb's reign.[116]

Habib argues that the postal system was essential for a large centralized territorial entity like the Mughal empire because news and orders had to be conveyed over great distances. The organization was essentially based on the twin methods of relay-runners and relay horses which were posted at various *dak chowkis* that had been set up along different routes throughout the empire. In one part of Gujarat alone, 94 Meoras were posted at the *chowkis* along the route from Khandap (Ajmer *suba*) to Ahmedabad and from there to Baroda and Broach. At least two Meoras were posted at each *chowki* because they had to be available round the clock. The Meoras were required to give a written undertaking that they would not carry along with the (official) *nalwas* the papers of (private) persons.[117] According to B. L. Bhadani,

113 Abul-Fazl, *Akbarnama*, vol. 2, trans. H. Beveridge (New Delhi: Low Price Publications, [1902–39] 1993), 427–8.

114 Channing, *Land Revenue Settlement of the Gurgaon District*, 30.

115 Abul-Fazl, *The Ain-i-Akbari*, vol. 1, 261–2.

116 Muhammad Hashim Khafi Khan, *Muntakhab-al Lubab*, vol. 1, trans. Anees Jahan Syed as *Aurangzeb in Muntakhab-al Lubab* (Bombay: Somaiya Publications, 1977), 147.

117 Irfan Habib, 'Postal Communication in Mughal India'. The letters that the couriers, whether on foot or mounted, transmitted, used to be put in a tube made of a section of hollow bamboo cane called *nalwa* (Irfan Habib, 'Postal Communication in Mughal India').

164 Dak Meoras were posted along the Agra–Ahmedabad route, out of whom 77 were stationed at the *chowkis*.[118] This shows that almost half of the Meoras remained on duty round the clock at the *chowkis* and presumably the remaining half always stood in reserve.

Dastur komwar, a set of documents pertaining to the Jaipur state, lists the names of more than 200 Meoras posted at *dak chowkis* on the routes from Delhi to Jaipur and from Jaipur to Agra.[119] Many of them were rewarded for their good services by the Amber state. For instance, Lalchand Meora and his son were known for their services as spies in the Mughal court during the reign of Aurangzeb.[120] Similarly, Khoja Avad Khan Meora was also rewarded with a *jagir* of three villages in *pargana* Jalalpur (Alwar *sarkar*) for his service by Aurangzeb.[121] Tara Meora and Ram Singh Meora were also rewarded with one village each in *pargana* Pahari and Bharkol on account of their services.[122]

The *Ain-i-Akbari* mentions that the monthly salaries of the Dak Meoras ranged from 100 to 120 *dams* (2½ to 3 rupees) during the reign of Akbar.[123] An early 18th-century *dastur komwar* also informs us that generally the Dak Meoras were paid monthly salaries ranging from 2 to 4 rupees.[124] However, it appears from the Rajasthani documents that the Dak Meoras were not paid equally; some got perquisites for delivering politically crucial communication. For instance, in 1714, Bhoja and Madho Meoras were paid 22 rupees by the *diwan* of Amber for brining a letter of Chhabela Ram from Allahabad.[125] Sunder and Chetan Meoras were paid 14 rupees for bringing a letter of Ruhla Khan (an imperial *mansabdar*) which assigned the *ijara* of the villages of *pargana* Chatsu to the Amber Raja.[126] Similarly, Hari Ram Meora and his ally—who brought a letter of an imperial *mansabdar* communicating that the zamindari rights of four *parganas*,

118 B. L. Bhadani, 'The Mughal Highway and Post Stations in Marwar', *Proceedings of the Indian History Congress* (Delhi, 1990), 141–55.

119 *Dastur komwar Mutfarkat*, vol. 23, VS 1774/1717 CE, 59–140.

120 *Arzdasht*, Mah Vadi 6, VS 1744/1687 CE.

121 *Arsatta, pargana* Jalalpur, VS 1744/1687 CE.

122 *Arsatta, pargana* Pahari, VS 1793/1736 CE.

123 Abul-Fazl, *The Ain-i-Akbari*, vol. 1, 261–2.

124 *Dastur komwar mutfarkat*, vol. 23, VS 1774/1717 CE, 59–140.

125 *Khatut-ahalkarn*, Asoj Sudi, VS 1771/1714 CE.

126 *Arzdasht*, Bhadva Vadi 13, VS 1740/1683 CE.

namely Averi, Bahatri, Niwai, and Fagi, were assigned to the Amber Raja—were paid extra money by the *diwan* of Amber.[127] Apart from monthly salary and perquisites for extraordinary services, the Dak Meoras were also given concessions in the payment of land revenue on their personal land holdings by the Mughal state. The *amils* were asked to implement the state orders for such concessions after receiving them attested by the *qazis*.[128] Bhoja and Laad Khan Meoras, for instance, were respectively assigned 10 and 14 *bighas* of revenue-free lands (*muwafik bighas*) in *pargana* Bharkol (Tijara *sarkar*).[129] But it is not clear whether the Dak Meoras got revenue-free land in lieu of their salaries or as extra in reward. However, upon their retirement from the service of the Mughal state, such concessions were automatically terminated.[130]

The Dak Meoras, like other Meos, came from the tribal background and their religious identity was in a state of flux. They found employment in the Mughal postal service socially and economically beneficial. From the economic point of view, they obtained a secure source of income by way of monthly salaries and other perquisites. Besides, they were also given concessions in the payment of land revenue on their personal land holdings. Socially, they now constituted a class superior to the ordinary Meo peasants. Therefore, whoever once got a job in the Mughal postal service always tried to induct his family members into it.[131] It seems that the Dak Meoras had always enjoyed an advantageous position in the Mughal state in terms of creating job opportunities for their sons and relatives. This is how they must have transmitted their professional knowledge and experience in the field of postal service and their loyalty and faithfulness to the

127 *Arzdasht*, Chait Vadi 1, VS 170/1683 CE.

128 *Arsatta, pargana* Kotla, VS 1722/1665 CE; *pargana* Jalalpur, VS 1722/1665 CE; *pargana* Bharkol, VS 1722/1665 CE; *pargana* Pahari, VS 1793/1736 CE.

129 *Arsatta, pargana* Bharkol, VS 1722/1665 CE.

130 *Chithi* to the *amil, pargana* Pahari, Asoj Vadi 9, VS 1804/1747 CE. Complaints were lodged by some Dak Meoras against the *amils* who denied them concessions in the payment of land revenue on their personal holdings. The *amils*, in turn, argued that the concession was valid till the Dak Meoras remained in the service of the Mughal state (*Chithi* to the *amil, pargana* Pahari, Asoj Vadi 9, VS 1804/1747 CE).

131 *Arzadasht*, Mah Vadi 6, VS 1740/1683 CE.

Mughal state to the succeeding generations. British ethnographers, too, had observed this spirit of fidelity among the Meos towards their masters.[132]

Due to their regular interaction with the Mughal court as well as other imperial authorities, the Dak Meoras found themselves closer to the Islamic culture and gradually began to follow certain Islamic customs and rituals associated with the Mughal court. The nature of the Islamic festivals and rituals was such that they involved a congregation of a large number of people. These festivals were Id-ul-fitr, Ramzan, Shab-e-barat, and the Urs of Sufi saint Khwaja Muinuddin Chishti, with a lot of people, including palace staff and the emperor's bodyguards, taking part in the celebrations.[133] In particular, the Urs of Muinuddin Chishti, celebrated in the Mughal court since the days of Akbar, witnessed the participation of scores of people from all classes such as nobles, officers, *khidmatiyyas*, bodyguards, and the Dak Meoras. They walked 228 miles from Agra to the tomb of Khwaja Saheb in Ajmer passing through the Mewat region. They carried the holy flag of the saint and a large number of people paid their respects to the flag on their way to Ajmer.[134] The Dak Meoras and *khidmatiyyas* reverently observed these festivals, and after retirement started celebrating these festivals in their own villages.[135] They even invited their relatives and the friends to take part in these festivals. They started inviting *qazis* to perform *nikah* (wedding ceremony) for their children and contracting marriages with Muslim peasants. Thus, in more ways than one, they started regarding themselves as part of the Muslim community. The *khatoot ahalkarans* also underline the role of *qazi* appointed by the Mughal state to resolve the disputes of the people. Devidas Harkara (spy) complained to the *diwan* of

[132] Major-General Sir John Malcolm, *The Political History of India from 1784 to 1823*, vol. 2 (London: John Murray, 1826), 174. Malcom says that the Meos happened to be faithful and courageous guards and servants to their masters.

[133] Muhammad Umar, *Muslim Society in Northern India during the Eighteenth Century* (Delhi: Munshiram Manoharlal, 1998), 145–55.

[134] *Arsatta, pargana* Wazirpur, VS 1771/1714 CE, VS 1774/1717 CE, VS 1776/1719 CE, VS 1777/720 CE, VS 1778/1721 CE, VS 1780/1723 CE.

[135] *Khatoot ahalkaran*, Asadh Sudi 4, VS 1780/1723 CE.

Amber that the *qazi* did not attend his own duties; rather, he visited the villages to perform *nikahs*. Devidas further stated that although the *qazi* got a salary of 240 rupees from the Mughal state, he was very greedy; and that he should have concentrated on his job. Finally, he pleaded with the *diwan* to speak to the *vakil* so that he could raise the issue at the Mughal court.[136]

As discussed earlier, after the Battle of Khanwa, the Khanzadas lost their principality; Mewat became part of the Mughal state while the Khanzadas became part of the Mughal nobility. With the decline of the Mughal empire, the socio-economic position of the Khanzadas also declined. Muhammad Makhdum, the author of *Arzang-i-Tijara*, states that they migrated eastwards, that is, to the adjoining states such as Awadh, Lucknow, and Bareilly.[137] A section of the Khanzadas left in Mewat cultivated fields as *khudkashta* peasants with the help of family labour, although they had never touched the plough before.[138] The social security of the Khanzadas was further threatened by the rising power of the Jats of Bharatpur state and the Naruka Rajputs of Alwar state in Mewat. In order to strengthen their social base, the Khanzadas thus began to enter into matrimonial relations with the former Dak Meoras who had acquired a Muslim identity by then. *Arzang-i-Tijara* also adds that earlier, Meos belonging to Gotwal and Duhlot clans had matrimonial relations with the Khanzadas.[139] Corroborating this, Channing writes that the Meos belonging to Ghatawasan, Paul, Narainwas, Kherlikhurd, and Mohammada Bas villages of *pargana* Firozpur Jhirka claimed that they were Khanzadas in the past, but merged their identity with the Meo community as a consequence of their matrimonial relations with the Meos.[140] However, this does not mean that all Khanzadas had matrimonial relations with the Meos, although certainly the matrimonial relations between some Khanzadas and Dak Meoras did encourage the Islamization of the Meo community. In fact, the Jagga records show that by the early 18th century, the Meos had begun to adopt Muslim names (see Table 3.1).

136 *Khatoot ahalkaran*, Asadh Sudi 4, VS 1780/1723 CE; Devidas cited the instance of Noor Khan Meora inviting the *qazi* to perform *nikah*.

137 Makhdum, *Arzang-i-Tijara*, 5.

138 Makhdum, *Arzang-i-Tijara*, 5.

139 Makhdum, *Arzang-i-Tijara*, 33.

140 Channing, *Land Revenue Settlement of the Gurgaon District*, 30.

Table 3.1 Genealogy of some Meo families

Family genealogy	*Gotra*	Name of the village	Date of the establishment of the village
1. Mansingh ↓ Umed Singh ↓ Mukhtiar Singh ↓ Maan Singh ↓ Salar Singh ↓ Rai Mal ↓ Mohammad Khan, Nahar Khan	Shaugan	Maacha	VS 1524/1467 CE
2. Chuhar Singh ↓ Loot Singh ↓ Todar Mal ↓ Mawasi ↓ Mohar Singh ↓ Mehrab Singh ↓ Imam Baksh, Mlekhan		Chuharpur	VS 1505/1448 CE
3. Pithusamal ↓ Jaswant Singh ↓ Hari Singh ↓ Dhan Singh ↓	Ratawat	Pathrai	VS 1532/1465 CE

(Cont'd)

Table 3.1 (*Cont'd*)

Family genealogy	*Gotra*	Name of the village	Date of the establishment of the village
Umrao Singh ↓ Khuda Baksh, Chote Khan			
4. Chand Singh ↓ Ranbir Singh–Bhan Singh ↓ Vir Bhan ↓ Amar Singh ↓ Mangal Singh ↓ Rustam, Ismail Khan	Singhal	Chandauli	VS 1532/1465 CE

Source: Jagga records, *pothi* no. 1.

As discussed earlier, Powlett in the late 19th century commented on the fragile and incomplete process of Islamization among the Meos, who, according to him, adopted Muslim names, but continued to worship Hindu village deities and observe several Hindu and Muslim festivals. Further, only eight out of 52 Meo villages in *pargana* Tijara had mosques.[141] Channing, too, made similar remarks about the Meos of Nuh-Firozpur Jhirka region:

> [T]hey have been very lax Muhammadans sharing in most of the rites and customs of their Hindu neighbours, especially such as are pleasant to observe, their principle of action seems to have been to keep the feasts of both religions, and the fasts of neither. Recently some Meos now even observe the Ramzan fast, build village mosques, say their prayers, and their wives wear trousers instead of Hindu petticoat—all signs of a religious revival.[142]

[141] Powlett, *Gazetteer of Ulwur*, 70.

[142] Channing, *Land Revenue Settlement of the Gurgaon District*, 37–8.

Although the process of Islamization among the Meos remained slow up to the early 20th century, it certainly created an Islamic identity of the Meos which distinctly separated them from other non-Muslim castes in the region.

There are two beliefs prevalent among the Meos regarding their Islamization. The first is that they converted to Islam under the influence of Salar Masud.[143] The second is that Khwaja Muinuddin Chishti, while passing through Mewat on his way to Ajmer, blessed them to become Muslims. These beliefs can be read as an attempt of the Meos to convey to the Islamic world that they should not be considered a lower category of Muslims because their Islamization was sanctified by renowned Sufi saints. Such postulations were constructed to attain religious legitimacy as Meos were the latest converts to Islam.

Colonial ethnographers, on the other hand, believed that the Meos adopted Islam due to the cruelties inflicted by Sultan Balban.[144] However, during Balban's reign, the Meos had neither become peasants nor formed a distinct community. Moreover, even Indo-Persian chroniclers like those of Barani and Minhaj Siraj do not state that Balban forcibly converted Meos to Islam. Others argued that the Islamization of Meos took place exactly during the period Akbar carried out the territorial division of Meo *pal*s. However, this view, too, lacks credibility because Akbar's religious policy was not discriminatory but all-inclusive. Yet others pointed out that the conversion of Meos to Islam occurred during the reign of Aurangzeb as a result of his bigoted religious policy that was prejudiced against

143 Abul-Fazl states that Salar Masud was one of the martyrs of the Ghaznavid army (*The Ain-i-Akbari*, vol. 1, 153). According to *Mirat-i-Masudi*, Salar Masud was the son of a sister of Mahmud of Ghazni and was born in 1015 in Ajmer. At the age of 16, he participated in the Ghaznavid invasions of Hindustan. He served in Mahmud's army and died at the age of 19. A number of significant events were thought to be associated with Masud's life, and he was worshipped by both Hindus and Muslims (Abdur Rahman Chisti, *Mirat-i-Masudi*, in *The History of India as Told by Its Own Historians*, vol. 2, eds H. M. Elliot and John Dowson [Delhi: Low Price Publications, 2001], 513–49).

144 Cunningham, *Report of a Tour in Eastern Rajputana in 1882–83*, 29–30. Channing adds that the ancestor of the Meos embraced Islam during the reign of Qutbuddin Aibak (1206–1210 CE) (*Land Revenue Settlement of the Gurgaon District*, 28).

non-Muslims.[145] There is no historical evidence to support this view either. In the Rajasthani sources, particularly the *dastur komwar*s and *arsatta*s, while there are no clear references to the Islamic identity of Meo peasants, there are some clues about their religious and social identity. It is, however, from the late 17th and early 18th centuries that references to the Dak Meoras indicate the beginnings of the process of Islamization of Meos in terms of their observance of certain Islamic rituals, such as *nikah*, burial, celebration of festivals such as Id, and adoption of Muslim names. This can also be viewed as changes in the cultural life of the Dak Meoras on account of their long service in the Mughal administration, as discussed earlier. These changes also spread the impact of Islam among the Meo peasantry. However, the religious identity of the Meos remained ambiguous, even as late as the mid-19th century, since the first statistical report prepared by the British in 1840 recorded that about one-third of the Meo population in *pargana*s Firozpur Jhirka, Nuh, and Taoru were unaware of whether they were Hindus or Muslims. Thus, it may be concluded that many among the Meos began to assume Muslim identity towards the end of the 18th century and this process continued up to the 20th century.

[145] J. Forbes Watson and John William Kaye, eds, *The People of India*, vol. 4 (London: W. H. Allen and Co. for the India Museum, 1869), Item 202. They think that the conversion of the Meos was 'probably the work of Sultan Firozshah Tughlaq in the 14th century, when so many tribes were forcibly made Mohammadans, and that Aurangzeb completed what was then begun'. The settlement report of 1878 puts the date of Meos' conversion somewhere around the time of Qutubuddin Aibak, while W. W. Hunter puts the date of conversion of the Meos at the time of Mahmud of Ghaznavi (Channing, *Land Revenue Settlement of the Gurgaon District*, 28).

4

RESOURCES OF MEWAT

APPROPRIATION AND DISTRIBUTION

THE RULING CLASS DERIVED THE BULK of its income by appropriating the surplus produce of the peasantry in the form of land revenue and other taxes. An inquiry into the salient features of the land revenue system and its working is called for in view of its central role in determining the pattern of agrarian relationships. The magnitude of land revenue and the mechanism of its appropriation shaped not only the relations between the various components of the ruling class but also those between the ruling class as a whole and the peasants. Moreover, the actual process of the distribution of land revenue demand among individual cultivators would also reveal both the relations among the various categories of peasants and the actual working of the village society.

I

Information from various documents, such as *arsattas*, *jamabandis*, and *dastur-al-amals* of various *parganas*, forms the empirical basis for investigation into the nature and magnitude of land revenue and other taxes. The *arsattas* provide details of the income and expenditure of the *parganas*. The information on revenue can be divided into three parts: the total collection (*muqararajama*), the expenditure (*kharch* or *minzalik*), and the arrears (*baqaya*). The amount of revenue collected from various taxes and cesses is divided into two separate categories, namely *muafiq-jamabandi* (revenue realized according to the assessment) and *siwai-jamabandi* (revenue realized from a variety of taxes other than the *mal-o-jihat*). The former is further subdivided into *mal-o-jihat* (*mal* or tax on crop and *jihat* cesses) and *sair-jihat* (a variety of agricultural and non-agricultural taxes).The *mal* (tax on crop) accounted for the major portion of revenue. The share of other taxes and cesses, such as *jihat* and *sair-jihat* in the total revenue, was small.

The *jamabandis* contain information about the methods of revenue assessment and the magnitude of *mal*, *jihat*, and *sair-jihat*. These documents were prepared *pargana*-wise and provided details of the revenue demand from each village under the Amber Raja's *khalisa* land.[1] However, they do not include the revenue figures of the villages held in *ijara*. Nevertheless, they are of immense value in computing the magnitude of land revenue demand on crops assessed under the *batai-jinsi* system and the magnitude of *jihat*.

The *dastur-al-amals* provide the schedules of land revenue rates for different crops. The rates or *dasturs* were prepared on the basis of a comprehensive prior survey of the nature of crops sown, the productivity of soil, the methods of irrigation used, the prevailing market prices, and the caste status of the peasant (and thereby his position in the rural social hierarchy).

This chapter attempts to ascertain the net burden of land revenue and other taxes on the peasants, the mode of revenue payment, the mechanism by which the revenue demand was distributed among the individual cultivators, and, finally, the relationship between the revenue demand and the actual revenue paying capacity of the cultivators. The information contained in the aforementioned documents enables us to study the magnitude and incidence of taxation at the level of both *pargana* and village. The total revenue demand at the level of village, the primary unit of revenue assessment, can be computed on the basis of a selective study of a few representative villages that

[1] The villages of Amber Raja's *tankhwa jagir* which were not sub-assigned by him to his servants constituted his *khalisa* land.

continued to be part of the *khalisa* land for the better part of the period under review. This method has the advantage of being more appropriate for the purpose of calculating the total burden of agricultural and non-agricultural taxes on the peasants. Moreover, in this case, it is possible to show whether or not there was any significant change in the level of revenue demand. An overall picture of the magnitude of taxes, however, can be drawn by comparing the results of the study of sample villages with the figures for the entire *pargana*.

It is quite evident from the *arsattas* that the rate of *mal* was not arbitrarily fixed. It was calculated on the basis of such factors as the quality of soil, the nature of crops sown, the methods of irrigation used, the prevailing market prices, and the caste of the cultivator. In accordance with these variable factors, the quantum of *mal* varied from *pargana* to *pargana*, from village to village within a *pargana*, and from peasant to peasant within a village.

Considering that soil productivity was an important determinant of the rate of *mal*, land was classified into several categories, namely *polachh* (continuously cultivated and never left fallow), *banjar* (uncultivated),[2] *magro* (hilly), and sandy. However, it is not clear whether the classification of land as *polachh* and *banjar* was based on the continuity of cultivation or the quality of soil. Revenue from the *polachh* land was fixed at 50 per cent of the produce for the majority of peasants, while revenue from the *banjar* land was fixed on an ascending scale constantly increasing for up to five years after which it was fixed at 40 per cent of the produce.[3] The revenue demand from the *polachh* land also varied according to the status of the cultivator in the rural social hierarchy. For instance, in *pargana* Atela Bhabra, the land revenue rate on the *polachh* land that produced one crop in a year was fixed at 25 per cent of the produce for the Shekhawat Rajput cultivators and 50 per cent of the produce for the *paltis*.[4]

According to the means of irrigation used, different revenue rates were applied to *barani* (rain-fed), *chahi* (well-irrigated), *nehri* (canal-irrigated), and *talabi* (tank-irrigated) lands. For instance, the rate of revenue for the *batai-jinsi* crops raised on lands irrigated by wells

[2] *Dastur-al-amal, pargana* Atela Bhabra, VS 1767/1710 CE and VS 1791/1734 CE.

[3] *Dastur-al-amal, pargana* Atela Bhabra, VS 1767/1710 CE.

[4] *Dastur-al-amal, pargana* Atela Bhabra, VS 1767/1710 CE.

(*chahi kuan*) in *parganas* Atela Bhabra and Mojpur was 40 per cent and 33 per cent of the produce respectively for different categories of cultivators.[5] The rate for crops raised on the *barani* lands in *pargana* Mojpur was fixed at 40–50 per cent of the produce, although slight variations appeared for different categories of cultivators.[6] The rates on the *chahi* and *barani* lands in *pargana* Khohri were 40 and 50 per cent of the produce respectively.[7]

The quality of crop sown was yet another factor which was taken into account while determining the rate of land revenue. As the returns from cash crops were higher than those from food crops, the former were assessed at higher rates. The prevailing market prices of various agricultural commodities were also taken into account while assessing the rate for a particular crop. The variations in the rate from one *pargana* to another were also due to price variations to some extent. Moreover, the caste status of a cultivator in a village was also considered while determining the rate of land revenue demand levied upon him. Thus, the revenue levied on the cultivators belonging to higher castes in a village—the *riyayati*—were assessed at concessional rates, while the cultivators of middle and lower castes designated as the *raiyati* were required to pay revenue at higher rates. The *raiyati* was required to pay *mal* at rates about 15–20 per cent higher than those levied upon the *riyayati*.[8] There also existed a separate *dastur* for the *gaveti* and the *pahi* cultivators.[9]

The land revenue was assessed and collected by two methods, namely *zabti* (*zabt*)[10] and *jinsi* (*batai*).[11] The *zabti* method was not

5 *Dastur-al-amal, pargana* Mojpur, VS 1780/1723; *pargana* Atela Bhabra, VS 1767/1710 CE.

6 *Dastur-al-amal, pargana* Mojpur, VS 1770/1713 CE.

7 *Dastur-al-amal, pargana* Khohri, H. 1049/1639–40 CE.

8 *Dastur-al-amal, pargana* Atela Bhabra, VS 1767/1710 CE; *pargana* Sonkhar-Sonkhari, VS 1773/1716 CE.

9 *Dastur-al-amal, pargana* Mojpur, VS 1770/1713 CE; *pargana* Khohri, H. 1049/1639–40 CE.

10 For the definition and working of the *zabt*, see Irfan Habib, *The Agrarian System of Mughal India 1556–1707*, 2nd rev. ed. (New Delhi: Oxford University Press, 1999), 200–19.

11 Under the *batai-jinsi* (*ghalla-bakshi*), a simple sharing of the harvested grain took place on the basis of shares agreed upon between the peasants and the state.

implemented in the entire Mewat region, and the peasants were given the option of paying revenue in cash or kind. The peasants usually paid revenue for cash crops according to the *zabti* system and for food crops according to the *batai-jinsi* system. However, this was not a rigid division, as some peasants opted for the *zabti* method even for some food crops. Under the *zabti* system, separate cash rates per *bigha* for different crops were prepared for each *pargana* and for each village within a *pargana*. Moreover, there prevailed different *zabti* rates for the same crop in different *parganas* and even different villages of the same *pargana*. The inter-*pargana* variation in the *zabti* rates was due to variations in the material conditions of agriculture and prices. Another factor for this variation was the difference in the quality of crops.

The most formidable problem in working out the magnitude of *mal* under the *zabti* system is that the *arsattas* and the *jamabandis* do not indicate the incidence of *mal* on the *zabti* crops in terms of the total produce. During the reign of Akbar when the *zabti* system reached the final phase of its evolution, the *zabti* rates or *dasturs* were prepared on the basis of an elaborate process called *jama-i-dah-sala* by taking into account yields, prices, and area statistics of last ten years.[12] From the available documents, it is not possible to get the requisite statistics to ascertain the ratio of the *zabti* rates to the total produce. It is, therefore, difficult to say whether the land revenue under the *zabti* system was fixed at one-third or half of the produce. On the other hand, sufficient information is available on the annual movement of the *zabti* rates which enables us to examine whether the *zabti* rates were stable, subject to periodic revision or modification, and whether there existed any correlation between the *zabti* rates and the movement of agricultural prices. An analysis based on this approach would also partly reveal the preference of the peasant for one of the two methods of land revenue assessment.

The *arsattas* and the *jamabandis* provide valuable information for determining the rate of *mal* where the revenue was assessed under the *batai-jinsi* system. For the crops assessed under this system, the

[12] Habib, *The Agrarian System of Mughal India*, 205–10. For a different interpretation of the *Ain-i-Akbari* on this aspect, see Shireen Moosvi, *The Economy of the Mughal Empire c. 1595: A Statistical Study* (Delhi: Oxford University Press, 1987), 95–101.

figures of the total produce for each crop and the respective shares of the *raiyat* and the state are specified. It is thus possible to calculate the percentage of produce collected by the state from the peasants in the form of land revenue. It may, however, be noted that the figures of produce and the revenue mentioned in the *arsattas* are for the entire *pargana*, and not for each village.

In order to ascertain the magnitude of *mal* for the *parganas*, figures from the *arsattas* and the *jamabandis* have been utilized. In the *jamabandis*, the figures of the total produce, the share of the state, and the share of the *raiyat* are mentioned separately for each village along with the quantity realized as *farah*. The information on the quantity of produce realized as *mal* from the villages selected as samples from each *pargana* has been taken from the *jamabandis*. The results at the *pargana* as well as the village level are as given in Tables 4.1–4.4a, 4.4b, and 4.4c.

From the available figures, it is clear that the rate of *mal* under the *batai-jinsi* varied from *pargana* to *pargana* in the Mewat region. It ranged from 28 to 48 per cent of the produce in the case of *kharif* crops and from 26 to 46 per cent in the case of *rabi* crops. Among the eight *parganas* listed in Table 4.1, Khilohra had the lowest rate of *mal* (about

Table 4.1 Average rate of *mal* in different *parganas* (*mal* as percentage of the total produce)

Name of the *pargana*	Year	*Kharif*		*Rabi*	
		Share of the *raiyat*	Share of the state	Share of the *raiyat*	Share of the state
Atela Bhabra	1664	52.0	48.0	62.7	37.3
Pindayan	1665	58.0	42.0	63.0	37.0
Mojpur	1714	65.3	34.7	54.0	46.0
Jalalpur	1718	70.0	30.0	72.0	28.0
Mandawar	1713	–	–	53.6	46.4
Khilohra	1718	72.0	28.0	74.0	26.0
Pahari	1716	53.4	46.6	–	–
Wazirpur	1749	64.0	36.0	65.5	34.5

Source: *Arsatta Muzmil*, *pargana* Atela Bhabra, VS 1721/1664 CE; *pargana* Pindayan, VS 1722/1665 CE; *pargana* Mojpur, VS 1771/1714 CE; *pargana* Jalalpur, VS 1775/1718 CE; *pargana* Mandawar, VS 1770/1713 CE; *pargana* Khilohra, VS 1775/1718 CE; *pargana* Pahari, VS 1773/1716 CE; *pargana* Wazirpur, VS 1806/1749 CE.

Table 4.2 *Mal* as percentage of the total produce in different villages in different *parganas*

Name of the *pargana*	Name of the village or *qasba*	Year	*Kharif*		*Rabi*	
			Share of the *raiyat*	Share of the state	Share of the *raiyat*	Share of the state
Atela Bhabra	*Qasba* Bhabra	1665	51.5	48.5	60.3	39.7
Atela Bhabra	Ransika	1664	60.4	39.6	60.4	39.6
Khohri	*Qasba* Khohri	1747	–	–	55.2	44.8
Khohri	Shamsirpur	1664	60.0	40.0	60.0	40.0
Jalalpur	*Qasba* Punkhar	1709	62.8	37.2	72.6	27.4
Chalkaliyana	Mithathal	1665	53.2	46.8	55.0	45.0

Source: *Jamabandi*, *pargana* Atela Bhabra, VS 1721/1664 CE, VS 1722/1665 CE; *pargana* Khohri, VS 1804/1747 CE, VS 1721/1664 CE; *pargana* Jalalpur, VS 1766/1709 CE; *pargana* Chalkaliyana, VS 1722/1665 CE.

Table 4.3 Land revenue under *batai-jinsi* system as percentage of total produce

Name of the *pargana*	*Palti*	*Pahi*	*Kamin*	Rajput/ *mahajan*/ Brahmin	*Patel*	*Chaudhari qanungo*	Quality of land
Kharif **crops**							
Atela Bhabra	50	33	40	25–33	40	25	*polachh*
Sonkhar-Sokhari	40–50	50	0	33	0	33	-do-
Narnol	50	–	–	–	–	–	-do-
Rabi **crops**							
Atela Bhabra	40–50	–	–	25–33	–	25	*polachh*, *vor* (irrigated by well and *dhenkhli*)
Sonkhar-Sokhari	40–50	50	–	33	–	33	-do-

(*Cont'd*)

Table 4.3 (*Cont'd*)

Name of the *pargana*	*Palti*	*Pahi*	*Kamin*	Rajput/ *mahajan*/ Brahmin	*Patel*	*Chaudhari qanungo*	Quality of land
Khohri	40–50	50	–	–	–	–	-do-
Narnol	40	–	–	–	–	–	-do-
Averi	40–50	–	–	25	–	25–33	-do-

Source: *Dastur-al-amal*, *pargana* Atela Bhabra, vs 1767/1710 CE; *pargana* Sonkhar-Sonkhari, vs 1773/1716 CE; *pargana* Narnol, vs 1803/1746 CE; *pargana* Khohri, vs 1723/1666 CE; *Chithi* to the *amil*, *pargana* Averi, Sawan Sudi 8, vs 1783/1726 CE.

Table 4.4a *Zabti* rates per *bigha* in *pargana* Mojpur (1714 CE)

Name of the crop	*Raiyat*		*Patel/Patwari/ Qanungo*		Rajput	
	Rupees	*Annas*	Rupees	*Annas*	Rupees	*Annas*
Kharif						
Kuri-varti	1	0	0	14	0	12
Makka (Maize), *Jowar* (Sorghum)	1	8	1	6	–	–
Kodon (Kodo millet)	1	6	1	4	1	0
Vani (Cotton)	2	8	2	6	2	4
San (Hemp)	2	8	–	–	–	–
Chola	1	0	0	14	–	–
Kaguni	1	8	1	2	–	–
Chari	0	12	–	–	–	–
Torai	2	12	–	–	–	–
Rabi						
Wheat	6	0	5	12	4	8
Barley	5	0	4	12	3	12
Gram	6	0	5	8	–	–
Sarson	5	0	4	12	3	12
Cheena (Common millet)	1	0	–	–	0	12
Tobacco	4	0	–	–	–	–
Baingan (Brinjal)	–	–	–	–	1	14
Tarkari (Vegetable)	2	0	–	–	–	–

Source: *Arsatta*, *pargana* Mojpur, vs 1771/1714 CE.

Table 4.4b *Zabti* rates per *bigha* in *pargana* Atela Bhabra (1728 CE)

Name of the crop	*Raiyat*		Rajput		*Muqaddam/ Chaudhari/ Patwari/ Patel/Qanungo*	
	Rupees	*Annas*	Rupees	*Annas*	Rupees	*Annas*
Kharif						
Vani	2	8	1	8	2	0
Baar/Ganna (Sugarcane)	2	2	1	6	1	11
Makka	1	4	0	12	1	0
Kaguni, Mandwa (Ragi)	1	8	1	4	1	8
Kuri	0	8	0	2	0	8
Tarkari	3	4	2	4	–	–
Rabi						
Tarkari, Muli (radish), *Kakari, Gajar* (carrot), *Baingan*	3	4	2	4	2	12
Cheena	0	8	0	6	–	–
Dodi (Opium)	2	0	1	8	–	–

Source: Arsatta, pargana Atela Bhabra, VS 1785/1728 CE.

Table 4.4c *Zabti* rates per *bigha* in *pargana* Wazirpur (1712 CE)

Name of the crop (*kharif*)	*Raiyat*		*Qanungo/ Chaudhari*	
	Rupees	*Annas*	Rupees	*Annas*
Vani	6	0	5	0
Baar	3	0	2	8
Jowar	1	10	1	6
Bajra (Bulrush, spiked millet)	1	3	0	14
Moth	1	1	0	12
Til	1	13	1	6
Neel (Indigo)	2	4	1	12
Chola	1	1	–	–
San	3	0	–	–
Mandwa	1	2	–	–

Source: Arsatta, pargana Wazirpur, VS 1769/1712 CE.

Table 4.4d *Zabti* rates per *bigha* in *pargana* Khohri (1713 CE)

Name of the crop (*kharif*)	*Raiyat*		*Qanungo/ Chaudhari*	
	Rupees	*Annas*	Rupees	*Annas*
Kuri-varti	1	0	0	10
Kodon	1	10	1	2
San	2	0	1	8
Baar	2	0	1	8
Chola	1	2	0	12

Source: *Arsatta*, *pargana* Khohri, VS 1770/1713 CE.

28 per cent in the case of *kharif* and 26 per cent in the case of *rabi* crops), whereas Atela Bhabra had the maximum average rate (about 48 per cent in the case of *kharif* and 37 per cent in the case of *rabi* crops). Further, the magnitude of *mal* was higher for *kharif* than for *rabi* crops, since *kharif* crops were rain-fed, while *rabi* crops required more inputs in the form of irrigation, and so on. The information from the *arsatta*s can also be corroborated by other documents. According to the *dastur-al-amal*s of different *pargana*s, the share of the produce demanded from the *raiyati* (non-privileged, ordinary) peasants under the *batai-jinsi* varied from 40 to 50 per cent,[13] while that demanded from the *riyayati* (privileged) peasants varied from 25 to 33 per cent.[14] On the whole, the figures given in the revenue records reveal that the rate of *mal* was not uniform. The share of state normally ranged between 25 and 50 per cent of the produce and this range of variation applied to both *riyayati* and *raiyati* peasants.

As noted earlier, in addition to *mal* the peasants were also required to pay a variety of taxes and cesses designated as *jihat*, *sair-jihat*, and *siwai-jamabandi*. The *jihat* taxes were exclusively collected from the peasants and merged into the *mal*. There was no uniform pattern in

13 *Dastur-al-amal*, *pargana* Khohri, VS 1723/1666 CE; *pargana* Atela Bhabra, VS 1767/1710 CE; *pargana* Sonkhar-Sonkhari, VS 1773/1716 CE.

14 *Dastur-al-amal*, *pargana* Khohri, VS 1723/1666 CE; *pargana* Atela Bhabra, VS 1767/1710 CE; *pargana* Sonkhar-Sonkhari, VS 1773/1716 CE.

the collection of *sair-jihat* and *siwai-jamabandi* across the *parganas*. The same tax would be listed under the category of *sair-jihat* in one *pargana*, while in others it would be classified as *siwai-jamabandi*. Consequently, the number of taxes under the heads *sair-jihat* and *siwai-jamabandi* varied from *pargana* to *pargana*.

The *jihat* taxes were levied under both *zabti* and *batai-jinsi* systems. They were assessed under two heads: (a) *lawazima*, particularly under the *zabti* system; and (b) *farah* under the *batai-jinsi* system. Taxes under the head *lawazima* were collected from the peasants to meet the expenses incurred in the measurement of land (including the perquisites of revenue officials who measured the fields). These were *jaribana, zabitana, rozina zabti, dohnimi zabti*, and *sarhi*. *Jaribana* was charged at the rate of 28 *dams* per *bigha*.[15] *Zabitana* was charged at the rate of 15 *dams* per *bigha*.[16] *Rozina zabti* was charged at the rate of one rupee for every 100 *bighas* of *zabti* land under cultivation in *pargana* Wazirpur[17] and 12 *annas* for every 30 *bighas* in *pargana* Khohri.[18] *Dohnimi zabti* was charged at the rate of one *taka* on each *zabti* rupee.[19] *Sarhi* was charged at the rate of half-a-*taka* on every 100 *zabti* rupees.[20] Six *annas* on every 100 *zabti bigha* were collected as *jihati-zabti*.[21] Under the *batai-jinsi* system, the *jihat* taxes were realized from the peasants to recover the expenses incurred in the collection of *mal*. These were *farah-sarina, takina* (cess collected in *taka*), *rozina-batai, bhara, lata-kharach, tulai*, and *kayali*. The *riyayati* cultivators were exempted from these cesses. The rates of *jihat* taxes under the *batai-jinsi* are given in Table 4.5.

Some of the taxes under the heads *sair-jihat* and *siwai-jamabandi* were agricultural in nature and others non-agricultural. Further, while most of the agricultural taxes were imposed on individual peasants,

15 *Jamabandi, pargana* Kotla, VS 1721/1664 CE.
16 *Jamabandi, pargana* Kotla, VS 1721/1664 CE.
17 *Arsatta, pargana* Wazirpur, VS 1779/1722 CE.
18 *Arsatta, pargana* Khohri, VS 1770/1713 CE.
19 *Jamabandi, pargana* Kotla, VS 1721/1664 CE.
20 *Arsatta, pargana* Pahari, VS 1773/1716 CE.
21 *Arsatta, pargana* Wazirpur, VS 1779/1722 CE.

Table 4.5 *Jihat* taxes under *batai-jinsi* system

Type of taxes	Rate of taxation
Farah-sarina	2–3 *sers*[22] for every *maund* of the state's share of produce
Takina and *bhara*	½–1 *taka*[23] for every *maund* of the state's share
Lata-kharach	1 *ser*[24] for every *maund* of produce
Rozina-batai	8 *annas*[25] for every 100 *maund* of produce
Tulai	10 *annas*[26] for every 100 rupee of *mal*
Kayali	¼ *ser*[27] for each *maund* of the state's share

some were levied on the village as a whole, that is, the village taken as the unit of assessment. Many non-agricultural taxes were levied on the artisans and the traders for carrying out commerce and artisanal production. The rest of non-agricultural *sair-jihat* and *siwai-jamabandi* taxes included transit duties, presentations, fines on various crimes, tax on fairs and mines, and so on. This study, however, focuses primarily on agricultural taxes.

The agricultural *sair-jihat* and *siwai-jamabandi* taxes were largely extracted from the peasants to recover various administrative expenses on the assessment and collection of *mal*. Several officials were recruited from among the influential sections of the sections of the rural society to carry out the regular assessment of revenue. The remuneration of these semi-government, hereditary officials

22 *Arsatta, pargana* Khohri, VS 1769/1712 CE; *pargana* Pahari, VS 1784/1727 CE; *pargana* Jalalpur, VS 1723/1666 CE. The rate was two *sers* per *maund* in *parganas* Pahari and Jalalpur and three *sers* per *maund* in *pargana* Chalkaliyana (*jamabandi, pargana* Chalkaliyana, VS 1722/1665 CE).

23 *Jamabandi, pargana* Kotla, VS 1721/1664 CE; *pargana* Chalkaliyana, VS 1722/1665 CE; *Arsatta, pargana* Mojpur, VS 1771/1714 CE; *pargana* Jalalpur, VS 1723/1666 CE.

24 *Arsatta, pargana* Khohri, VS 1721/1664 CE; *Chithi* to the *amil*, Kartik Vadi 4, VS 1781/1724 CE.

25 *Arsatta, pargana* Khohri, VS 1768/1711 CE.

26 The rate was more or less uniform in all *parganas*.

27 *Jamabandi, pargana* Chalkaliyana, VS 1722/1665 CE.

working in various capacities, namely *bhomias*, *qanungos*, *patwaris*, *muqaddams*, and *chaudharis*, was thus realized from the peasants in the form of taxes. Table 4.6a indicates the types of taxes and the rates at which they were levied:

Table 4.6a *Sair-jihat* and *siwai-jamabandi* taxes levied to meet the expense of remunerating village-level officials

Types of taxes	Rate
Bhom or *bhomi*	3 per cent[28] of *mal*
Qanungo	1.25 to 2 per cent[29] of *mal*
Patwari	1.5 per cent[30] of *mal*
Muqaddami	1.6–3.0 per cent[31] of *mal*
Chaudharai	1.25–2.0 per cent[32] of *mal*

Other taxes which covered the cost of remunerating other officials are given in Table 4.6b.

Apart from these cesses, the other taxes are as follows (Table 4.6c):

Some of these taxes were exclusive to the *zabti* method of assessment. Among these a particular tax was quite heavy in magnitude and was named differently in different *parganas* depending upon the rate of taxation: *pichotra* (5 per cent of every *zabti* rupee) in *pargana*

[28] *Arsatta, pargana* Gazi ka Thana, VS 1794/1737 CE; *pargana* Bharkol, VS 1774/1717 CE; *pargana* Mojpur, VS 1771/1714 CE; *pargana* Pindayan, VS 1792/1735 CE. In *pargana* Khohri, however, the rate of *bhomi* was 2 and 2.5 per cent of the *mal* on lands under *zabti* crops and lands held in *ijara* respectively (*Arsatta, pargana* Khohri, VS 1770/1713 CE; *Arzdasht, pargana* Khohri, Vaishakh Sudi 7, VS 1769/1712 CE).

[29] *Arsatta, pargana* Wazirpur, VS 1773/1716 CE, VS 1802/1745 CE; *pargana* Jalalpur, VS 1777/1720 CE.

[30] *Chithi* to the *amil, pargana* Khohri, Mah Sudi 1, VS 1804/1747 CE.

[31] *Jamabandi, pargana* Kotla, VS 1721/1664 CE; *Chithi* to the *amil, pargana* Khohri, Mah Sudi 1, VS 1804/1747 CE.

[32] *Chithi* to the *amil, pargana* Khohri, Mah Sudi 1, VS 1804/1747 CE.

Table 4.6b *Sair-jihat* and *siwai-jamabandi* taxes levied to meet the expense of remunerating other officials

Type of taxes	Rate
Diwan-dasturi (cess levied to meet expenses on maintaining the office of *diwan*)*	1 per cent[33] of *mal*
Sadir-o-warid (perquisite collected to entertain those who visited the village as travellers, pilgrims, or strangers in general)	0.5–1.0 per cent[34] of *mal*
Rozina-tappadari (cess levied to recover the daily allowances paid to the *tappadar*)	16 *takas* for every 90 *zabti bighas*[35]
Chak-sehna and *ghughri-sehna* (cess levied to recover the allowances paid to watchmen employed to look after the crops assessed under the *batai-jinsi* system)	1 *ser* per *maund*[36] (for ordinary peasant); ½ *ser* per *maund*[37] of produce (for *chaudhuri, patel, qanungo*, and *patwari*). In cash, it was calculated at the rate of 2.5 per cent of the *mal*.

Note: * The *riyayati* cultivators were exempted from paying this tax.

33 *Arsatta, pargana* Wazirpur, vs 1779/1722 CE.

34 The rate of *sadir-warid* was eight *annas* in *parganas* Wazirpur and Pindayan; one rupee in *pargana* Khohri; and 12 *annas* in *pargana* Pahari (*Arsatta, pargana* Wazirpur, vs 1779/1722 CE; *pargana* Pindayan, vs 1787/1730 CE; *pargana* Khohri, vs 1770/1713 CE; *pargana* Pahari, vs 1791/1734 CE). See N. A. Siddiqi, 'Land Revenue Demand under the Mughals', *Indian Economic and Social History Review* 2, no. 4 (1964): 373–80.

35 *Arsatta, pargana* Pindayan, vs 1787/1730 CE.

36 *Chithi* to the *amil, pargana* Piragpur, Asoj Vadi 8, vs 1786/1729 CE; *pargana* Khohri, Fagun Vadi 12, vs 1790/1737 CE.

37 *Chithi* to the *amil, pargana* Piragpur, Asoj Vadi 8, vs 1786/1729 CE; *pargana* Khohri, Fagun Vadi 12, vs 1790/1737 CE.

Table 4.6c Miscellaneous *sair-jihat* and *siwai-jamabandi* taxes

Type of taxes	Rate
Contribution to *malba* (common financial pool of the village)*	1.25 per cent of *mal*[38]
Farah-dahaani (*farah* cess assessed at the rate of 10 *annas* per 100 rupees of *mal*)*	10 *annas* for every 100 rupees of *mal*[39]
*Sikka-mabarak** (cess on the celebration of the Urs of Khwaja Muinuddin Chishti)	12 *takas* for every 100 rupees of *mal*[40]
Tawai-parkhai (cess on weighing of grain)*	8 *annas* for every 1,000 rupees of *mal*[41]
Aghori (cess on the hides of dead animals)	1 rupee for each 500 rupees of *mal*[42]
Ghiwai (cess levied in the event of non-payment of loan [*taqavi*] forwarded by the state to the needy peasants)	1 *taka* for every rupee of *taqavi*[43]
Water tax (cess levied on land irrigated by canals and streams)	4–5 per cent of *mal*[44]

Note: *The *riyayati* cultivators were exempted from paying these taxes.

Jalalpur,[45] *sadhathothra* (8.5 per cent of every *zabti* rupee) in *pargana* Wazirpur,[46] and *satotra* (7 per cent of ever *zabti* rupee) in *pargana*

38 *Arzdasht*, Bhadva Sudi 10, VS 1787/1730 CE. *Chithi* to the *amil*, *pargana* Atela Bhabra, Asoj Sudi 2, VS 1801/1744 CE; *pargana* Piragpur, Bhadva Sudi 5, VS 1801/1744 CE; *pargana* Atela Bhabra, Vaishakh Sudi 14, VS 1769/1712 CE. In *pargana* Atela Bhabra, it was charged at the rate of one *ser* per *maund*.

39 *Arsatta*, *pargana* Wazirpur, VS 1779/1722 CE.

40 *Arsatta*, *pargana* Wazirpur, VS 1771/1714 CE.

41 *Arsatta*, *pargana* Khohri, VS 1770/1713 CE.

42 *Arsatta*, *pargana* Khohri, VS 1768/1711 CE.

43 *Arsatta*, *pargana* Wazirpur, VS 1802/1745 CE.

44 *Arsatta*, *pargana* Khohri, VS 1790/1733 CE; *pargana* Pahari, VS 1791/1734 CE.

45 *Arsatta*, *pargana* Jalalpur, VS 1723/1666 CE.

46 *Arsatta*, *pargana* Wazirpur, VS 1779/1722 CE.

Khohri.[47] In addition, the peasants had to pay taxes on bullocks, cows, buffalos, and goats at the rate of half-a-*taka*[48] per animal.

A large number of other such taxes levied upon the peasantry are as follows:

(a) *Salami* (salutation fee) and *bhent* (present): these cesses had to be paid regularly to the visiting *pargana* officials such as *faujdars*, *amils*, and *amins*. The amount of such taxes varied across *parganas*. For instance, in *parganas* Khohri and Pahari, it was 2½ and 2 rupees respectively,[49] while in *pargana* Wazirpur it was as low as 1 rupee.[50]
(b) *Virar waqia-nawis*: a cess collected from individual peasants to remunerate the *waqia-nawis* (news-writer) and ranging from 8 *annas* to 1 rupee 8 *annas*, depending on the size of the village.[51] The *riyayati* cultivators were exempted from this tax.[52]
(c) *Hasil kotwal*: a cess collected from every village to remunerate the *kotwal* (police chief) of the *pargana*[53]
(d) *Charai*, *ghas charai*, or *hasil ghas charai*: cess levied on the use of pasture land for grazing cattle[54]
(e) *Hasil chak-chithi*: cess levied to meet the expenses incurred by the *amil*'s office in its administrative duties. This was charged at the rate of 2 *annas* per village.[55]
(f) *Hasil jhupari*: house tax charged at the rate of 12 *annas* per *jhupari*[56]
(g) *Hasil nyota*: cess on royal marriage paid by individual peasants and levied in the villages of the Amber Raja's *watan jagir*

47 *Arsatta*, *pargana* Khohri, vs 1723/1666 CE.

48 *Arsatta*, *pargana* Jalalpur, vs 1723/1666 CE.

49 *Arsatta*, *pargana* Khohri, vs 1769/1712 CE; *pargana* Pahari, vs 1788/1731 CE.

50 *Arsatta*, *pargana* Wazirpur, vs 1802/1745 CE.

51 *Arsatta*, *pargana* Pindayan, vs 1792/1735 CE.

52 *Arsatta*, *pargana* Pindayan, vs 1792/1735 CE.

53 *Arsatta*, *pargana* Pahari, vs 1788/1731 CE.

54 *Arsatta*, *pargana* Khohri, vs 1770/1713 CE.

55 *Arsatta*, *pargana* Wazirpur, vs 1779/1722 CE; *pargana* Khohri, vs 1768/1711 CE.

56 *Arsatta*, *pargana* Pindayan, vs 1792/1735 CE.

Since some of these taxes were levied upon the entire village community as a unit, the burden had to be apportioned out among individual peasants. However, the sources are silent about the mechanism of distribution of this tax burden. It is difficult to posit any connection between the resources of each individual peasant and his contribution to the *malba* out of which these taxes were paid. Given the nature and degree of social stratification and the power structure within the village, it is very likely that the dominant groups and high-caste peasants were able to shift their burden of taxes on to the shoulder of the smaller peasantry. Taken together, these taxes thus considerably added to the tax burden of the *raiyati* peasants.

An enormous economic burden on the peasantry was constituted by *peshkash*, although customarily they were not supposed to bear it. The *peshkash* was realized by the Mughal state from territories with almost every form of administration in the region, namely *watan*, *jagir*, and *ijara*. As per imperial rules, it was to be paid to the *subedar* and *faujdar* from the treasury of the Amber rulers. But instead of paying it out of their own resources, the rulers transferred the entire burden on to the peasantry. The *patels*, *patwaris*, and *chaudharis* were made responsible for its collection through the imposition of an additional tax called *virar*. What criterion was adopted by the administration for determining its magnitude in different *parganas* is not clear, although one document, however, mentions that it was to be collected at the rate of 2 per cent of the *hasil* (land revenue) of each village.[57]

The total burden of agricultural taxes upon the peasantry can be ascertained if we calculate the tentative amount of agricultural taxes under different heads in relation to the *mal*. This method enables us to compute the proportion of produce taken away from the peasants in the form of *mal* and other taxes. Under the *zabti* system, there is no clear information that can help estimate the magnitude of land revenue as a share of the total produce. However, if we assume that the revenue under the *zabti* system was collected at the rate of one-third of the produce—as was the practice in those areas of the Mughal empire where the *zabti* system was in operation—the total burden of agricultural taxes under the *zabti* system can be worked out by adding to it the burden of other agricultural taxes in terms of

57 *Arsatta*, *pargana* Pindayan, vs 1792/1735 CE.

the total produce. The other agricultural taxes under the *zabti* system amounted to 17–22 per cent of the *mal*. Thus, the total revenue demand under the *zabti* system roughly amounted to be about 50–5 per cent of the total produce. The Rajasthani documents suggest that under the *batai-jinsi* system, the share of the state was 40–50 per cent of the total produce, and the other cesses formed 12–15 per cent of the *mal*.

Thus, the total surplus realized from the peasants on an average was about 50–5 per cent of the produce under both *zabti* and *batai-jinsi* systems. The land revenue demand was regressive, as its burden fell more heavily on the smaller peasants who could produce only on a limited scale and mainly for self-consumption. Its regressive nature is further established by its application on the basis of the caste status of individual peasants and in inverse proportion to the revenue-paying capacity of the cultivator. The land revenue system thus further intensified the economic differentiation between the richer and the poorer sections of the peasantry. That the majority of the peasants found it difficult to meet the revenue demand in full is clear from repeated appeals and petitions made by the *raiyat* against the burden of land revenue and other agricultural taxes. The growing inability of the peasants to pay the land revenue and their resistance to increasing tax burden are well documented in the sources.

The other important point that emerges from the examination of the *arsattas* is that there was a growing tendency on the part of the peasants to pay revenue even for food crops according to the *zabti* system. The increasing preference of the peasants for the *zabti* system was due to, perhaps, the relative stability of the *zabti* rates per *bigha* during the late 17th and early 18th centuries when agricultural prices were rising constantly. In such a situation, the *zabti* system tended to be more advantageous to the peasants who were able to get some benefit from the price rise.

II

The period from 1389 to 1527 marks a new phase in the history of Mewat, in which new *qasbas* emerged as a result of the formation of the new Khanzada chiefdom in the region. After the death of Firozshah Tughlaq (1389), the new chiefdom was formed in the Mewat region by the Khanzadas with the help of the former Firozi slaves, and it survived till the Battle of Khanwa (1527), after which the region was brought under the Mughal administrative system.[58]

On account of their past experience as military men and *iqta* holders, the former Firozi slaves were given important positions in the Khanzada chiefdom. This can be inferred from the fact that they were also called Khanzads (later, they were commonly spoken of as Khanzadas). Having a fluid social hierarchy, the former Firozi slaves soon organized themselves as the military elite of the new chiefdom and merged their social identity with that of the original Khanzadas; the state, too, assigned them villages in lieu of their remuneration. This fact is borne out by the Jagga records which mention that many new villages were established and settled by the Khanzadas from 1389 to 1527 in the vicinity of Tijara and Firozpur Jhirka.[59] A later-19th-century Archaeological Survey of India report shows that the Khanzadas had built the mosques in many villages and paid much attention to increasing agricultural production.[60] To expand the arable area, the woods were cleared and more lands were brought under the plough. Eventually, many new *qasba*s emerged as a result of the increased surplus generated by agrarian growth in the region. Some *qasba*s also emerged as centres of commerce due to growing indigo and cotton production.

The *qasba*s that rose in the periphery of Tijara, the capital town of the Khanzadas lying on the main trade route between Delhi and Amber, were Indori, Sarheta, Bhindusi, Manda, Shahbad, Fatehabad, Tuglaqpur, and Salarpur.[61] The Khanzadas resided in these *qasba*s; therefore, the traders used to bring such commodities as were required by the new ruling class. Basically, these *qasba*s served as the hinterland for Tijara, supplying foodgrains to the ruling class of the

58 See Chapter 1.

59 Jagga records, *pothi* no. 1, in personal possession of Jagdish, son of Shri Ghasi Ram Jagga, village Khuteta Kalan, *tehsil* Ramgarh, district Alwar, Rajasthan.

60 Cunningham, *Report of a Tour in Eastern Rajputana in 1882–3*, 10–22.

61 Sheikh Muhammad Makhdum, *Arzang-i-Tijara* (Urdu) (Agra: Akhbar, H. 1290/1873 CE, trans. [Hindi] Anil Joshi, Alwar, 1989), 3–5.

Khanzadas and their soldiers. The existence of old mosques in these *qasbas* points to the concentration of Muslim population during the Khanzada rule. Besides, Tijara was also a religious centre for Hindus and Jains, as *Arzang-i-Tijara* mentions that there were many old Hindu and Jain temples there during the Khanzada rule. Most of the Hindus and Jains belonged to the trading class; and Tijara, even during the later Mughal period, must have witnessed interaction between different religious communities.[62]

After the political and administrative integration of Mewat into the Mughal state by Akbar, many more towns and *qasbas* emerged and served as hinterland for the main trading centres such as Delhi, Agra, Alwar, Tijara, Sanganer, Averi, Baswa, and Rajgarh. These *qasbas*, like those of the preceding Khanzada period, developed as a result of the agrarian surplus produced by the peasants. The majority of these *qasbas* happened to be the headquarters of different *parganas* in which revenue officials and troops of the *faujdar* used to reside. Therefore, these *qasbas* became administrative centres, revenue-paying units, and sub-station centres of army—all rolled into one.

We do not have much information about the agricultural production of Mewat prior to the reign of Akbar. For the first time, the *Ain-i-Akbari* provides us with detailed information on agricultural production in both *kharif* and *rabi* seasons during the reign of Akbar. The *Ain-i-Akbari* enumerates 41 crops raised in Mewat in a year, suggesting that the peasants of Mewat grew not only food crops but also cash crops such as indigo (*neel*), cotton (*kapas*), sugarcane (*baar* or *ganna*), and oilseeds (*sarson* and *tilhan*).[63] An *arsatta* of the late 17th century mentions 32 *kharif* crops and 34 *rabi* crops raised in *pargana* Khohri.[64] The main feature of agriculture in the region in the 17th century was the production of a multiplicity of food and cash crops. That the cash crops yielded high value clearly suggests that the increasing demand of traders must have encouraged the peasants to grow them and sell them in the nearby *qasbas*.

Cultivation of indigo (Tables 4.7a–4.7c) was particularly impressive in *parganas* Kotla, Bisru, Umra-Umari, Ujina, Pahari, and Khilohra,

62 Makhdum, *Arzang-i-Tijara* (Urdu), 44–5.

63 Abul-Fazl, *The Ain-i-Akbari*, vol. 2, 76, 78, 105, 108, 114, 117.

64 *Arsatta*, *pargana* Khohri, vs 1722/1665 CE.

Table 4.7a Area (*zabti bighas*) under cultivation of cotton, sugarcane, and indigo in *pargana* Wazirpur

Year (CE)	Cotton	Sugarcane	Indigo	Total cultivated area in *zabti bighas*
1712	37	28	31	456
1714	78	228	17	3,692
1717	329	60	20	2,417
1720	161	88	56	2,787
1722	123	161	28	3,552
1725	355	123	130	6,269
1729	375	323	07	4,516
1745	204	228	40	5,946
1747	476	172	53	4,695
1748	272	231	59	5,152
1749	462	172	58	4,203

Source: *Arsattas* of years mentioned.

Table 4.7b Area (*zabti bighas*) under cultivation of cotton and indigo in *pargana* Khohri

Year (CE)	Cotton	Indigo	Total cultivated area in *zabti bighas*
1664	3,416	364	98,746
1666	804	615	55,739
1716	1,203	202	13,453
1728	552	125	11,955
1733	–	451	18,381
1741	1,073	393	47,792
1743	–	245	15,460
1744	–	168	9,195

Source: *Arsattas* of years mentioned.

all in Tijara *sarkar*.[65] The *Ain-i-Akbari*, too, suggests that indigo was produced in many *parganas* of Tijara *sarkar*. Although indigo used to be cultivated in the Mughal *subas* of Multan, Lahore Malwa, Allahabad, and Awadh, the indigo of Mewat and Bayana was considered superior.

65 Irfan Habib, Rajasthan Economic Map, in *An Atlas of the Mughal Empire* (Delhi: Oxford University Press, 1982).

Table 4.7c Area (*zabti bighas*) under cultivation of cotton and indigo in *pargana* Gazi ka Thana

Year (CE)	Cotton	Indigo	Total cultivated area in *zabti bighas*
1730	1,919	3,030	15,359
1731	1,403	1,414	8,008
1734	1,570	2,984	16,304
1735	1,861	3,028	10,783
1737	2,530	3,087	17,995
1740	656	968	8,610
1741	1,415	2,636	13,189
1742	910	1,895	10,057
1745	753	875	13,268
1747	1,092	628	10,525
1748	1,195	709	8,326

Source: *Arsattas* of years mentioned.

The *arsattas* provide us with *pargana*-wise statistical data of indigo cultivation in Mewat. In 1665, 29,631.5 *maunds* of indigo were produced in *pargana* Kotla.[66] In 1666, indigo was produced on 615 *bighas* in *pargana* Khohri;[67] on 494 *bighas* (out of a total cultivated area of 1,139 *bighas*) in *pargana* Pahari;[68] and only on 31 *bighas* (out of a total 456 *bighas*) in *qasba* Wazirpur.[69] The volume of indigo trade in the 16th and 17th centuries was quite high, but declined in the early 18th century partly because there was a reduction in the demand for Indian indigo in the international market and partly because there was a decline in indigo cultivation.[70]

Cotton (Tables 4.7a–4.7g) was largely produced in the localities of Firozpur Jhirka, Nuh, Kotla, and Punahana. The cotton of Firozpur valley was considered the best; the yield from the area amounted to 3½–6½ *maunds* per acre even as late as the late 19th century.[71] The

66 *Arsatta*, *pargana* Kotla, VS 1722/1665 CE.

67 *Arsatta*, *pargana* Khohri, VS 1723/1666 CE.

68 *Arsatta*, *pargana* Pahari, VS 1723/1666 CE.

69 *Arsatta*, *pargana* Wazirpur, VS 1723/1666 CE.

70 See Chapter 2 and tables 4.7b and 4.7c.

71 F. C. Channing, *Land Revenue Settlement of the Gurgaon District* (Lahore: Central Jail Press, 1882), 62–3.

Table 4.7d Area (*zabti bighas*) under cultivation of cotton in *pargana* Jalalpur

Year (CE)	Cotton	Total cultivated area in *zabti bighas*
1666	53	223
1691	19	239
1711	309	4,208
1716	87	1,811
1718	205	2,684
1720	207	1,951
1723	312	2,568
1735	54	828
1738	683	5,990
1739	269	3,268

Source: *Arsattas* of years mentioned.

Table 4.7e Area (*zabti bighas*) under cultivation of cotton in *pargana* Pindayan

Year (CE)	Cotton	Total cultivated area in *zabti bighas*
1722	203	1,022
1729	185	1,991
1730	946	4,614
1732	794	4,084
1735	544	3,004
1749	211	2,191

Source: *Arsattas* of years mentioned.

Table 4.7f Area (*zabti bighas*) under cultivation of cotton in *pargana* Mojpur

Year (CE)	Cotton	Total cultivated area in *zabti bighas*
1722	517	3,702
1722	450	2,716
1730	1,187	4,112
1732	852	4,685
1735	325	3,850
1749	353	4,219

Source: *Arsattas* of years mentioned.

Table 4.7g Area (*zabti bighas*) under cultivation of cotton in *pargana* Pahari

Year (CE)	Cotton	Total cultivated area in *zabti bighas*
1735	556	11,394
1741	127	2,016
1742	136	469

Source: Arsattas of years mentioned.

arsattas also provide us with statistical data of cotton production in many *parganas* of Mewat. In *pargana* Khohri, the cotton production amounted to 3.5 per cent of the total production in 1664[72] and the share rose by up to 1 per cent in 1716.[73] In *parganas* Wazirpur and Jalalpur, cotton production constituted 14–17 per cent of the total production in 1717.[74] In *parganas* Gazi ka Thana, Pindayan, and Mojpur, it amounted to 18, 20, and 28 per cent, respectively, of the total production in 1730.[75] It seems that the high productivity of cotton in these *parganas* was due to soil quality and better irrigation. Further, the productivity of cotton was apparently much higher in *qasbas* than in villages. For instance, in *qasba* Jalalpur the share of cotton in the total production was 23.75 per cent in 1665.[76] In *qasba* Pindayan, the area under cotton cultivation was 24.34 per cent of the total cropped area in 1720.[77] In 1665, 306 *maunds* of cotton were sold to the *mahajans* in *qasba* Kotla.[78] The statistical data show that cotton cultivation did not decline in the early 18th century because the demand for cotton in the local markets did not fall. And it is this high local demand that sustained the peasants' keen interest in growing cotton.

Sugarcane (Table 4.7a) was also an important cash crop grown on the banks of Kotla Lake and in Firozpur Jhirka valley, but largely

72 *Arsatta, pargana* Khohri, VS 1721/1664 CE.

73 *Arsatta, pargana* Khohri, VS 1773/1716 CE.

74 *Arsatta, pargana* Wazirpur, VS 1774/1717 CE; *pargana* Jalalpur, VS 1774/1717 CE.

75 *Arsatta, pargana* Gazi ka Thana, VS 1787/1730 CE; *pargana* Pindayan, VS 1787/1730 CE; *pargana* Mojpur, VS 1787/1730 CE.

76 *Arsatta, pargana* Jalalpur, VS 1722/1665 CE.

77 *Arsatta, pargana* Pindayan, VS 1777/1720 CE.

78 *Arsatta, pargana* Kotla, VS 1722/1665 CE.

produced in the villages of Wazirpur and Khohri *parganas*.[79] The peasants used to prepare the raw sugar (*gur*) from sugarcane in their villages and sell it to the *qasbas*.[80]

In every *qasba* there lived *mahajans* who used to buy cash crops directly from the farmers. Even the state's share in the produce, in the form of land revenue paid in kind by the farmers, was sold to these local *mahajans* by the state officials. For instance, Tatra and Harikishan Mahajans of *qasba* Pahari purchased 3,798 *maunds* of grain from the peasants.[81] Similarly, Karamchand and Chattra Mahajans of *qasbas* Punkar and Pindayan purchased 1,400 *maunds* of *rabi* crops from the peasants.[82] The peasants sold *til, moong, moth,* and *urad* to the *mahajans* of *qasba* Jalalpur.[83] There are many more such references to peasants selling their produce to the *mahajans*. In many cases, the *mahajans* purchased cash crops, such as cotton and indigo, in advance from the farmers. For instance, in 1641, the *mahajans* of Sanganer purchased 30 *maunds* of indigo in advance from the farmers at the rate of 25 rupees per *maund* in *pargana* Kotla.[84] In 1683, the *mahajans* of Hindon purchased 75 *maunds* of indigo in advance from the farmers of Mewat.[85] Thus, during the Mughal period, the peasants of each village had direct relations with the *mahajans* of the nearest *qasba*, who not only purchased agricultural produce but also extended loans (*taqavi*) to needy peasants at the time of sowing and harvesting and in times of scarcity, on behalf of the state. The *mahajans*, therefore, played a vital role in the economic life of countryside in Mewat. The traders from far-off regions, too, used to come to the main towns of Mewat to purchase indigo and cotton. For instance, in 1698, the Baloch traders of *qasbas* Bhera and Kasab in Punjab (Pakistan), who brought 800 camels laden with saltpetre (*phitkari*) for the Amber

79 *Arsatta, pargana* Wazirpur, vs 1770/1713 CE, vs 1774/1717 CE, vs 1769/1712 CE, vs 1771/1714 CE.

80 *Arsatta, pargana* Khohri, vs 1722/1665 CE; *pargana* Wazirpur, vs 1777/1720 CE.

81 *Arsatta, pargana* Pahari, vs 1796/1739 CE.

82 *Arsatta, pargana* Pindayan, vs 1723/1666 CE.

83 *Arsatta, pargana* Jalalpur, vs 1723/1666 CE.

84 *Arzdasht,* Sawan Sudi 3, vs 1698/1641 CE.

85 *Arzdasht,* Posh Sudi 7, vs 1740/1683 CE.

Raja, purchased cotton from the *qasbas* of Mewat on their way back.[86] Pelsaert also mentions that the *qasbas* of Mewat exported 1,000 bales of indigo annually.[87]

In many *qasbas* of Mewat, oilseed crushers (*ghanna telis*) for extracting oil from oil seeds were found. For instance, there were 17, 10, 7, 6, 5, and 4 oilseed crushers in Mojpur, Pindayan, Pahari, Harsana, Mandawar, and Wazirpur *qasbas* respectively.[88] The oilseed crushers were set up and operated by oilmen (*telis*) who sold oil to traders and paid a cess called *hasil ghana teli* at the rate of two rupees and four *annas* per crusher to the state.[89] The peasants from the nearby villages, too, brought oil seeds to the *qasbas* to extract oil for personal consumption.

In some villages of Mewat, peasants set up their own sugarcane crushers (*leharis*) for extracting juice from sugarcane to make raw sugar. For instance, 30 sugarcane crushers were set up by the peasants of six villages in *pargana* Wazirpur.[90] The peasants had to pay a cess (*hasil gur ganna*) at the rate of four rupees per crusher to the state.[91] The *mahajans* used to buy raw sugar from the peasants. However, sugarcane was not grown much by the peasants in Mewat due to lack of irrigation facilities.

The *mahajans* not only purchased the rural produce in the *qasbas*, but also themselves engaged in cultivation. According to information obtained from the *arsattas*, although the *mahajans* mostly lived in the *qasbas*, they engaged in farming, along with trade. For instance, Harkishan, Khusaliram, Sitaram, and Tara Mahajans in *qasba* Pahari;[92] Rekha and Doda Mahajans in *qasba* Harsana;[93] Govardhan Mahajan

[86] *Arzdasht*, Fagun Sudi 4, VS 1755/1698 CE.

[87] Francisco Pelsaert, *Jahangir's India: The Remonstratie of Francisco Pelsaert*, trans. W. H. Moreland and P. Geyl (Cambridge: W. Heffere, 1925), 10–14.

[88] *Arsatta*, *pargana* Mojpur, VS 1787/1730 CE; *pargana* Pindayan, VS 1792/1735 CE; *pargana* Pahari, VS 1799/1742 CE; *pargana* Harsana, VS 1792/1735 CE; *pargana* Mandawar, VS 1722/1665 CE; *pargana* Wazirpur, VS 1770/1713CE.

[89] *Arsatta*, *pargana* Pahari, VS 1799/1742 CE.

[90] *Arsatta*, *pargana* Wazirpur, VS 1770/1713 CE.

[91] *Arsatta*, *pargana* Wazirpur, VS 1774/1717 CE.

[92] *Arsatta*, *pargana* Pahari, VS 1792/1735 CE, VS 1798/1741 CE.

[93] *Arsatta*, *pargana* Harsana, VS 1787/1730 CE; *pargana* Harsana, VS 1792/1735 CE.

in *pargana* Pindayan;[94] and Chattra and Karamchand Mahajans in *qasba* Atela Bhabra[95] were engaged in both cultivation and trade.

Sometimes, the local *mahajans* trading in foodgrains exercised monopoly over trade. For instance, a complaint was lodged with the Amber Raja against the *mahajans* of *qasba* Averi that they bought foodgrains from all the traders coming from outside and sold them dear to the consumers in times of scarcity. The traders were summoned to the court and asked to maintain uniformity in prices. The traders who violated this order were to be punished with five lashes each.[96]

Rajasthani documents mention that the *mahajans* had their shops in the *qasbas*. Some of them, known as *sarrafs* and *bohras*, were engaged in issuing *hundis* (bills of exchange), although their activities were centred mainly in towns. The *sarrafs* were mainly engaged in writing and discounting *hundis*, money-changing, insurance of goods, and, to some extent, accepting deposits. The *bohras* were also engaged in the transmission of funds and issuing of *hundis*, as well as money-lending and trade. All of them were involved in trade directly or indirectly.[97] For example, Kussal Singh Lahani, Sabal Singh Lahani, Ramdas Lahani, Syoram Lahani, Prannath Lahani, Chattardas Lahani, and Lakhmidas Lahani were the chief *sarrafs* in Mewat who were engaged in the transmission of funds and issuing of *hundis* to the traders[98] and had enough influence on local trade. Among them, Syoram Lalani of *qasba* Manoharpur was such a prominent trader that at his death the Amber Raja personally expressed condolence.[99] In Mewat, the *mahajans* were related to the Muhars, Khandelwals, Saravagis, and Lalanis—all sub-castes of *banias*—who mainly traded in foodgrains.[100]

94 *Arsatta, pargana* Pindayan, VS 1792/1735 CE.

95 *Arsatta, pargana* Atela Bhabra, VS 1780/1723 CE, VS 1782/1725 CE.

96 *Arzdasht*, Asoj Vadi 12, VS 1751/1694 CE.

97 G. D. Sharma, 'Indigenous Banking and the State in the Eastern Rajasthan during the Seventeenth Century', *Proceedings of the Indian History Congress*, 40th Session, Waltair, 1979, 332–441.

98 *Arzdasht*, Posh Sudi 9, VS 1742/1685 CE.

99 *Arzdasht*, Bhadva Vadi 3, VS 1741/1684 CE; Mangsir Sudi 7, VS 1745/1684 CE.

100 *Tozi dastur komwar*, bundle no. 3, VS 1774–1990/1717–1933 CE, Jaipur State Archives.

The *mahajans* had trade relations with the big traders to whom they sold their goods transported by the *banjaras*. The *banjaras* belonged to special tribes whose hereditary occupation was to transport and trade in various commodities. They lived in camps called *tandas* with their own oxen in the open fields. Sometimes, they were hired by the merchants, but most commonly they were merchants themselves, buying grain, rice, pulses, and salt cheap, and selling them dear. Their caravans were accompanied by armed men for the security of scarce and high-value merchandise. They possessed hundreds of bullocks who were fed in the pastures falling on the trade routes. For this, the state extracted a cess called *hasil ghas charai* from the *banjaras* at the rate of 5 rupees per 100 bullocks.[101] Sometimes, fights broke out between the *banjaras* and farmers on account of the former feeding their bullocks on the standing crops (*zirayati*) of the latter. For instance, in 1664, Charandas Banjara, carrying salt from Shambar, fed his bullocks on the standing crops of *mauza* Kheri on the way; this led to a fight between the *banjaras* and farmers resulting in serious injuries to both sides.[102] Similarly, the *banjaras* and farmers of *mauza* Kalwara fought over the issue of crop damage by the former's cattle, resulting in the death of one Bhimsen Patel from that *mauza*. The *banjaras* were arrested by the *faujdar*'s troops and forced to submit an undertaking promising not to damage standing crops in future.[103]

In the medieval period, the only means to transport merchandise in Mewat was either bullocks owned by the *banjaras* or camels. However, bullock carts were also used to carry goods from villages to nearby *qasbas*, but not for long-distance trade. The geographical location of Mewat was such that the Delhi–Jaipur and Delhi–Agra trade routes passed through it. Therefore, several small feeder routes in Mewat were connected with these twin major routes. One such route passed from Gurgaon to Firozpur Jhirka via Sohna and Nuh. A second one between Hodal and Firozpur Jhirka passed through Punhana. A third one joined Firozpur with Tijara. A fourth one connected Bisru and Firozpur Jhirka passing through Pahari. Two other routes joined Firozpur Jhirka with the Delhi–Jaipur route, the Nowgong–Ramgarh–Alwar route, and

101 *Arsatta, pargana* Khohri, VS 1722/1665 CE, VS 1773/1716 CE.

102 *Arzdasht*, Asoj Sudi 13, VS 1751/1694 CE.

103 *Arzdasht*, Posh Sudi 5, VS 1756/1699 CE.

the route going towards Tijara. There were several minor routes in Alwar *sarkar* that merged into the Delhi–Jaipur route. One of them ran from Kishangarh to Alwar; another one started from Lakshmangarh and reached Malakhera via Bhojpur and joined Delhi–Jaipur route. There was one more route from Bhojpur to Rajgarh. *Qasba* Rajgarh fell between Delhi–Jaipur route; hence, it was connected with several smaller routes. Some minor trade routes passed from the *qasbas* of Baswa, Macheri, Lakshmangarh, and so on, to Rajgarh. Thus, several small trade routes were scattered throughout medieval Mewat and joined the two major trade routes and thus bore considerable significance for rural and inter-regional trade.[104]

III

Abul-Fazl mentions that in some *qasbas* of Mewat, the horses of the Mughal cavalry used to be trained. These *qasbas* were Nuh, Taoru, Firozpur Jhirka, Ghasera, Kot-Qasim, Ujina, and Indori.[105] By the 18th century, *qasba* Ramgarh in Alwar *sarkar* had emerged as the main centre for the training of cavalry horses and hence was known as Tabela Ramgarh.[106] In 1763, the total number of horses in Tabela Ramgarh was 2,278.[107] The horses, once trained, were meant to be dispatched to different parts of Mughal India for induction in the cavalry. For instance, 50 horses in 1683 and 30 more horses (19 Turki and 11 Khanzada) in 1684 had been sent to the Deccan.[108] Such horse-training centres of Mewat thus had great military importance for the Mughal state. The training of cavalry horses required a large number of artisans and trainers, most of whom must have been part of the local population.[109] However, with the decline of the Mughal empire, the demand of cavalry horses also declined and the horse-training centres of Mewat lost their importance. This is corroborated by the fact that

104 Channing, *Land Revenue Settlement of Gurgaon District*, 152, 153; Powlett, *Gazetteer of Ulwur* (London: Trubner & Co., 1878), 79–80.

105 Habib, Rajasthan Economic Map.

106 *Arzdasht*, Fagun Vadi 10, VS 1741/1684 CE.

107 *Arsatta, pargana* Ramgarh, VS 1820/1763 CE.

108 *Arzdasht*, Fagun Vadi 6, VS 1740/1683 CE.

109 For instance, the Mirasi caste, known as trainers of cavalry horses, live(d) in the Mewat region.

a new village named Chhappra was founded on the site of a training centre in Tijara in 1800.[110]

During the Mughal period, *qasba* Nuh was a famous centre for salt production. Although Sambhar in Rajasthan was the biggest salt-production centre, Nuh supplied salt to the nearby *qasbas* of Haryana and the Ganga–Yamuna Doab. According to the late 19th-century settlement report of Gurgaon district, adjoining *qasba* Nuh were some villages, namely Kherla, Ranila Khurd, Sampal, Malab, Firozpur Namak, Adhar Bai, Dundaheri, Salaheri, Untka, Firozpur Namak, and Salamba, which, too, manufactured salt.[111] These villages annually produced 1,200 *maunds* of salt, priced at 25 rupees per 100 *maunds*.[112] The *banjaras* carried out the salt trade,[113] just as they carried out trade in other articles. Hukumchand was a famous salt trader of *qasba* Nuh who exported salt to the neighbouring region in the late 18th century.[114] The Mughal state, on its part, charged a cess called *hasil aghori* from salt manufacturers.[115]

As mentioned in Chapter 2, at many places in the Aravali hills that surround Mewat, iron and copper were extracted during the medieval period. According to the late 19th-century gazetteer of Alwar by the British settlement officer Major P. W. Powlett,

> The manufacture of iron was in former times [i.e., Mughal period] a great industry in the [Alwar] State [i.e., Alwar and Tijara *sarkars*], as is testified by the large hillocks of slag which are to be found in all directions; but it has fallen off greatly of late years, the value of the native iron having been greatly lessened by the large quantities imported from Europe.

110 *Bandhak* no. 6, *granthank* no. 83, Non-archival Records of Alwar State, Rajasthan State Archives, Bikaner.

111 A. Fraser, 'Appendix L', in *Statistical Report of Zillah Gurgaon*, 57.

112 Fraser, *Statistical Report of Zillah Gurgaon*, 57. Two pits are necessary for the manufacture of salt by evaporation from brine raised from the wells. The size of each pit, on an average, was about 120 feet by 60 or about 1.5th of an acre. The cost of digging each pit, together with the expenses on repairing, filing, cleaning, etc., was about 196 rupees per annum (Fraser, *Statistical Report of Zillah Gurgaon*, 57).

113 *Arzdasht*, Chait Sudi 2, VS 1767/1710 CE.

114 Fraser, *Statistical Report of Zillah Gurgaon*, 57.

115 *Arsatta*, *pargana* Khohri, VS 1722/1665 CE. In fact, emperor Shahjahan issued a farman in 1643 to immediately stop the illegal production of salt since it had been causing a loss of revenue (Bhardwaj, 'Qasbas in Mewat in the Medieval Period').

Formerly, there were 200 smelting furnaces, but there are now only 37 at work, which are calculated to turn out 18,500 maunds (660 tons) a year.[116]

The *Arzang-i-Tijara*, too, mentions sites of iron-smelting furnaces in many *qasbas* of Mewat. Of these, Tehala and Nayagaon near *qasba* Rajgarh had the oldest furnaces dating back to the reign of Alauddin Khalji.[117] The other sites were Akbarpur, Parthipura, Baleta, and Dantia in *pargana* Alwar, where iron ore was extracted from the hills and smelted in furnaces.[118] The site of Gola ka Baas in *pargana* Gazi ka Thana had very rich iron mines from which great quantities of iron ore were extracted and smelted in furnaces.[119] Iron ore was also available in the hills of Firozpur Jhirka and Tijara.[120]

Traders came to these sites to buy smelted iron and carried it on camels or bullock carts to the *qasbas*. Blacksmiths (*lohars*) bought iron from these *qasbas* in order to make agricultural tools for peasants. Blacksmiths in certain *qasbas* also specialized in making war weapons. For instance, in the *qasbas* of Ramgarh and Macheri, some such blacksmiths manufactured firelocks (guns, known as *dhamaka*), both flint (*tradar*) and match (*chabdar*).[121] The blacksmiths of *qasbas* Jalalpur, Mojpur, Wazirpur, and Baswa manufactured local guns called *ramchangi* and small cannons called *rahakalla*.[122] Both state officials and the rebel *bhomias* purchased these weapons from the blacksmiths. In fact, the Mughal state reportedly asked these blacksmiths to submit undertakings that they would not make war weapons for and sell them to the rebel *bhomias*.[123] Despite this, the *bhomias* continued to procure war weapons from these blacksmiths, even by force at times. For instance, Churaman Jat captured the blacksmiths of *qasbas* Jalalpur and Wazirpur and took them to his *thoon* (fortress) to manufacture war

116 Powlett, *Gazetteer of Ulwur*, 76–7.

117 Makhdum, *Arzang-i-Tijara*, 57.

118 Makhdum, *Arzang-i-Tijara*, 51.

119 Makhdum, *Arzang-i-Tijara*, 59.

120 Fraser, *Statistical Report of Zillah Gurgaon*, 57.

121 *Arsatta, pargana* Jalalpur, vs 1777/1720 CE; *pargana* Wazirpur, vs 1774/1717 CE. These blacksmiths were Kanhi Ram, Keso Ram, and Chatra Lohar of *qasbas* Jalalpur and Wazirpur respectively.

122 *Arzdasht*, Jeth Vadi 1, vs 1761/1704 CE; Jeth Vadi 3, vs 1761/1704 CE.

123 *Arzdasht*, Kartik Sudi 14, vs 1760/1703 CE.

weapons for the Jats.[124] The blacksmiths of *qasba* Narwar sent 11 *rahakallas* to Kishna Naruka, a zamindar who had rebelled against the Amber Raja.[125] Francis Buchanan who stayed in India in the late 18th and early 19th centuries pointed out that there was a group of blacksmiths in towns that made swords, spears, knives, and guns, especially for the rural markets.[126] Thus, the region's iron ore was important for agriculture and weaponry and was also exported to the adjoining regions.

Besides iron mines, there were many copper mines in the Aravali hills of Mewat. An *arzdasht* names several sites of copper-smelting in region. These sites were in the hills of Surehati, Jamrauli, Akoda, and Muhi villages of the Alwar *sarkar*.[127] Among these, the richest site was in the Khohdariba hill of *pargana* Rajgarh.[128] The coppersmiths used to smelt copper with the help of familial labour. Powlett's report mentions the presence of many Mughal-period copper-smelting furnaces in region and cites British officer Major Cadell's observations:

> The richest copper-mine in the Ulwur State is that of the Dariba hill ... but copper ore is found in many other parts of the branch of the Aravelli Hills ...; and several ancient copper mines are to be found which were worked and abandoned centuries ago ... The average annual out-turn of copper ... is becoming less year by year, owing to the influx of copper from Europe and of British India copper coin. The value of the indigenous copper has [thus] greatly diminished.[129]

124 *Arzdasht*, Jeth Vadi 1, VS 1761/1704 CE. The *faujdar* of Amber Raja informed the *diwan* that the blacksmiths of *qasba* Shawari had made *rahakallas* and *ramchangis* for the rebel Jats. These blacksmiths were subsequently arrested by the *faujdar*.

125 *Arzdasht*, Kartik Sudi 14, VS 1760/1703 CE.

126 Tapan Raychaudhuri and Irfan Habib, eds, *The Cambridge Economic History of India*, vol. 1: c. 1200–c. 1750 (Cambridge: Cambridge University Press, 1982), 280.

127 *Arzdasht*, Fagun Vadi 11, VS 1738/1681 CE.

128 Makhdum, *Arzang-i-Tijara*, 57.

129 Powlett, *Gazetteer of Ulwur*, 82–3. Powlett further cites Major Cadell's views on the mode of copper-manufacturing in the late 19th century:

> The manufacture is carried on in thatched sheds, which are generally in a very dilapidated state. The ore is chipped out of the solid rock with hammer and chisel; and, having been beaten with hammers into powder, is mixed with double its weight of powdered iron slag. This mixture is then made into small cakes with an equal quantity of cow-dung; and, after being roasted in a fire made of

The *arzdasht*s inform that Thathera, a caste of artisans in *qasba* Kalyanpur, manufactured images of goddesses and decorative articles and vessels from copper.[130] The Thatheras requested the Amber Raja to allot land to live to those artisans who came from the neighbouring areas to work in the *qasba*. These artisans exported their copperware to the towns of Alwar, Rajgarh, and Tijara.[131] However, the copperware, being high-priced, could be purchased by the rich sections of the society, that is, members of the ruling class, traders, *sahukar*s (moneylenders), and zamindars, not by the peasants. Nevertheless, not only did the availability of copper in the region provide livelihood to a large number of artisans, but was also important for the Mughal state whose currency was made from this metal.

It is clear from the foregoing discussion of the region's economy that the *qasba*s of Mewat performed varied functions: many emerged as *pargana* headquarters; some had strategic importance as centres for weapon manufacturing, coin minting, or training of cavalry horses; and others became centres of trade and manufacturing that also established linkages with villages in that they procured agricultural produce and raw materials for artisanal production from the villages and provided the peasants with articles of domestic and agricultural use. Further, it was the agricultural surplus generated by the Meo peasants which was instrumental in the formation of *qasba*s and

---

grass and cow-dung, is placed, like the iron ore, in the smelting furnace, in alternate layers with charcoal. When the ore is melted, the furnace cylinder is broken down, and the mass of copper which has collected at the bottom, after being allowed to cool, is lifted out. It is then taken to another shed, and is placed in an open charcoal fire, where it is melted a second time with the aid of the bellows, which is worked by two men standing, and which is opened and closed at the proper moment by the man who also attends to the fire. It is then poured into a mound in bars, and out of these bars the copper currency of the State is coined ... Thirty-two families, comprising eighty-eight men, women and children, derive their principal means of subsistence from this industry; and during the rainy season, when the furnaces are not worked, they cultivate twenty-two acres of land. (Powlett, *Gazetteer of Ulwur*, 83)

130 *Arzdasht*, Sawan Sudi 4, VS 1721/1664 CE.

131 *Arzdasht*, Sawan Vadi 6, VS 1723/1666 CE. Alwar, an important town housing the headquarters of Alwar *sarkar* during the Mughal period and situated on the Delhi–Jaipur trade route, was famous for its woollen carpets, glass articles, and copper mint (Raychaudhuri and Habib, eds, *The Cambridge Economic History of India*, 282).

growth of a prosperous town economy based on artisanal production and intra- and inter-regional trade in the Mewat region.

Thus, Mewat from the 16th century onwards witnessed significant agricultural and commercial growth. Its effective administrative integration with the Mughal state system and its strategic location between Agra–Delhi and Amber regions, together with the agricultural growth, transformed it into a centre for agricultural and non-agricultural production as well as trade in grains, cash crops such as indigo and cotton, salt, iron, and copper, although from the late 17th-century disruptions in trade caused by the depredations of Rajputs and Jats did adversely affect the region's economy.

IV

The information on the prices of principal food crops grown in Mewat has been taken from the *arsattas* of five *parganas*, namely Khohri, Gazi ka Thana, Jalalpur, Atela Bhabra, and Piragpur. The *arsattas*, however, do not provide information for all the *parganas* nor for all the years in the period under study. Further, they furnish data on prices of food crops only. The prices in the records are the actual sale prices of food crops collected as revenue at short intervals and given in terms of quantity per rupee. For a comparative study, the prices of all food crops have been converted into rupees per *maund*. Considering the variation in the weight of a *maund* in different *parganas*, the prices have been calculated taking one *maund* as equal to 40 *sers*.

The prices of principal food crops of the five *parganas* are given in Tables 4.8a–4.8e.

Apart from the information on actual prices of all food crops in the *arsattas*, the *arzdashts* and *chithis* have numerous references to the movement of prices. These price movements had two important economic implications: first, prices fluctuated in response to supply and demand, and second, price fluctuations affected economic activity and differently impacted different sections of the rural society.

The movement of prices of principal food crops did not follow a uniform pattern during the period under study. During the 1660s, the prices were abysmally low—a fact borne out by the *arsattas* and

Table 4.8a Prices (in rupees) of *rabi* crops per *maund* in *pargana* Khohri

Crops (*rabi*)	1712	1713	1716	1733	1741	1743	1744	1747
Wheat	1.42	1.61	1.86	1.77	1.32	1.72	1.17	1.41
Barley	1.08	1.15	1.36	1.25	1.07	1.12	–	1.04
Gram	0.96	1.15	1.23	1.37	1.06	–	–	1.07
Gochani (mixture of wheat and gram)	–	–	–	1.36	1.19	1.66	1.07	1.09
Gojaro (mixture of wheat and barley)	–	–	1.83	1.30	1.16	1.33	1.02	1.02
Sarson	2.90	–	2.24	2.50	1.77	1.50	1.81	1.31
Masoor (lentil)	0.87	–	1.08	1.05	1.00	1.80	1.02	1.08
Matar (peas)	–	1.15	–	1.05	–	–	–	–
Aurhari	–	1.00	–	1.18	1.14	1.41	1.06	–
Vatla	–	–	1.26	1.16	1.08	1.22	–	1.01
Bejhari (mixture of gram and barley)	–	–	–	1.25	1.06	1.25	0.96	1.07

Source: Arsattas of years mentioned.

Table 4.8b Prices (in rupees) of *kharif* and *rabi* crops per *maund* in *pargana* Jalalpur

Crops (*Kharif*)	1666	1689	1691	1711	1716	1718	1720	1723	1735	1737	1739
Bajra	0.39	0.50	0.60	0.64	1.35	1.60	1.52	1.12	1.23	1.86	0.61
Jowar	0.37	0.37	0.43	0.57	1.18	1.29	1.42	1.05	1.03	1.68	0.55
Moong	0.42	0.50	0.50	0.57	1.39	1.79	1.60	1.35	1.23	2.07	0.84
Moth	0.34	0.37	0.47	0.45	1.35	1.66	1.51	1.08	1.02	1.86	0.57
Urad	0.40	0.38	0.50	0.57	1.36	1.67	1.54	1.25	1.02	2.57	0.58
Til	0.87	1.30	0.89	1.73	3.36	3.30	2.37	2.07	2.35	3.19	1.32
Crops (*Rabi*)	**1666**	**1689**	**1691**	**1711**	**1716**	**1718**	**1720**	**1723**	**1735**	**1737**	**1739**
Wheat	–	0.70	0.77	0.73	1.21	1.25	2.10	1.86	1.40	2.50	0.87
Barley	0.40	0.38	0.56	0.44	0.83	0.84	1.29	1.51	1.06	1.82	0.50
Gram	0.39	0.40	0.42	0.46	0.64	0.80	1.57	1.66	1.04	2.50	0.71
Sarson	–	0.84	0.53	1.05	0.96	1.36	1.81	1.50	–	2.33	1.32
Aurhari	–	0.35	0.39	–	0.94	0.71	0.84	1.43	–	1.94	0.57

Source: Arsattas of years mentioned.

Table 4.8c Prices (in rupees) of *kharif* and *rabi* crops per *maund* in *pargana* Gazi ka Thana

Crops (*Kharif*)	1730	1731	1734	1735	1737	1740	1741	1742	1743	1747	1748
Bajra	0.97	2.53	1.38	1.38	1.86	0.61	0.70	1.43	1.05	0.74	0.77
Jowar	0.95	2.64	1.15	1.25	1.78	0.50	0.65	1.25	0.73	0.66	0.74
Guwar	0.69	1.70	0.80	0.83	1.29	0.50	0.58	1.08	0.66	0.63	0.54
Moth	0.97	2.54	1.18	1.22	1.94	0.50	0.67	1.50	1.04	0.94	0.81
Urad	0.91	2.33	1.22	1.38	2.42	0.61	0.71	1.59	1.37	1.32	0.82
Moong	1.07	–	1.44	1.47	2.62	0.67	0.71	2.06	–	1.41	1.12
Til	2.50	4.50	3.23	2.88	3.48	1.94	1.89	2.67	2.11	1.71	2.13

Crops (*Rabi*)	1730	1731	1735	1737	1740	1741	1742	1743	1747	1748	1750
Wheat	1.30	1.94	1.27	2.05	0.95	0.96	1.40	1.35	1.31	1.08	0.88
Barley	0.81	1.86	1.05	1.54	0.45	0.65	1.09	0.84	0.75	0.77	0.68
Gram	0.86	–	1.05	–	0.59	0.75	1.47	1.33	1.25	0.83	0.91
Sarson	2.54	4.75	1.66	2.41	1.07	1.28	2.09	1.60	1.00	1.42	1.22
Bejhari	0.83	–	1.05	–	0.51	0.70	1.26	1.02	–	0.90	0.74
Gochani	0.96	–	1.16	–	0.71	0.85	1.38	–	–	–	–
Gojaro	–	–	1.14	1.97	0.63	0.80	–	1.05	–	–	–

Source: Arsattas of years mentioned.

corroborated by other sources too.[132] The evidence clearly suggests that a glut of foodgrains in the *qasbas* caused such downward mobility of prices. This glut, in turn, may be attributed to the reasonably good harvest which might have led to a situation in which the supply of foodgrains outstripped the demand. In 1666, when the Mughal emperor moved his camp from Agra to Delhi, the *pargana*-level officials in Mewat expected that the establishment of the imperial camp would lead to an increase in the demand for grains from the region.[133] The prices tended to stabilize between 1670 and 1690,[134] but thereafter witnessed a sharp increase, an increase that was marked in the last decade of the 18th century. In fact, prices of almost all commodities more than doubled during this decade.

132 Amber Records, Asoj Sudi 9, VS 1723/1666 CE; Chait Vadi 6, VS 1722/1665 CE; Mah Vadi 6, VS 1722/1665 CE.

133 Amber Records, Mangsir Vadi 12, VS 1723/1666 CE.

134 *Arzdasht*, Kartik Vadi 13, VS 1741/1684 CE.

Table 4.8d Prices (in rupees) of *kharif* and *rabi* crops per *maund* in *pargana* Atela Bhabra

Crops (*Kharif*)	1664	1711	1712	1728	1730	1731	1733	1734	1736	1737	1740	1741	1742
Bajra	0.42	0.42	1.02	1.07	1.14	2.96	1.12	1.54	1.86	2.81	1.15	0.80	1.34
Jowar	0.37	0.36	0.88	1.04	1.00	2.71	1.02	1.41	1.50	2.61	0.63	0.67	1.23
Moth	0.53	0.41	0.88	1.05	1.00	3.06	1.09	1.50	2.17	2.95	0.78	0.76	1.65
Moong	0.79	0.50	1.00	1.25	1.05	3.22	1.23	1.57	2.67	3.93	1.07	1.18	2.27
Til	1.82	1.41	2.50	3.37	3.60	7.54	3.25	–	–	5.07	3.07	–	3.40
Guwar	–	–	1.00	0.62	0.65	–	0.73	0.72	1.08	1.49	0.41	–	0.92

Crops (*Rabi*)	1664	1711	1730	1731	1733	1734	1736	1737	1740	1741	1742
Wheat	080	0.65	1.34	2.31	1.42	1.53	1.88	2.91	1.04	1.07	1.57
Barley	0.48	0.44	1.04	1.69	1.08	1.24	1.48	2.22	0.78	0.79	1.23
Gram	0.71	–	1.05	–	1.31	1.49	2.24	4.02	1.00	–	–
Sarson	1.10	0.67	2.84	6.21	2.35	2.44	3.05	3.22	1.59	–	2.80

Source: Arsattas of years mentioned.

Table 4.8e Prices (in rupees) of *kharif* and *rabi* crops per *maund* in *pargana* Piragpur

Crops (*Kharif*)	1725	1728	1730	1732	1734	1735	1736	1737	1740	1741	1742
Bajra	1.28	1.08	1.13	1.19	1.58	1.61	1.95	2.83	0.68	0.75	1.35
Jowar	1.14	1.04	1.08	1.11	1.42	1.44	1.51	2.66	0.64	0.71	1.29
Moth	1.29	1.05	1.06	1.11	1.53	1.44	2.12	2.96	0.75	0.73	1.74
Til	–	3.50	3.50	4.69	4.81	3.88	–	4.88	2.86	–	3.64
Guwar	0.64	0.61	0.67	0.77	0.78	0.81	1.25	1.39	0.38	0.48	0.90

Crops (*Rabi*)	1730	1732	1734	1735	1736	1737	1740	1741	1742
Wheat	1.31	1.41	1.56	1.75	1.83	2.88	0.95	1.09	1.56
Barley	0.97	1.07	1.19	1.43	1.45	2.24	0.68	0.79	1.22
Gram	1.02	1.09	1.61	1.53	1.97	4.04	0.84	1.00	–
Sarson	2.65	2.47	2.47	2.41	2.70	3.19	1.38	1.57	2.80

Source: Arsattas of years mentioned.

The steep rise in the price level from the last decade of the 17th century onwards was due to a shortfall in the supply of foodgrains.[135] The shortfall might have been partly caused by the drought of 1694–8 and the resultant poor state of cultivation.[136] It is evident from a number of documents that owing to crop failure in Mewat, the prices of foodgrains rose drastically.[137] For instance, in 1694, the *amil* in his letters to Amber Raja informed that the crops had been destroyed on account of famine; that there was an acute shortage of foodgrains in the local markets; that the peasants had nothing to eat and a large number of them had died because of starvation while many had migrated to Mathura and Ajmer in search of food; that the prices of foodgrains had been shooting up every day; and that the trade in foodgrains had been hampered seriously as very few grain traders had

[135] *Arzdasht*, Asoj Vadi 2, VS 1751/1694 CE.

[136] *Arzdasht*, Kartik Vadi 2, VS 1753/1696 CE; Asadh Vadi 7, VS 1755/1698 CE.

[137] *Arzdasht*, Asoj Vadi 7, VS 1751/1694 CE; Asoj Vadi 1, VS 1751/1694 CE; Asoj Vadi 9, VS 1751/1694 CE; Kartik Vadi 3, VS 1751/1694 CE; Asoj Vadi 6, VS 1751/1694 CE.

been visiting the markets of the region.[138] The year 1695, in particular, was one of crop failures in most *parganas* of Mewat, and this resulted in soaring prices.[139] Further, there was insufficient rainfall during the years 1694–8, 1704–5, 1709, 1716–17, and 1724 which adversely affected agricultural production. The increase in the prices of foodgrains during these decades can largely be attributed to a shortfall in their supply in the local markets.[140] The prices continued to rise in the first quarter of the 18th century due to crop failures in certain years. Another factor that contributed to price rise was an increase in the demand for foodgrains due to continuous military expeditions against the Jat rebels and disruption in the inter-regional trade in foodgrains.

The extent to which sudden shortages and glut of foodgrains in the market affected the price levels and trade in foodgrains can be seen from the documentary evidence of 1683. The traders encouraged by low market prices purchased 10,000 *maunds* of foodgrains in the hope of a price rise in the near future. However, in the coming year due to good monsoon, the agricultural output increased and the prices of foodgrains declined further. In distress, the grain traders complained to Amber Raja Bishan Singh that they could not withstand this loss.[141]

A general rise in the price level is discernible from the year 1712 when the prices of foodgrains in many *parganas* registered a sharp increase and thereafter never came down. It appears from Tables 4.8a–4.8e that the trend in the movement of prices of foodgrains in the five sample *parganas* was not uniform during the period from 1712 to 1750. In *parganas* Atela Bhabra, Piragpur, and Jalalpur, the prices registered a steep rise, whereas in *parganas* Gazi ka Thana and Khohri, the rise was gradual.[142]

Irfan Habib has attributed the stability of prices between 1665 and 1710 to the decline in currency supply and the subsequent rise in prices

[138] *Arzdasht*, Asoj Vadi 7, vs 1751/1694 CE; Asoj Vadi 1, vs 1751/1694 CE; Asoj Vadi 3, vs 1751/1694 CE; Asoj Vadi 6, vs 1751/1694 CE.

[139] *Arzdasht*, Asoj Vadi 6, vs 1752/1695 CE.

[140] *Arsattas* of the aforementioned years, *parganas* Khohri, Jalalpur, Mojpur Pahari, Gazi ka Thana, Pindayan, Atela Bhabra, and Piragpur.

[141] *Arzdasht*, Jeth Sudi 5, vs 1741/1784 CE.

[142] See Tables 7(a) to 7(i).

after 1710 to the cumulative effect of increase in currency supply.[143] The price movement in the *parganas* of Mewat was greatly influenced by the demand and supply situations prevalent in Agra and Delhi. The bulk of surplus foodgrains from these *parganas* was exported to Agra and Delhi. The constant demand for foodgrains from these two prosperous and populous urban centres thus largely affected the movement of agricultural prices in the region and contributed to the rise in prices.[144]

The other factor that caused the upward price movement was the disturbances created by rebellious zamindars (*bhomias*) in the region that adversely impacted the intra- and inter-regional trade and the production of foodgrains. Rajasthani documents of late 17th and early 18th centuries inform us that rural and long-distance trade in this region was quite disturbed, as both trade routes and traders were rendered insecure by agrarian revolts and depredations of the *bhomias*. Most acts of looting and extortion of traders were committed by Rajput *bhomias* and Jats and only a few by the Meos. For instance, in 1685, the Lalani traders of Manoharpur[145] and traders of Averi[146] were looted. In 1686, 17 bullock carts of Lalani traders were looted before they could reach Sanganer.[147] In the same year, the Baloch traders of *qasbas* Bhera and Khushab (Pakistani Punjab), who, with their 800 camels laden with saltpetre, were on the way to Sanganer in order to purchase cotton, were prohibited from advancing further from Kotputli towards Sanganer on account of the threats of robbery by the Rajputs.[148] In 1694, some grain traders were captured by the Panchanot and Jadon Rajput *bhomias* who demanded a huge ransom and *rahdari* (road tax).[149] In 1695, the traders of the villages of *pargana* Chatsu were looted by Sardar Singh Rajawat and his men.[150] In 1703, Santokhram, a trader from Meham (Haryana), while travelling from

143 Raychaudhury and Habib, eds, *The Cambridge Economic History of India*, 376.

144 Amber Records, Bhadva Sudi 8, VS 1769/1712 CE.

145 *Arzdasht*, Chait Sudi 8, VS 1742/1685 CE.

146 *Arzdasht*, Asadh Sudi 15, VS 1742/1685 CE.

147 *Arzdasht*, Mah Vadi 2, VS 1743/1686 CE.

148 *Arzdasht*, VS 1743/1686 CE.

149 *Arzdasht*, Posh Vadi 2, VS 1751/1694 CE.

150 *Arzdasht*, Fagun Sudi 5, VS 1752/1695 CE.

Sanganer along with his stock, was robbed of 1,000 rupees and goods worth 1,500 rupees.[151] In 1718, the men of Dalel Singh Rathor looted 11 carts on the way from *qasba* Chatsu to Gohana (Haryana).[152] Rajput *bhomias* Sardar Singh Rajawat and his son, and Dalel Singh Kilanot often robbed the traders of their stocks of salt and *gur*.[153]

Recurrent plundering and resultant apprehension and fear among the traders led to the closure of insecure trade routes and reduced commercial traffic, thereby heavily disrupting trade. For instance, in 1709 the routes and highways of Amber, Sanganer, Dausa, Fagui, and Mauzabad were closed due to disturbances, and as a result the movement of the *banjaras* and traders of the Brij region was ceased. The *faujdars* and *amils* were ordered to make adequate arrangements for the security of the trade routes.[154] Jagjivan Ram Pancholi, the *vakil* of Amber, posted at the Mughal court in Shahjahanabad (Delhi), wrote a letter to the *diwan* of Amber stating that the state was incurring heavy economic losses in terms of *hasil* due to the immobility of traders and *banjaras* on account of their fears of being robbed, and therefore strict arrangements must be made for their security.[155] In 1709, Amber Raja asked the traders of Delhi to send clothes for a royal wedding in Amber and provided them full security on the way.[156] On account of the looting of traders by the Rajputs in the villages of *pargana* Chatsu, the movement of people was stopped.[157] The news of the plunder of traders travelling through *pargana* Malrana by the Rajputs reportedly aroused fear among the traders and halted their movement.[158]

Like the Rajput *bhomias*, the Jats, too, were involved in such predatory activities. For instance, in 1717 they looted 23 vehicles laden with wheat and belonging to the *sahukars* of Shahjahanabad while they were on their way to Agra.[159] In the wake of the seizure of Alwar by the Jats, trade routes to Mewat were closed down and traders were

151 *Arzdasht*, Kartik Sudi 14, vs 1760/1703 CE.

152 *Arzdasht*, Jeth Vadi 11, vs 1775/1718 CE.

153 *Arzdasht*, Jeth Vadi 2, vs 1760/1703 CE.

154 *Arzdasht*, Mangsir Sudi 15, vs 1766/1709 CE.

155 *Arzdasht*, Mangsir Sudi 12, vs 1766/1709 CE.

156 *Arzdasht*, Mah Sudi 10 vs 1766/1709 CE.

157 *Arzdasht*, Fagun Sudi 2, vs 1752/1695 CE.

158 *Arzdasht*, Posh Sudi 5, vs 1774/1717 CE.

159 *Arzdasht*, Posh Sudi 5, vs 1774/1717 CE.

reluctant to enter Mewat apprehending robbery by the Jats.[160] In 1708, Bhikaridas, the *amil* of Amber, informed the Amber Raja that Churaman Jat had entered into a secret pact with Rahimullah Khan, the *naib faujdar* of Mathura, promising to give the latter half of whatever would be looted from the traders.[161]

The imperial *jagirdars*, on their part, complained to the Mughal emperor that the trade route between Akbarabad (Agra) and Shahjahanabad (Delhi) was badly disturbed by the Jats, and hence the traders were scared to travel on that route.[162] The *amil* of Amber informed the Amber Raja that apprehending the illegal demands of the rebel Rajput and Jat *bhomias* for large sums of money in the form of arbitrarily raised *rahdari* and other levies, the grain merchants from other areas were no longer visiting Mewat; and that the commercial activities in the region had come to a standstill as the caravans of *banjaras* were recklessly attacked and plundered by the rebels.[163] Commenting upon this abysmal situation, the *amil* further stated that the traders had become totally helpless and unless the state provided them security of life and property from the rebel *bhomias*, it would not be possible for them to trade in Amber.[164] In 1712, the *vakil* of Amber, in a letter from Delhi, stated that owing to the widespread disturbances created by the Meos in the Mewat and Rewari regions, the prices of foodgrains had suddenly gone up in Agra.[165]

As mentioned earlier, there is little documentary evidence for depredatory activities by the Meos amidst plenty of references to robberies by the Rajputs and Jats. However, this does not imply that the Meos were not involved in plundering activities against traders. Since the caravans of traders and *banjaras* were protected by armed escorts on their journeys, overpowering and robbing them required stronger and larger forces that the militarily well-organized Rajputs and Jats could only command. Hence, it was perhaps not feasible

160 *Khatoot ahalkaran*, Mah Vadi 4, VS 1775/1718 CE; 500 horsemen of the Jats lay in hiding to loot the traders.

161 *Arzdasht*, VS 1715/1708 CE.

162 *Arzdasht*, Mangsir Vadi 2, VS 1744/1686 CE.

163 *Arzdasht*, Posh Vadi 7, VS 1743/1686 CE; Kartik Sudi 13, VS 1742/1685 CE; Jeth Vadi 1, VS 1761/1704 CE.

164 *Arzdasht*, Mangsir Vadi 9, VS 1769/1712 CE.

165 *Vakil's* Report, Mangsir Vadi 9, VS 1769/1712 CE.

for the Meos who were weaker in military organization to maintain such large forces. This explains scant references to looting of traders and *banjaras* by the Meos. It seems that the Meos rather indulged in petty cattle-lifting, a task relatively easier than conducting organized plunder.

Thus, various interrelated factors appear to have contributed to the steep rise in agricultural prices during the period under study. The sharp annual fluctuations in agricultural production greatly affected the short-term trends in price movement. Decline in production in the region without any corresponding decline in the local demand for foodgrains due to continuous military expeditions against the rebel Jats and Rajput *bhomias* created a situation of relative scarcity of foodstuffs leading to a price rise. If we take into account the short-term price movements, it appears that prices soared every time harvests were poor and slumped when production rose above the average. Grain prices responded to fluctuations in demand over periods even shorter than the entire harvest year. However, these changes reflected conditions prevalent in a particular locality at a given period of time and hence were purely local phenomena.

Trade malpractices on the part of grain dealers also led to short-term downward and upward trends in the prices of foodgrains. In times of scarcity, the grain traders tried to raise the grain prices by hoarding stocks. In 1694, there was a general complaint against big grain traders that they prevented small traders from purchasing grains in the market of Averi.[166] Local officials also sometimes misused their official position to manipulate price movements. This is evident from the example of Sujan Singh Rajawat, the *faujdar* of *pargana* Bahatri, who was accused of buying and selling large quantities of grain through his local agents and preventing small traders from buying grain. The latter, in turn, strongly protested against the monopolistic attitude of such big traders and corrupt officials.[167]

The sharp regional variations in the prices of foodgrains were negated by the costs of transport. At times, the traders happened to buy grain cheap in more distant regions, but the difference in prices were balanced by the high cost of transport. Some short-term

166 *Arzdasht*, Asoj Vadi 12, VS 1751/1694 CE.
167 *Arzdasht*, Asoj Vadi 13, VS 1751/1694 CE.

movements of prices also followed changes in currency supply. The sagging tendency of prices in the early 18th century has been attributed to a decline in the supply of silver and gold from 1711 to 1750.[168] It can be argued that the response of the peasants to price movements was not automatic and certainly not positive. It was more likely to be 'negative' in the technical sense of the term, that is, to induce a decline of output when prices were high and a rise in output when they were low. However, as noted earlier, the *zabti* system based on separate cash rates for different crops was not applied to the entire region under study due to its geographical limitations. It existed alongside the *batai* system, allowing peasants the option to pay land revenue either in cash or in kind. The usual practice of the peasants was to pay in cash in the case of cash crops and opt for crop-sharing (*batai*) in the case of food crops. The small peasants who constituted the majority of rural population and primarily concentrated on the cultivation of food crops had two immediate concerns: first, to maintain a minimum subsistence level; and second, to pay the land revenue. As such, they were far less concerned about the changes in price levels than the rich peasantry was. It was the upper strata of peasantry that benefitted the most from an upward trend in price movement. Moreover, the relative stability in the movement of *zabti* rates in a situation when prices were moving up further benefitted this strata.

V

This section is devoted to a critical appraisal of the functioning of land revenue system in the region. The Rajasthani documents testify to the attempts made to collect revenue from the peasants far beyond the officially sanctioned customary limits. The arbitrary imposition of additional illegal or non-customary taxes by both the Amber rulers and the local authorities led to a marked discrepancy between the customary land revenue demand and the actual revenue collection, and meant an enormous increase in the tax burden on the peasants which, in turn, eventually affected the level of agricultural production adversely. Further, the documents point to a deterioration in the

168 Raychaudhuri and Habib, eds, *The Cambridge Economic History of India*, 360.

functioning of land revenue administration on account of continuous revolts by the *bhomias* against the Amber rulers and imperial *jagirdars*, as well as incessant infighting and rivalry among the *bhomias* themselves. The exploitation of peasants reached a stage at which they were forced to abandon cultivation and desert their villages. Flights of peasants from land became widespread from the middle of the 17th century. Interestingly, the phenomenon was not confined to a particular unit of administration, that is, imperial *jagirs* or *watan jagirs* of the Amber Raja. Rather, it cut across all *parganas* of Mewat.[169] As the situation in one administrative unit of the region was hardly better than that in another, it is extremely doubtful whether the peasants got any respite by resorting to inter-*pargana* migration. The high-handedness of the state officials also contributed to the worsening of the economic plight of the peasantry.

In 1712, the Raja of Amber received the zamindari rights, that is, right to collect revenue, of the *parganas* Firozpur Jhirka and Tijara from the imperial *mansabdars*. When he appointed two of his *amils*, Gopinath and Anup Singh Wakavat, to collect land revenue from these *parganas*, the Meo peasants of these *parganas* opposed the new *amils* to such an extent that they refused to pay the revenue. At this, the *faujdar*'s troops arrested a large number of Meo peasants, brought them to the *amil*'s office, and put them in prison. The *amil* released them when they submitted an undertaking promising that in future they would pay revenue to the Amber state. Notwithstanding this, the Meo peasants and *patels* of the two *parganas* submitted a petition at the Mughal court in Shahjahanabad. In the presence of Munim Khan, *diwan* of the Mughal state, they pleaded: 'Our territory falls in the *jagirs* of the imperial *mansabdars*. Therefore, we are the *raiyati* [peasants] of the Mughal emperor. The state of Amber [*sarkar*] tries to impose various kinds of taxes upon us. We are in stress; therefore, we have approached you with our plea; kindly help us.' Having heard the petition of the Meo peasants, the emperor directed Munim Khan to appoint imperial *amils* in place of the *amils* of Amber state.[170] Similarly, in 1683, the Meo peasants of *pargana* Firozpur Jhirka and

[169] *Arzdasht*, Sawan Vadi 6, VS 1762/1705 CE; Asoj Vadi 9, VS 1751/1694 CE; Kartik Vadi 3, VS 1751/1694 CE.

[170] *Arzdasht*, Asadh Sudi 2, VS 1769/1712 CE; Asadh Vadi 7, VS 1769/1712 CE.

Milakpur had submitted a petition at the Mughal court emperor complaining against the levy of non-customary taxes by the Amber state. According to the report sent by Devidas, a *harkara* (spy), to the Amber Raja:

> The *raiyati* of *pargana* Firozpur and Milkpur has become stubborn; no one can make them understand. It has stopped down to pig-headedness and treachery. Their refusal to pay certain taxes is daily causing us a great deal of loss. The *raiyati* of these *parganas* had gone to Delhi to plead before the Mughal emperor. After hearing their plea, the emperor has waived off *jajiya* tax [or *jizya*, a tax on non-Muslims] and ordered that *jajiya* be extracted from the *jagirdar* instead of the *raiyati*. Apart from this, the *raiyati* also refuses to pay *nyota* and *gara* [tax on cart]. The *diwan* of the Mughal *darbar* has sent a letter to the *ukil* [or *vakil*, 'lawyer' of the Amber state posted at the Mughal court] stating that the *raiyati* of the *pargana* of Firozpur Jhirka and Milakpur had approached the emperor with a complaint against the Amber state. Therefore, try to pacify the *raiyati* and get a contract of conciliation signed by it.[171]

The report clearly shows that the Meo peasants were well aware of the fact that their villages were part of the *jagir* assigned to the imperial *mansabdar*, not that of the Amber Raja's *watan jagir*; and that the *mansabdar*, in turn, had assigned the right to revenue collection from their villages to the Amber Raja by way of *ijara* (revenue farming). Thus, whoever happened to be their *jagirdar*, they could precisely understand that the Mughal emperor was their highest appellate authority, and that the Amber Raja had no legitimate right to collect non-customary cesses from them. Therefore, they did not lodge their complaint with the imperial *mansabdar* or the Amber Raja, but with the Mughal emperor himself. In 1712, when the imperial *mansabdar* Sarfaraz Khan Badshahzada assigned the *ijara* of *pargana* Firozpur Jhirka that was part of his *jagir* to the Amber chief Mirza Raja Jai Singh, the Meo peasants in protest submitted a petition at the Mughal court. In it they argued that under the cover of such practices as *ijara* the Amber ruler imposed many kinds of illegal and non-customary taxes, and pleaded that the emperor put pressure on the imperial *mansabdars* to desist from assigning the *ijara* of their *jagirs* to the Amber Raja and cancel the title deed or agreement.[172]

[171] *Khatoot ahalkaran*, Mah Vadi 6, vs 1740/1683 CE.

[172] *Arzdasht*, Bhadva Vadi 11, vs 1769/1712 CE.

In this context, Shail Mayaram's contention that the Meos were perpetually and uncompromisingly against the state, whether Mughal or Rajput,[173] is evidently ahistorical, as it ignores the multiple forms of negotiations and interactions between the Meos and the state. Historically, no peasant community, however defiant and rebellious, could afford to engage with the state by way of physical resistance alone. In normal times, it would find ways and means of negotiating with the state and expressing its grievances before its authorities to get concessions and relief. Petitioning was thus an important 'weapon of the weak' in the hands of the Meo peasants.[174] Faced with the frequent imposition and coercive collection of non-customary taxes by the Amber officials, the Meo peasants, together with their *patels*, often appealed to the Mughal emperors against the high-handedness of the Amber Raja's officials. And on many occasions, they indeed received concessions and relief from the emperors. This shows that the Meo peasants did have faith in the justice administered by the Mughal state.

The widespread disturbances caused by the depredations of rebellious Rajputs, Jats, and Meos in the Mewat region, while disrupting trade, added to the woes of the peasantry. Not only did such disturbances adversely affect the agricultural production, but the Rajput *bhomias* also resorted to forcibly exacting numerous illegal cesses from the peasants. For instance, an *arzdasht* of 1675 reported that the peasants belonging to five villages of *pargana* Mojpur had run away due to the disturbances created by the Naruka Rajput *bhomias*.[175] In another *arzdasht* of 1685, the *amil* reported to the Amber Raja that the Naruka, Kilanot, and Panchnot *bhomias* were illegally collecting *dastur-chaudharai* and other taxes from the peasants in *parganas* Mandawar, Naharkhoh, Punkhar, Bharkol, Umarni, Sonkhar-Sonkhari, and Hasanpur.[176] Yet another *arzdasht* of 1685 reported that the *bhomias* plundered four lakh rupees from the *jagirs* of the imperial *mansabdar* and prevented the peasants and *patels* from paying *hasil*

173 Mayaram, *Against History, Against State*, 120.

174 James C. Scott, *Weapons of the Weak: Everyday Forms of Peasant Resistance* (Delhi: Oxford University Press, 1990).

175 *Arzdasht*, Asoj Sudi 7, VS 1732/1675 CE.

176 *Arzdasht*, Bhadva Vadi 7, VS 1742/1685 CE; Asadh Vadi 5, VS 1742/1685 CE.

(land revenue) to the *jagirdars*.[177] Further, in order to throw the work of revenue collection out of gear, the rebel *bhomias* either killed the *patels* and *patwaris* in a number of *parganas* or held them in captivity.

The harassment and illegal exactions by the *bhomias* assumed such an alarming proportion that many villages were deserted.[178] For instance, the *amil* of an unspecified *pargana* informed the Amber Raja that most of the peasants had left their villages out of fear of the Rajput *bhomias*. The efforts were made to rehabilitate these villages and 2–4 *asamis* (peasants) were induced to reside in each village, but owing to the disturbances sufficient number of *asamis* could not be roped in and, consequently, the production could not be increased up to the expected level. The revenue realized in the current season was hardly comparable with that in the previous years. Moreover, the peasants were in no position to meet the burden of such additional taxes as *tehsildari, bhent, salami, lakri,* and *ghas*. In the recent past, the *pargana* had been fully populated and well cultivated to the extent that the peasants were able to shoulder the burden of all these taxes.[179] As mentioned earlier, some of these taxes were levied upon the village as a unit and the amount due from the village was divided among individual peasants or paid out of the *malba* to which each peasant was expected to contribute his share. However, the flight of peasants in large numbers from the villages created a particularly distressing situation for the remaining few peasants who were called upon to shoulder the entire tax burden notwithstanding their dwindling resources and numerical strength. They thus protested against these taxes and threatened to migrate if the payment was insisted upon.

As is evident from the reports of the *amils*, the villages facing peasant emigrations became thinly populated and the remaining residents—usually 2–4 *asamis* in each village—could not afford to meet the burden of common village taxes and other levies. Apprehending that they might be required to shoulder this entire burden, these peasants suffered from the feeling of insecurity. The peasants who had migrated petitioned to the *amil* stating that they were willing to return to their homestead villages if the administration was prepared

177 *Arzdasht*, Asadh Vadi 5, vs 1742/1685 CE.

178 *Arzdasht*, Jeth Vadi 2, vs 1746/1689 CE; Sawan Vadi 9, vs 1745/1688 CE.

179 *Arzdasht*, Fagun Sudi 9, vs 1752/1695 CE.

to concede their demand for the waiver of *tehsildari* and other taxes. The *amil* recommended that *tehsildari* be revoked in order to facilitate their rehabilitation, but at the same time suggested that henceforth the peasants pay taxes in accordance with the *dastur-al-amal*.[180] We can infer from this particular recommendation that hitherto the revenue demand was made in contravention of the *dastur-al-amal*. However, the extent to which the recommendations of the revenue officials were implemented in practice is but a matter of conjuncture. The available evidence, however, indicates that this migration of peasants continued unabated, as the various local authorities continued to levy additional taxes on the peasants, while demanding the customary taxes at exorbitant rates.[181] Although the magnitude of tax burden on the helpless peasantry varied, what is undisputable is the fact that it assumed alarming proportions everywhere.

The expansion of the *bhom* rights of the Amber chief in new areas led to the increasing tax burden on the peasantry and unrest, as reflected in their recurrent complaints and protests. In 1665, the peasants of *parganas* Khohri, Khilohra, Baroda-Meo, and Rewari decided to visit Delhi in order to submit their joint petition to the emperor against the high-handedness of the *jagirdars*, *ijaradars*, and their agents, and seek redressal of their grievances.[182] In the same year, many peasants of *parganas* Kotla and Mandawar approached the *diwan* of Amber in order to seek reduction in land revenue rates.[183] In 1714, the peasants of *parganas* Atela Bhabra and Piragpur requested the *diwan* of the Amber state for exemption from the new *bhomi* tax which was being imposed on them.[184] In the same *pargana*, in 1724 the peasants refused to pay *lata-kharach* at the rate of 2 *sers* per *maund*,[185] as it was in excess of the customary rate of one *ser* per *maund*. In 1709, the peasantry of *pargana* Kot-Qasim protested against the levy of *serino* tax at the rate of 4 *sers* per *maund* which exceeded the customary rate

180 *Arzdasht*, Fagun Sudi 9, VS 1752/1695 CE.

181 See Tables 5a to 5c.

182 Amber Records, Fagun Sudi 2, VS 1722/1665; Chait Sudi 3, VS 1722/1665 CE.

183 Amber Records, Vaishakh Vadi 1, VS 1722/1665; Asadh Vadi 6, VS 1722/1665 CE.

184 *Arzdasht*, Sawan Sudi 3, VS 1771/1714 CE.

185 *Chithi* to the *amil*, *pargana* Atela Bhabra, Kartik Vadi 4, VS 1781/1724 CE.

of one *ser* per *maund* according to the *dastur-al-amal*.[186] In *parganas* Averi and Bahatri, the *sahnas* who were appointed in the villages by the *amils* and *amins* were found demanding *ghughri* and *sahngi* cesses at exorbitant rates from the peasantry in utter disregard of the *dastur-al-amal*. Therefore, the Amber Raja issued a decree (*parwana*) that every *sahna* was to be appointed on the recommendation of the *bakshi* not by the *amils* and *amins*.[187] In 1737, in *pargana* Atela Bhabra when the *ijaradar* tried to increase the land revenue demand beyond the customary limit, the peasants refused to pay the same.[188] Among the peasant communities, it is the Meos who bore the brunt of tax burden the most. Thus, in 1665 the Meo peasants of 12 villages of *pargana* Khohri complained to the Amber Raja that they were being coerced into paying land revenue and other cesses at a higher rate as compared to the Ahir peasants in the same villages.[189]

The other cause of the peasants' discontent was the frequent demand for *peshkash* on various pretexts by the members of the ruling class, that is, *subedars*, *faujdars*, or imperial *jagirdars*.[190] The *peshkash* was not a customary levy on the peasants; it was over and above the normal revenue demand. It was collected from various sections of the rural society in various forms. By and large, it was extracted, often coercively, from the peasants, *patels*, and the *patwaris* under the head of *virar*. *Virar* is a broad category of taxes under which a variety of specified and unspecified taxes that did not form part of the regular *jamabandi* were collected from the peasants and hereditary village officials by the local authorities to meet their contingent expenditures and make up for deficient revenue collection. A number of documents illustrate the further deterioration in the economic condition of the peasantry as a result of the levy of *virar*. For instance, in one of his letters, the *diwan* of Amber informed the Amber Raja that the peasants of Mewat had come to the court in his absence and expressed their inability to pay the various *virar* taxes. The *diwan* further stated that

186 *Arzdasht*, Jeth Vadi 6, vs 1746/1709 CE.

187 *Arzdasht*, Bhadva Vadi 14, vs 1783/1726 CE.

188 *Chithi* to the *amil*, Chait Sudi 8, vs 1794/1737 CE.

189 *Chithi* to the *amil*, *pargana* Khohri, Asadh Vadi 8, vs 1722/1665 CE.

190 *Chithi* to the *amil*, *parganas* Khohri and Mojpur, Vaishakh Sudi 9, vs 1795/1738 CE; *Arzdasht*, Fagun Sudi 14, vs 1749/1692 CE.

he had tried to convince the *patels*, but the latter stuck to their position and were not prepared to go back without seeking exemption from *virar*. The peasants pleaded that a devastating drought had completely ruined their crops leaving them without any means of subsistence and with dim prospects of the next harvest. They emphasized that the revenue-paying capacity of the villages had already been adversely affected due to the flight of peasants in large numbers. They further argued that in the past they had never defaulted in paying revenue, but under the exceptionally adverse circumstances they should at least be exempted from the various *virar* taxes, such as *kawayara, waqai-nawis,* and *baqaya* (arrears).[191] In 1692, the *patels* and peasants from the villages of *pargana* Khohri lodged a complaint at the Amber court against the levying of *virar*, arguing that it was unfair on the part of the Raja to demand a heavy *virar* from the poor peasants in order to meet the expenses of his impending military expedition against the Jat rebels.[192]

In the entire region of Mewat, the peasantry, *patels*, *patwaris*, and *chaudharis* came together to oppose the *peshkash*. They collectively sent petitions to the Amber Raja for the revocation of the *peshkash*.[193] A wide divergence between the amount of *peshkash* demanded from the peasants and their actual capacity to meet the demand can be seen from an instance of the year 1738. The *patels* and peasants belonging to the *parganas* Khohri and Mojpur went to Delhi and sought audience with the emperor. They reported to the emperor that the sum of 17,300 rupees demanded from them as *peshkash* was not only unjust but totally beyond their capacity to pay. They were able to convince the emperor of their plight and the demand was considerably reduced at his instance. They were asked to pay just 2,000 rupees as *virar*.[194] The incident reveals the degree of extortion the peasants faced.

The growth of *ijara* system in Mewat after the death of Mughal emperors Aurangzeb and Bahadur Shah further intensified the exploitation of peasantry. The increase in the practice of assigning

[191] *Arzdasht*, Sawan Sudi 13, VS 1750/1693 CE.

[192] *Arzdasht*, Fagun Sudi 14, VS 1749/1692 CE.

[193] *Arsattas*, *parganas* Pindayan, Mojpur, Bharkol, Mandawar and Naharkhoh, VS 1806/1749 CE.

[194] *Chithi* to the *amil*, *parganas* Khohri and Mojpur, Vaishakh Sudi 9, VS 1795/1738 CE.

the *ijara* or revenue collection rights of the *jagirs* to various powerful local bidders such as the Amber Raja and Churaman Jat was the direct result of a crisis in the *jagirdari* system. The growing power of the rebellious *bhomias* belonging to various segments of the Kachhwaha Rajput clan in the region made it extremely difficult for the *jagirdars* to collect land revenue in their *jagirs* in Mewat compelling them to resort to farming out their *jagirs*.[195]

The Amber chief subleased the areas secured in *ijara* to his kith and kin with a view to consolidate his hold on these territories. The sub-*ijaradars* were the *bhomias*, *chaudharis*, *qanungos*, and *mahajans*, and the majority were the members of Kachhwaha sub-clans. As sub-*ijaradars*, they were required to pay a lump sum amount as *peshkash* to the Amber Raja. Quite often, the *bhomia ijaradars* indulged in over-assessing the revenue; they even forced the *patels* and peasants to make good the revenue losses they suffered in the wake of crop failures. The high-handedness of the *ijaradars* can be gauged from several instances. In *pargana* Niwai, the Rajawat *bhomia ijaradar* held the *patels* in captivity to make up for a shortfall of 3,000 rupees in revenue and released them only on the condition that they would collect the amount from the peasants.[196] The *ijaradars* in *parganas* Niwai and Malrana were accused of collecting unauthorized dues on some pretext or the other. The peasants of several *parganas* in Mewat frequently lodged their complaints with the Amber Raja against the high-handedness of the *ijaradars*.[197] The peasants of *pargana* Khohri even pleaded with the Raja not to grant the *ijara* of their villages.[198]

The peasants were harassed in other ways as well. If any robbery occurred within the jurisdiction of any *ijaradar* or *faujdar*, he was obliged to apprehend the culprits and recover the booty. He was not always successful in doing so, but the *patel* of the village where the crime was committed was held responsible for apprehending the culprits, failing which he was required to compensate the loss. Eventually, the burden of compensation fell on to the shoulders of

[195] S. P. Gupta, 'Ijara System in Eastern Rajasthan', in *Medieval India: A Miscellany*, vol. 2 (Aligarh Muslim University, 1972), 263–8.

[196] *Arzdasht*, Kartik Sudi 14, VS 1760/1703 CE; Asoj Vadi 12, VS 1761/1704 CE.

[197] *Arzdasht*, Mah Vadi 8, VS 1789/1732 CE; Chait Sudi 13, VS 1795/1738 CE; Kartik Sudi 4, VS 1803/1746 CE.

[198] *Dehai-ferhashti*, *pargana* Khohri, VS 1775/1718 CE, VS 1718/1661 CE.

the helpless peasants. For instance, in 1703, in *pargana* Chatsu, when 2,300 rupees were stolen by the thieves from three villages, the *faujdar* deputed his men to catch the thieves, and the *patels* of three affected villages gave an undertaking to the effect that they would produce the thieves within 20 days, failing which the money would be collected from them. The *patels* were unable to trace the thieves within the stipulated time, and it was decided that the loss would be made up by the *patels* and peasants. The peasants, however, resisted this move and complained to the *subedar* that they were being forced to pay *virar*, when the thieves did not even belong to their villages.[199]

All these aforementioned instances, therefore, clearly establish the fact that the normal functioning of the land revenue system was considerably hampered and adherence to customary norms was no longer the order of the day. Under these conditions, it became inevitable that the actual burden of taxes on the peasantry crossed the customary limits and reduced the small peasants to dire straits. The increase in the number and frequency of peasant complaints over time suggests that the administrative control over local elements had become so lax that the over-exploitation of the peasantry at the hands of the local authorities grew with the passage of time. The refusal to concede the illegal revenue demands of the authorities or non-payment of land revenue on the part of the peasants due to unavoidable reasons caused them further harassment. Unable to withstand the ever-increasing burden of taxes and the tyranny of the authorities, many peasants resorted to migration. For instance, it was reported to the Amber Raja that in each *pargana* only 40–50 villages were populated.[200] The desertion of villages by the peasants in large numbers had a far-reaching impact on the agrarian economy. In many *parganas* of Mewat, the area under cultivation declined drastically as a result of such large-scale desertions.

The oppression of the peasants at the hands of the revenue-appropriating ruling class and various other local authorities was not confined to Mewat; it was a widespread phenomenon affecting the neighbouring territories of Amber state as well.[201] In view of this, it

[199] *Arzdasht*, Kartik Sudi 14, VS 1760/1703 CE.

[200] *Arzdasht*, Kartik Sudi 14, VS 1760/1703 CE.

[201] This region included the *parganas* of Chatsu, Malrana, Saner, and so on. See *Arzdasht*, Asoj Vadi 5, VS 1742/1685 CE; Chait Sudi 1, VS 1740/1683 CE; Kartik Vadi 14, VS 1744/1687 CE; Bhadva Vadi 14, VS 1783/1726 CE.

is difficult to accept the French traveller Francois Bernier's statement that the peasants were heavily taxed and over-exploited in the imperial territory and fled to the areas controlled by the chieftains.[202] The increasing inability of the imperial *jagirdars* to realize revenue from the recalcitrant *bhomias* led to a tussle between these two elements of the ruling class, further aggravating the crisis. In this ensuing struggle for the appropriation of surplus, the peasants were inevitably the casualty. Not only was the burden of revenue demand becoming heavier for them, its regressive nature was also heightened by the almost total collapse of the land revenue administration at the local level and the inability of the imperial authority to contain the tyranny of zamindars and *jagirdars*. With the revenue-paying capacity of the peasants thus severely affected, the revenue collection in the region drastically declined. Desperate attempts by the revenue-appropriating authorities to compensate the loss of revenue by further rack-renting the already shrinking number of peasants in the villages created a serious crisis of production in the region.

VI

Our sources contain a great deal of information about the impact of famines and droughts on the life and conditions of the peasants. The absence or shortfall of rain caused crop failures which, in turn, created famine conditions in rural society. The twin phenomena of droughts and famines were recurring features of socio-economic life in the Mughal period, and Mewat was no exception. The sources highlight the consequences of frequent crop failures and famines: destitution of peasantry, their inability to undertake cultivation, the cultivable land falling into disuse, the migration of peasants to less affected areas and consequent depopulation of their native villages, steep rise in the prices of agricultural commodities, and decline in the state share of revenue. The prospects of agricultural decline created panic in the rural society, forcing the state to intervene by way of various relief measures, which, however, were not always sufficient to alleviate the miseries of ruined peasants and aid the process of

[202] Francois Bernier, *Travels in the Mogul Empire, A. D. 1656–1668*, ed. and trans. A. Constable (repr., New Delhi: Munshiram Manoharlal, 1983), 205.

recovery of agricultural production. Nevertheless, from the point of view of the state, such relief measures were necessary for restoring the long-term revenue-paying potential of the peasants. It was this concern of the state that the *amil* as its local agent frequently articulated in his reports to the Amber Raja.

The documents *arzdasht*s, *chithi*s, and *parwana*s contain graphic descriptions of the impact of droughts on the rural society. The droughts severely affected the normal life of the peasants in different *pargana*s, although its intensity varied from area to area and from time to time. For instance, describing the drought conditions in *pargana* Bahatri in 1687–8, the *amil* informed the Amber Raja about the hardships that the demoralized *raiyat*s had to bear on account of non-availability of food.[203] In *pargana*s Jalalpur, Gazi ka Thana, Mojpur, Bharkol, Khilohra, Umarni, Piragpur, Atela Bhabra, Pahari, Averi, Bahatri, and many other unspecified ones, the normal functioning of the village society was severely disrupted during the drought years. An *arzdasht* of 1693 refers, among other things, to peasants leaving for the royal court to plead for exemption from land revenue, in view of their extreme impoverishment brought about by the droughts.[204] From this, it can be deduced that at least in the areas held as *jagir*s, the imperial *jagirdar*s tried to extract revenue from the peasants even in such extreme conditions of scarcity. Other documents also testify to a similar state of affairs.[205] In one case, a sympathetic *amil* expressed his dismay and helplessness at the phenomenon of peasants struck by scarcity and starvation and urged the authorities not to press for the collection of *hasil*.[206]

Depopulation and desertion of villages was the natural outcome when drought and starvation persisted. Unable to face hardships, the peasants ultimately took the extreme decision of leaving their villages to search for food and evade the payment of land revenue. There are numerous references in the sources to peasant migrations, and

203 *Arzdasht*, Kartik Sudi 13, VS 1743/1686 CE; Bhadva Vadi 11, VS 1743/1686 CE; Kartik Sudi 11, VS 1742/1685 CE; Kartik Vadi 3, VS 1742/1685 CE.

204 *Arzdasht*, Sawan Sudi 13, VS 1750/1693 CE.

205 *Arzdasht*, Sawan Vadi 6, VS 1762/1705 CE; Sawan Vadi 3, VS 1775/1718 CE; Asoj Vadi 6, VS 1751/1694 CE; Kartik Sudi 10, VS 1751/1694 CE; Jeth Vadi 8, VS 1751/1694 CE.

206 *Arzdasht*, Asoj Vadi 6, VS 1751/1694 CE; Kartik Sudi 10, VS 1751/1694 CE.

depopulation and ruination of villages. The *amils*, faced with such a situation, strongly recommended exemption from or relaxation in the land revenue burden as the best way to persuade the peasants to stay in their villages.[207] They also stressed the urgency of granting loans to the peasants so that they could mobilize resources to cultivate the land again.[208] It was in the interest of the state to ensure that the peasants did not leave their villages, and, at times, it was also able to make successful intervention in terms of actual relief measures. In one *arzdasht*, the *amil* wrote to the Amber Raja that he and other local officers had somehow managed to persuade the peasants to stay in their villages by promising them loans from the state.[209]

However, it was not always possible to mobilize adequate resources and check peasant migrations during famines. In such cases, the revenue proceeds were eventually affected. The *amil* observed in one case that the prospects of a good *rabi* crop were bleak in the face of peasants leaving their villages. That the spectre of depopulated and ruined villages haunted the revenue-extracting authority despite the abundance of land is clearly discernible from the *arzdashts*. However, a qualification needs to be made here. Our evidence suggests that the peasants did not readily resort to migration to escape starvation and hardship. The prospects of losing one's position in the social hierarchy of the village in the event of emigration meant that the peasants often looked upon emigration as one of their last strategies of survival. In many cases, they offered to stay on in the villages, in lieu of minimum resources, such as seeds, ploughs, and cattle that could enable them to till the land again and ensure their mere survival. In one instance, the *amil* particularly underlined the importance of cattle in agriculture production and averred that if the peasants were forced to sell their cattle to pay revenue, it would ultimately prove counter-productive and cause a fall in the amount of land revenue in future.[210] The survival

[207] *Arzdasht*, Kartik Sudi 3, vs 1751/1694 CE; Sawan Vadi 6, vs 1762/1705 CE; Sawan Vadi 3, vs 1775/1718 CE; Jeth Sudi 1, vs 1775/1718 CE; Bhadva Vadi 11, vs 1743/1646 CE; Kartik Sudi 13, vs 1743/1686 CE.

[208] *Arzdasht*, Asadh Sudi 15, vs 1743/1686 CE; Asoj Vadi 12, vs 1752/1695 CE; Sawan Vadi 6, vs 1762/1705 CE; Jeth Sudi 1, vs 1775/1718 CE; Sawan Vadi 3, vs 1775/1718 CE.

[209] *Arzdasht*, Asoj Sudi 2, vs 1751/1694 CE; Asoj Vadi 8, vs 1751/1694 CE.

[210] *Arzdasht*, Kartik Sudi 11, vs 1742/1685 CE; Kartik Vadi 3, vs 1742/1685 CE.

of cattle at the disposal of peasants, therefore, was indispensable to the continuance of agricultural operations. The *amil* noted that in times of scarcity, the peasants often consumed the seeds and were left with no seeds for raising crops.[211] Thus, in many cases, the state was urged to provide peasants with seed loan.[212] Despite such appeals to the state by the *amils*, the state often failed to check the frequency of migrations which increased with every spell of drought and famine.[213]

The peasants' miseries were aggravated in the drought years by the rising prices of foodstuffs and their critical dependence on the village *bohra*. Even in normal years, the land revenue system, based, as it was, on cash payment, worked to the detriment of the majority of peasants. Since the peasants had to raise cash at the time of harvest to pay the land revenue, they had to sell a large part of their produce in the market. However, the prices of agricultural commodities were lower at the time of harvest than in the lean season due to the increased supply of foodgrains. This led to a vast difference between the prices at which they sold their harvested produce and those at which they had to buy foodgrains when the glut situation in the market was over. Unable to buy foodstuffs at high prices, they had to borrow money from the moneylender at high rates of interest. If this was the situation in normal years, it was far worse during years of crop failures, when their own produce was either meagre or almost nil. The resultant price rise was, then, due to shortfall in supply. The *amil* reported the *bohras*' reluctance or inability to lend money[214] to the pauperized peasants, their reluctance to even visit the famine-stricken areas,[215] and, interestingly, even the impoverishment

211 *Arzdasht*, Asadh Sudi 15, vs 1743/1686 CE.

212 *Arzdasht*, Kartik Sudi, 13, vs 1743/1686 CE; Bhadva Vadi 11, vs 1743/1686 CE; Jeth Sudi 1, vs 1775/1718 CE; Sawan Vadi 3, vs 1775/1718 CE.

213 *Arzdasht*, Fagun Sudi 12, vs 1746/1689 CE; Asoj Vadi 6, vs 1751/1694 CE; Kartik Sudi 10, vs 1751/1694 CE; Jeth Vadi 8, vs 1751/1694 CE; Kartik Sudi 3, vs 1751/1694 CE; Asoj Sudi 2, vs 1751/1694 CE; Asoj Vadi 8, vs 1751/1694 CE; Sawan Vadi 6, vs 1762/1705 CE; Sawan Vadi 3, vs 1775/1718 CE.

214 *Arzdasht*, Kartik Sudi 13, vs 1743/1686 CE; Bhadva Vadi 11, vs 1743/1686 CE; Asadh Sudi 15, vs 1743/1686 CE.

215 *Arzdasht*, Kartik Sudi 13, vs 1743/1686 CE; Bhadva Sudi 11, vs 1743/1686 CE.

of many *bohras* themselves.[216] The moneylender, as we have seen, was an integral part of the rural society. In times of scarcity, he particularly became a much sought-after person. At times, even the local authorities requested him to lend money or foodgrains to the needy peasants in both normal and abnormal years.[217]

Sometimes, the peasants did succeed in borrowing resources such as ploughs and seeds from the moneylender during the drought years.[218] But more often than not, the intensity of drought was so high and the extent of the consequent agricultural dislocation so large that small moneylenders were not found equal to the task of lending money and resources to all the needy peasants. Moreover, they did not want to take any undue risk in times of instability. In such a situation, the local authorities and peasants were both on the lookout for a big moneylender with large resources at his disposal.[219] Despite its best efforts, the administration could not always provide the services of a resourceful *bohra* who could rescue the peasants from starvation.[220] The absence of credit made the destitution of peasants irremediable. Unable to withstand the cumulative effects of starvation and ruination and to till their land or clear their revenue dues, the peasants eventually left their villages.

Eventually, the process of agricultural decline set in as more and more land remained uncultivated due to peasant migration. Most of the abandoned land could not be brought under cultivation for many years due to the slow rehabilitation of the deserted villages. Moreover, the cost of agricultural operations escalated in the season following the drought, since more ploughing and irrigation was required and new wells had to be dug. The *arzdashts*, time and again, emphasized the need for digging new wells if the next crop (*rabi*) was to be protected from the vagaries of weather.[221] Thus, the adverse effects of famines and droughts did not remain restricted to the *kharif* season; they could

[216] *Arzdasht*, Kartik Sudi 13, VS 1743/1686 CE; Bhadva Vadi 11, VS 1743/1686 CE.

[217] *Arzdasht*, Asoj Vadi 6, VS 1751/1694 CE; Kartik Sudi 10, VS 1751/1694 CE.

[218] *Arzdasht*, VS 1756/1699 CE.

[219] *Arzdasht*, Sawan Vadi 6, VS 1762/1705 CE.

[220] *Arzdasht*, Asoj Vadi 12, VS 1752/1695 CE.

[221] *Arzdasht*, Kartik Sudi 13, VS 1743/1686 CE; Bhadva Vadi 11, VS 1743/1686 CE; Asoj Sudi 2, VS 1751/1694 CE; Asoj Vadi 8, VS 1751/1694 CE.

invariably spill into the next season unless remedial measures were undertaken by the state. In the face of financial constraints, often, agricultural recovery without state assistance was not possible, as was repeatedly stressed by the revenue officials. A series of consistently good harvests alone could have restored conditions of normalcy in the near future.

Droughts and famines also significantly altered the demographic pattern of the rural society and brought about instability in the caste and class composition of peasantry in numerical terms, in the famine-stricken villages. It is very difficult to speculate about the extent of depopulation caused by deaths during famines, as sources are often silent about this. Nevertheless, the fact of depopulation is well established. The population of many villages affected by droughts would decline causing, among other things, labour shortage. It was also anticipated that the peasants who left their villages might never return and new peasants had to be settled in the affected villages. This was not unusual, as is evident from the *arzdasht*s which show that the settlement of *pahi*s in the depopulated villages was encouraged when the original settlers had not returned.

The *arzdasht*s also make it clear that while many old villages were getting deserted, attempts were made to resettle new villages. Many old villages were repopulated with new peasants at the state initiative. In one instance, the land of 10 ruined villages was first handed over to *pahi* peasants from other villages for cultivation on a purely temporary lease and then eventually to *palti* peasants from another village who were then permanently settled in this village which now acquired a new name.[222] In another instance, a ruined village was repopulated with the help of a Brahmin colonizer.[223] In yet another instance, a Rajput colonizer resettled a ruined village by shifting peasants from his original territory (*vasi*).[224] Another *arzdasht* informed the Amber Raja that peasants belonging to the Ahir caste were brought into many newly settled villages.[225]

It is difficult to assess the balance between the twofold processes of ruination of old villages, and settlement of new ones and resettlement

222 *Arzdasht*, Jeth Sudi 5, VS 1742/1685 CE.

223 *Arzdasht*, Jeth Sudi 5, VS 1742/1685 CE.

224 *Arzdasht*, Jeth Sudi 15, VS 1784/1727 CE.

225 *Arzdasht*, Fagun Sudi 12, VS 1746/1689 CE.

of old ones by new peasant groups with different economic and caste backgrounds. But it is not unreasonable to assume that such processes would have significantly altered the demographic pattern of the peasant society, as also its caste and class composition.

Equally important for the analysis of famines and droughts is the impact of these phenomena on the state and the state's response. The sources, especially the *arzdashts*, shed a great deal of light on the state's response at the local level to conditions of scarcity and famine in the villages. Although the medieval state emphasized the strict subordination of the peasantry, the peasants were valued as an indispensable asset to the state in view of their revenue-paying potential. The phenomenon of desertions and migrations that a famine situation created was often viewed with great apprehension by the ruling authorities. The state's basic interests thus lay in keeping the peasants tied to their villages as far as possible. Despite this basic and primary consideration, one does not find a consistent and long-term policy of relief in the medieval period.

For the region under study, one finds a shift in the policies and attitude of the ruling authority represented by the Amber Raja in the 17th and 18th centuries. Till the end of the 17th century, the Amber Raja was an imperial *jagirdar* who because of the uncertainty of his tenure was not inclined to pursue any long-term policy of agricultural development. Thus, one finds an inadequate infrastructure to cope with the famine problem. There was lack of adequate irrigational facilities with the number of existing wells not being very large. The failure of rains would immediately hit the rain-fed crops (*kharif*) and there would be hardly any scope for *rabi* cultivation which depended on artificial irrigation. Similarly, the shortage of fodder meant that cattle were the first to perish. Both excavation of wells and replacement of cattle needed considerable investment which majority of the *raiyat* could not afford to provide on their own. In fact, one finds instances of many peasants sinking to the status of majors (labourers) on account of the loss of their cattle.[226] Loans from outside agencies such as *bohras* were not immediately forthcoming, as they were often willing to provide loans only in conditions of stability.

[226] *Yaddashti Hal Bail, pargana* Mauzabad, vs 1723/1666 CE.

The Amber Raja, because of his short-term interests, that is, realization of revenue due from his *jagirs*, was not willing to provide adequate loans for relief from his own resources, despite being aware of crop failures, misery of peasants, and migrations. It is also possible that the *jagirdars* were not granted *takhfif* in case the *jama* declined due to natural calamities. Hence, they tried to collect the revenue even in conditions of crop failure and near-starvation of peasants. The indifference of the state to the suffering of peasants is evident from the fact that the administration attempted to extract revenue even when it would have threatened their very survival. There is hardly any reference to the Mughal emperor or his representative (*subedar, diwan-i-suba*) showing any concern for the peasantry or coming forward with any relief for them. It means that either the imperial administration wilfully neglected the plight of peasantry in the areas held as *jagirs*, or the *jagirdars* themselves deliberately concealed such conditions from the emperor or prevented them from being reported to him.

In any case, one finds a marked change in the attitude of the Amber Raja after about 1715 or so. By that time, following a period of continuous territorial expansion, he had developed a long-term interest in the area. The state officials were then not merely showing concern but also coming forward with concrete relief measures, that is, loans, construction of wells, and so forth. In one instance, when the peasants were unable to pay land revenue to the state due to Maratha depredations, the Amber *diwan* in his letter to the Maharaja maintained that if the peasants were forced to pay arrears of land revenue continuously it would erode their faith in the government, and the country would be ruined because ultimately, as he put it, 'the peasants were the basis of the state'.[227] In 1757, the state even borrowed 7,000 rupees from the *bohras* and distributed the amount among the *raiyat* of *pargana* Chatsu at the time of scarcity. The *raiyat* were, however, particularly induced not to desert the villages.[228] The awareness on the part of the state that the best way to ensure the collection of adequate revenue was to conserve the peasants' ability to pay taxes is clear. Hence, such extreme measures as imposing excessive land revenue burden that would provoke peasant migrations or rebellions were to be avoided.

227 *Arzdasht*, VS 1799/1742 CE.

228 *Chithi* to the *amil*, Asoj Vadi 5, VS 1814/1757 CE.

In cases of extreme food scarcity and drought, land revenue demand was reduced and other necessary relief measures were undertaken by the state. However, the state assistance in form of agricultural loans (*taqavi*) to the peasants came more readily during the normal years. This was motivated by the state's desire to enhance revenue. Moreover, the state also expected the timely repayment of these loans along with interest. In normal years, these loans were given to the peasants to enable them to excavate new wells and buy seeds and ploughs.[229] The *amils* also pleaded that these loans would bring additional benefits in the form of huge amounts of interest collected from the peasants.[230]

It is difficult to speculate whether the state loans were frequent or occasional. But the local officials were quite aware about their need in conditions of drought for improving as well as restoring agricultural production. Their arguments in favour of these relief measures were: (a) if the relief was not granted in periods of stress, the peasants would be left with no option but to sell their cattle which would, in turn, affect agricultural production and hence the revenue (*hasil*);[231] (b) in normal conditions, the moneylenders were available to grant loans to the peasants, but in times of droughts and famines the state was expected to assume this role;[232] and (c) if the peasants were allowed to become destitute to the extent of threatening their very survival, they would leave their villages.[233] However, these pleas of local officials were not always heard. The state made its own calculations in deciding the appropriateness and timing of extending relief measures to the affected peasants.

Despite the concern expressed by the local officials and the relief measures undertaken by the state in the later period, one should not

[229] *Arzdasht*, Kartik Sudi 13, VS 1743/1686 CE; Bhadva Sudi 11, VS 1743/1686 CE; Asadh Sudi 15, VS 1743/1686 CE; Sawan Sudi 13, VS 1750/1693 CE; Asoj Vadi 12, VS 1752/1695 CE; *Chithi* to the *amil*, Jeth Vadi 2, VS 1792/1735 CE; Sawan Vadi 15, VS 1786/1729 CE.

[230] *Arzdasht*, Asoj Sudi 2, VS 1751/1694 CE; Asoj Vadi 8, VS 1751/1694 CE; Fagun Sudi 12, VS 1746/1689 CE; Sawan Vadi 6, VS 1762/1705 CE; Asadh Sudi 15, VS 1743/1686 CE.

[231] *Arzdasht*, Kartik Sudi 11, VS 1742/1685 CE; Kartik Vadi 3, VS 1742/1685 CE.

[232] *Arzdasht*, Kartik Sudi 13, VS 1743/1686 CE; Bhadva Vadi 11, VS 1743/1686 CE; Asadh Sudi 15, VS 1743/1686 CE.

[233] *Arzdasht*, Asoj Vadi 6, VS 1751/1694 CE; Kartik Sudi 10, VS 1751/1694 CE; Asoj Sudi 2, VS 1751/1694 CE; Asoj Vadi 8, VS 1751/1694 CE.

exaggerate its role in providing relief. On some occasions, it is clear that the peasants did not find these measures adequate.[234] There remained a gap in the actual requirement of the peasants and the relief provided. The processes of migration, depopulation, and agricultural devastation thus remained a reality which the state could not control completely.

[234] *Arzdasht*, Kartik Sudi 13, VS 1743/1686 CE; Bhadva Vadi 11, VS 1743/1686 CE; Asoj Sudi 8, VS 1751/1691 CE.

5

THE *BHOMIAS*

IN THE MEWAT REGION, the overwhelming majority of zamindars were called *bhomias*. The term *bhomias* is derived from the Sanskrit word *bhumi* (the Persian term *bum* also means earth or land).[1] In the Rajasthani documents, the term *bhumi* is used as a synonym of the term 'zamindari', and the holders of *bhumi* are called *bhomias*. The *bhomias* constituted a privileged class in the rural society, enjoying hereditary superior rights in land as well as its produce. Being thus economically privileged, they, on the whole, commanded a high social status in the rural society. However, in the Rajasthani documents, the term *bhomia* has been used exclusively for the zamindars of Rajput clans, and not for zamindars of other castes such as the Meos and Jats.

Despite the fact that the *bhomias* were a socially dominant class, they could claim a subordinate share in the peasants' surplus produce. The share of the *bhomias* in the *parganas* of Mewat varied between 2½ and 3 per cent of the produce. For instance, in *parganas* Gazi ka Thana, Mojpur, Harsana, Bharkol, and Pindayan, the *bhomias*' share in the produce was 3 per cent,[2] while, in *pargana* Khohri, the rate of

[1] Irfan Habib, *The Agrarian System of Mughal India, 1556–1707*, 2nd rev. ed. (New Delhi: Oxford University Press, 1999), 139.

[2] *Arsatta, pargana* Gazi ka Thana, VS 1794/1737 CE; *pargana* Bharkol, VS 1774/1717 CE; *pargana* Mojpur, VS 1771/1714 CE; *pargana* Pindayan, VS 1794/1737 CE; *pargana* Harsana, VS 1792/1735 CE.

bhom cess was 2–2½ per cent of the produce.[3] The other privilege extended to the *bhomias* was that the lands personally cultivated by them were considered *riyayati* or concessional holdings and assessed at considerably lower rates of revenue than were the lands of ordinary cultivators. According to the *dastur-al-amal*, the *bhomias* had to pay 25 per cent of the total produce as land revenue.[4] But the originally assessed revenue from the *bhom* land was quite nominal, as is evident from *arsatta bhomi*. In the *bhom* land, the *zabti* rate remained constantly one *taka* per *bigha*. In some *parganas*, for example, Pindayan, it was even less.[5] Under the *batai-jinsi* system, the state share in the produce from the *bhom* land was merely one *ser* per *maund*. Thus, the magnitude of the actual share of gross produce appropriated by the *bhomias* was considerable, and hence they were able to generate enough marketable surplus.[6] Besides, they were exempted from a number of cesses and paid many of the cesses at highly concessional rates. For instance, the contribution to *malba* (common financial pool of the village) was not realized from them, whereas the peasants had to pay one per cent of the land revenue as contribution to *malba*.[7] The *bhom* cess per *jhupri* was one *taka*, while in general it was 12 *annas* per *jhupri*.[8] The *bhomias* exercised their proprietary rights over land in various ways. In some cases, they rented out their lands to tenants and *pahi* cultivators on different terms and conditions and appropriated *malikana* from them.[9] In many cases, they employed full-time agricultural labourers known as *halis* (ploughmen) and *vasidars* for the cultivation of their personal landholdings.[10]

3 *Arsatta, pargana* Khohri, VS 1770/1713 CE.

4 See Chapter 4.

5 *Arsatta bhomi, pargana* Pindayan, VS 1806/1749 CE.

6 S. P. Gupta and Shireen Moosvi, 'Bhomi in the Territories of Amber c. 1650–1750', in *Proceedings of the Indian History Congress*, 32nd session (Jabalpur, 1970), 353–9.

7 See Chapter 4.

8 Gupta and Moosvi, 'Bhomi in the Territories of Amber'.

9 *Chithi* to the *amil, pargana* Piragpur Atela, *Mangsir Sudi* 10, VS 1792/1735 CE.

10 *Chithi* to the *amil, pargana* Khohri, Chait Sudi 9, VS 1785/1728 CE; Chait Vadi 6, VS 1795/1735 CE. Kishan Singh Naruka had his own *vasi* in village Kaithwara of *pargana* Khohri, where *vasidars* belonging to the Ahir caste were

In addition to collecting the *bhomi* tax or *dastur bhomi*, the *bhomias* were also entitled to many other customary cesses. For instance, the peasants of *pargana* Mandawar had to pay cesses such as *dhol*, *nyota*, and *kotri bhomi ki* to the *bhomias*.[11] These customary rights enabled the *bhomias* to appropriate a substantial part of the produce. But they even attempted to increase their share in the surplus at the cost of the state as well as the peasants. They resorted to levying new imposts on the peasants, at times far beyond the customary limits, and at the same time tried to evade the payment of *hasil* to the state. A variety of other customary privileges attached to the *bhom* right made it both socially and economically a highly valuable tenure for them. Perhaps, it was due to this fact that there was a growing tendency on the part of many members of the leading Rajput clans to extend their *bhom* rights by way of either usurpation or conversion of the *raiyati* area into *bhom*.[12]

The struggle for the acquisition, retention, and expansion of the *bhom* right was a constant feature of the rural society in Mewat during the period under study. It had several implications for the rural society. First, it became a major factor in producing tensions between different groups. Second, it led to a significant alteration in the power structure within the rural society, the worst sufferers in the process being the Khanzadas and the Meos who eventually were reduced to the status of petty zamindars and *khudkashta* peasants.

Those *bhomias* who felt assured of the stability and permanence of their tenure started playing a crucial role in the growth of agricultural production in their *bhom* villages. They, in many cases, became a dependable source of agricultural equipments and loans for the needy peasants. The growing economic dependence of a large section of the peasantry on the *bhomias* in the context of increasing monetization of

---

employed. Rao Kaliyan Singh Naruka had his *vasi* in village Bhurpahari of *pargana* Pindayan where *vasidars* belonging to the other castes were employed (*Arzdasht*, Vaishakh Vadi 5, vs 1773/1716 CE; *Arsatta, pargana* Pindayan, vs 1722/1665 CE).

11 *Arsatta, pargana* Mandawar, vs 1787/1730, 1793/1736 CE. The amount of these cesses is not given in the *arsattas*, but it is clear from the documents whether they were regular cesses or not.

12 *Chithi* to the *amil, pargana* Alwar, Asadh Sudi 3, vs 1783/1726 CE.

rural economy was apparent. They also stood surety on behalf of the poor and needy peasants for contracting agricultural loans from the state and the moneylenders.[13] This positive role enabled the *bhomias* to acquire a considerable hold over the countryside.

The pattern of distribution of zamindaris in the *parganas* of Mewat among various castes/clans, as mentioned in the *Ain-i-Akbari*, is given in Table 5.1.

It is clear from Table 5.1 that by the end of the 16th century, most of the *parganas* of Alwar *sarkar* were under the possession of the Khanzada and Meo zamindars. The Rajput zamindars belonging to various clans had some pockets and enclaves in some *parganas* of

Table 5.1 Zamindaris in Alwar *sarkar* (43 *mahals*)

Caste of the zamindars	Number of *parganas* held entirely under zamindari	Number of *parganas* held partially under zamindari	Total number of *parganas*
Khanzadas of Mewat	10	8(1/2)	18
Meo	5	7(1/2)	12
Kachhwahas	1	–	1
Baqqals	2	–	2
Bargujars	2	1(1/2)	3
Rajputs	1	1(1/2)	2
Chauhans	4	–	4
Amas and Duars	–	1(1/2)	1
Meenas	1	–	1
Sayyids	–	1(1/2)	1
Gujjars	–	1(1/2)	1
Mahats	1	–	1
Abbasis	1	–	1
Jats	1	–	1
Other castes	2	–	2

Source: Abul-Fazl, *The Ain-i-Akbari*, vol. 2, 202–3.

[13] Dilbagh Singh, 'The Role of the Mahajans in the Rural Economy in Eastern Rajasthan during the 18th Century', *Social Scientist* 2, no. 10 (1974): 20–31.

Alwar *sarkar*. Other castes did not hold any substantial zamindaris in the Alwar *sarkar*.

In Tijara *sarkar*, the Meo zamindars possessed the most extensive territories under their control (Table 5.2). They were followed by the Khanzadas, Thathars, and Gujjars in terms of the area under their zamindari jurisdiction. While the Khanzadas were the erstwhile ruling class of Mewat, as mentioned earlier, the origin of the zamindaris of the Thathars can be traced back to the time of Balban who assigned them military posts in Mewat.

The majority of *parganas* in Sahar *sarkar* were controlled by the Meo zamindars (Table 5.3). The Jats and the Ahirs were the other dominant zamindari castes. The zamindars of the Thathars were insignificant.

Table 5.2 Zamindaris in Tijara *sarkar* (18 *mahals*)

Castes of the zamindars	Number of *parganas* held entirely under zamindari	Number of *parganas* held partially under zamindari	Total number of *parganas*
Khanzadas of Mewat	1	3(1/2)	4
Meos	12	2(1/2)	14
Thathars (Afghans)	1	2(1/2)	3
Gujjars	–	1(1/2)	1

Source: Abul-Fazl, *The Ain-i-Akbari*, vol. 2, 203–4.

Table 5.3 Zamindaris in Sahar *sarkar* (4 *mahals*)

Castes of the zamindars	Number of *parganas* held entirely under zamindari	Number of *parganas* held partially under zamindari	Total number of *parganas* held under zamindari
Meos	2(1/3)	2(1/2)	4
Jats	2(1/3)	–	2
Ahirs	2(1/3)	–	2
Thathars	–	1(1/3)	1

Source: Abul-Fazl, *The Ain-i-Akbari*, vol. 2, 206.

The Meos and Khanzadas did not possess any zamindari rights in Narnol and Rewari *sarkars*. The historical roots of these zamindaris can clearly be traced to the movements and settlement patterns of various castes and clans. The zamindaris of members of the same clan were generally contiguous, lending credence to the tradition that the zamindari rights of a clan over an area originated from the dominance gained over that area by the ancestors of that particular clan.[14] However, considerable reshuffling in the zamindari rights held by various castes and clans in the course of historical developments was a feature of the medieval Indian society.

During the 17th century, we find a significant change in the position of Meo and Khanzada zamindars: they gradually lost their pre-eminence to the Kachhwaha Rajputs with the creation of new zamindaris and enlargement of the existing ones by the various segments of the Kachhwaha clan. The Jats also gained zamindaris at the expense of the Meos and Khanzadas. Thus, around 1600, the Meos and Khanzadas who hitherto had more zamindaris in the Alwar, Tijara, and Sahar *sarkars* were gradually replaced by the Rajput and Jat zamindars who were able to make successful encroachments upon their domains and reduce many of them to the rank of *khudkashtas* or ordinary peasant proprietors.

The emergence of the Kachhwaha zamindaris in Mewat was perhaps due to the influence gained by the Amber chiefs of the Kachhwaha clan at the Mughal court as a result of their alliance with Akbar. From the second half of the 17th century, the Kachhwahas systematically used their political leverage to expand their territorial possessions in Mewat by carving out new zamindaris in the *parganas* contiguous to their *watan jagir* and displacing the pre-existing Meo and Khanzada zamindars. The Mughal politico-administrative policies, too, were responsible for the loss of superior land rights of the Khanzadas and Meos, since the Mughals regarded the Rajputs as more reliable and worthy supporters than the Meos and the Khanzadas.[15] The initial hostility of Hasan Khan Mewati towards the Mughals, perhaps, also led to the neglect of the Khanzada chiefs of Mewat.

[14] Irfan Habib, 'The Social Distribution of Landed Property in the Pre-British India', *Enquiry*, old series, no. 12 (1965): 21–75.

[15] A. R. Khan, *Chieftains in the Mughal Empire during the Reign of Akbar* (Shimla: Indian Institute of Advanced Study [IIAS], 1977), 102–4.

In 1643, the Amber Raja was assigned *jagirs* in 14 *mahals* (*parganas*) of Mewat, most of which were, in turn, sub-assigned by him to his own clansmen,[16] particularly the Naruka Rajputs. In 1650, Karat Singh (Amber chief Jai Singh's son) was appointed *faujdar* of Mewat by the emperor on the ground of political expediency and was specifically instructed to crush the Meo and Jat rebels of the region. Under his jurisdiction came 44 *parganas*; among them 37 *parganas* were in the Alwar, Tijara, Rewari, and Narnol *sarkars*.[17]

Thus, the upper echelons of the rural society in Mewat witnessed a considerable reshuffling in the superior land rights of different castes and clans. The Meos and the Khanzadas came out as the casualties of changes in the caste/clan composition of the zamindaris. This fact assumes further significance in that the Meos were also the dominant peasant castes and, in terms of numerical strength, constituted the largest single caste group among the peasantry. In the process, traditional caste links between the Meo zamindars and the peasants must have been eroded to a considerable extent. To what extent it affected the functioning of the rural society and the pattern of relationship between the new Rajput zamindars and the Meo peasants needs to be examined in depth.

The homogeneous character of the Meo peasants in the villages of Mewat was altered by the establishment of the zamindari rights of other castes and clans. The new zamindars encouraged the settlement of peasants belonging to other castes, particularly the Jats, Ahirs, and Gujjars, in the hitherto Meo-dominated villages. This led to the growth of a heterogeneous and composite peasant population in the villages of Mewat. As a result of these developments in the rural society of Mewat, a tussle ensued between the Rajput zamindars and the vanquished Meo zamindars on the one hand, and between the Meo peasants and the Rajput zamindars on the other. The implications of this two-dimensional conflict in the rural society and its impact on the economy of the region form the subject matter of this chapter.

[16] *Arzdasht*, Mah Vadi 5 and 7, vs 1746/1689 CE; Mangsir Sudi 3, vs 1761/1704 CE.

[17] S. Nurul Hasan, 'Further Light on Zamindars under the Mughals: A Case Study of (Mirza) Raja Jai Singh under Shahjahan', in *Proceedings of the Indian History Congress*, 39th session (Hyderabad, 1978), 497–502.

The Rajasthani documents throw considerable light on the creation of new *bhom* rights during the late 17th and early 18th centuries in Mewat. The latter part of the reign of emperor Aurangzeb witnessed a considerable alteration in the caste and clan composition of the zamindars in the region. This reshuffling of the zamindari rights was a two-way process: both from above and from below. First, the Amber Raja (who was a leading noble of the Mughal court) aspired to extend his *watan jagir* into Mewat by taking over the zamindari rights from the region's many *zortalab* (recalcitrant or rebellious, i.e, non-revenue-paying) zamindars with the tacit support of the Mughal emperor. The emperor's support was motivated by the desire to establish law and order in the region which was infested by such 'rebel' zamindars. It may be noted that it was a continuation of the traditional policy of the Mughals vis-à-vis the zamindars, whereby the recalcitrant zamindars in a particular region were ousted and replaced by loyal ones. Second, many new village-level zamindaris came into existence through either a settlement of new villages or rehabilitation of old, ruined villages.

Apart from the operation of these two forces, the *bhom* rights were also created by the members of dominant clans in the hitherto *raiyati* villages through sheer use of force or usurpation of the *bhom* rights belonging to other clans. There are numerous references to the Amber Raja acquiring *bhom* rights over various *parganas* of Mewat during the latter half of the 17th century. However, this process passed through several stages. In the initial stage, he strengthened his administrative control by acquiring *thanedari* rights (by way of establishing police *chowkis*) over many *parganas* of Mewat that he obtained from the *faujdar* of Mewat on the pretext of restoring law and order. He used the *thanedari* rights as a means to further consolidate his position in the region. Upon the successful consolidation of his position in the region, he was able to further pressurize the Mughal authorities to transfer the zamindaris of these *parganas* to him. In 1702, he got the zamindari of *parganas* Jalalpur, Bharkol, Khilohra, Mojpur, and Vadhera.[18] Initially, he had been given the *thanedari* of these *parganas* and, later, the zamindari rights on the recommendation of the *faujdar* of Mewat.

[18] *Arzdasht*, Mangsir Sudi 14 and 15, VS 1759/1702 CE.

Next, the Amber Raja managed to acquire the zamindari of 14 more *mahals*[19] and later another seven *parganas*.[20] However, these *mahals* or *parganas* are not named in the documents. In 1712, he further secured the zamindari of *pargana* Khohri.[21] This move of his brought him in conflict not only with the Rajputs of his own clan, particularly the Naruka *bhomias*, but also with the Jat and Meo zamindars. The tussle between the Amber Raja and these zamindars found manifestation in the open defiance of his authority by the rebels. The Narukas, already a dominant clan in the Alwar *sarkar*, were the most powerful among the rebels. They not only succeeded in protecting their existing land rights but also eventually emerged as the potential *bhomias* in various *parganas* of Mewat by the latter part of Aurangzeb's reign.[22] Up to the mid-17th century, the Narukas had limited *bhom* rights which they had acquired by subjugating petty zamindars of erstwhile castes/tribes with the cooperation of the Amber Raja. In the process, however, some Naruka *bhomias* became so powerful as to threaten the Raja's authority and the latter was compelled to check their growing strength. They raised the banner of rebellion against all levels of authorities, that is, their own clan chief (the Amber Raja), the imperial *khalisa* officials, and the imperial *jagirdars* or *mansabdars*. Towards the closing years of Aurangzeb's reign, they thus came to be reckoned as the most turbulent rebels.

A majority of the Naruka *bhomias* did not have any legitimate *bhom* rights. When the Amber Raja obtained the *parganas* of Mewat as part of his *tankhwah jagir* from the Mughal emperor, a number of Narukas gained employment as troopers of the Raja who had now turned into an imperial *mansabdar*. As remuneration, they were sub-assigned villages as *jagir* by the Raja. Thereafter, it became a constant endeavour of such Naruka Rajput *jagirdars* to convert their *jagirs*, irrespective of their size, into *bhoms* or zamindaris. Once these *parganas* were transferred from the *jagir* of the Amber Raja to other imperial *mansabdars*, the sub-assignees stood to lose the villages sub-assigned to

19 *Arzdasht*, Mangsir Sudi 3, VS 1760/1703 CE.

20 *Arzdasht*, Jeth Vadi 1, VS 1761/1704 CE.

21 *Arzdasht*, Vaishakh Sudi 7, VS 1769/1712 CE.

22 *Arzdasht*, Mangsir Sudi 14, VS 1759/1702 CE; Vaishakh Vadi 3, VS 1760/1703 CE; Bhadva Vadi 5, VS 1760/1703 CE.

them. But many Naruka sub-assignees, instead of giving up their sub-assignments, tried to establish their *bhom* rights in the villages that they been holding as sub-assignees. This brought them into conflict with the Amber Raja as well as the imperial *mansabdars* who were assigned *jagirs* in these *parganas* of Mewat. The state officials such as *faujdars* and *amils* repeatedly lodged complaints against the Narukas for forcibly establishing their *bhom* rights. For instance, in his report (*arzdasht*) of 1702, the *faujdar* of *pargana* Bahatri complained to the Amber Raja that these Narukas were trying to justify their illegally acquired *bhom* rights in many *parganas* of Mewat.

The genesis of the conflict is clearly illustrated in the aforementioned report. It states that many villages of the *parganas* acquired by the Amber Raja as *jagir* in 1643 from the Mughal emperor were sub-assigned to the *thakurs* (the Kachhwaha Rajputs, particularly the Narukas) for settling their claims to remuneration. When the *jagirs* of these *parganas* were transferred from the Raja, some of the *thakurs* left, while others remained in the villages sub-assigned to them. Some of the Narukas even got the *ijara* of these villages from the new *jagirdars* and continued living there. When disturbances caused by the Jats gathered momentum in the villages of Mewat, these opportunist *thakurs* withheld the entire *hasil* (land revenue). The report further stressed that although they were behaving as de facto zamindars, their zamindari *amals* had yet to get the legal sanction from the requisite authority, and that the political turmoil in the region and the resultant laxity of the imperial administration only made them bolder. But the Narukas contested this official claim and argued that in 1689 they had got the zamindari of Jalalpur, Bharkol, and other *parganas* of Mewat with the consent of village-level officials such as *muqaddams*, *chaudharis*, and *qanungos*, and on the recommendation of the imperial *faujdar* of Mewat. The Amber Raja's officials, in turn, dismissed these claims as spurious. They asserted that whenever the *faujdar* of Mewat was transferred, these *thakurs* (Narukas) created disturbances in their villages: they would send their men to every village with five coloured flags, establish their own *thanas* (police posts) there, and start collecting *rahdari* (road tax) and other zamindari taxes from them.[23] In fact, following similar methods, the Narukas gradually

[23] *Arzdasht*, Mangsir Sudi 15, VS 1759/1702 CE.

extended their *bhom* rights over many *parganas* of Mewat during the period under study.

The *faujdar* of Bahatri and the author of the aforementioned *arzdasht* reporter thus highlighted the circumstances in which new zamindari claims were made over a vast area in Mewat without any official sanction. The *thakurs*, as the *jagirdars* of the Amber Raja, converted the villages sub-assigned to other troopers into *bhom*. At the same time, they also refused to fulfil their obligations as soldiers of the Raja. The *arzdasht* and other documents testify to the fact that by illegally carving out zamindaris, they gradually consolidated their position in the region. In order to protect and enforce their zamindari claims, the Naruka *bhomias* constructed *garhis* (fortresses) in the villages and then forced the *raiyat* and traders to pay zamindari, *rahdari*, and other taxes. For instance, according to the *amil*'s report dated 1685, the Naruka *bhomias* constructed their *garhis* in the villages of 14 *mahals* that constituted the *jagirs* of imperial *mansabdars* in Mewat, and forcibly collected the *bhomi* cess from their villages.[24] This became a widepsread phenomenon in the Mewat region during the period under study.

The Amber state took punitive actions against the recalcitrant Naruka *bhomias*, yet at times the combined resistance of the Naruka *bhomias* against the state was so strong that all efforts to subdue them proved abortive. There are numerous references to the demolition of Amber Raja's *thanas* and physical assaults on his officials and servants by the Naruka *bhomias*. The inability of the local authorities to successfully meet the challenge of *bhomias* is an index of the growing ineffectiveness of the administrative machinery. One Naruka chief, Rao Hathi Singh, and his men declared their zamindari rights in all the villages of *parganas* Bharkol and Jalalpur and refused to surrender the zamindari *amal* of these villages to the Amber Raja.[25] Naruka *bhomias* such as Kishan Singh, Karan Singh, Gaj Singh, Uday Singh, Devi Singh, Sawai Ram, Anand Ram, Fauju Singh, and Daulu Singh became so powerful that acting in unison, they moved freely in the villages of *parganas* Mojpur, Alwar, Bharkol, Hasanpur, Pindayan, Khilohra, Umarni, Todathek, Naharkhoh, Nanawar,

[24] *Arzdasht*, Asadh Vadi 5, VS 1792/1685 CE.

[25] *Arzdasht*, Mangsir Sudi 15, VS 1759/1702 CE.

Sonkhar-Sonkhari, and Bahatri.[26] Strong attachment to hereditary territorial rights which was a characteristic feature of the Rajput polity prompted the leading members of Kachhwaha sub-clans to convert their temporary *jagir* assignments into *bhom*. The Narukas thus were bent upon fulfilling their ambitions to the detriment of the interest of their clan chief (the Amber Raja).

The Rajasthani documents are relatively silent on the activities of the Meos and Khanzada zamindars, although, as mentioned earlier, there is some evidence to suggest that the number of Meo and Khanzada zamindars was declining and so was their influence, in the wake of a tremendous growth of new zamindaris of the Naruka Rajput *bhomias*. Although the Meos put up stiff resistance to this encroachment upon their traditional land rights, they appear to have been fighting a lost battle. For instance, in 1712, when the Amber Raja got the zamindari of *pargana* Khohri, the Meo zamindars revolted against this move,[27] but had to retreat and finally give up their claims in the face of the Raja's superior military strength. In many cases, the Meo zamindars were also removed on administrative grounds. For instance, in 1684, the Meo zamindars of *pargana*s Mojpur, Bharkol, and Punkhar of Alwar *sarkar* were expelled on the ground of non-payment of land revenue to the state.[28] In 1740, the Meo zamindars in the villages of Neekatpura, Bhada, Todarpur, Pran Nath, Vaisachh, Jai Singh Pura, and Ram Singh Pura of *pargana* Khohri were also deprived of their zamindaris on the ground of their failure to deposit the land revenue to the *jagirdar*.[29] Many Meo zamindars were ousted from their zamindari on account of seditious activities. For instance, the Pahat Meo zamindars of *pargana*s Kama and Pahari were expelled for their alliance with Jats. The *amil*, in his report to the Amber Raja, alleged that Dura Meo, zamindar of the Pahat Meo *pal*, and other Pahat Meos joined hands with the Churaman Jat, the Raja's enemy.[30]

26 *Arzdasht*, Mangsir Sudi 15, VS 1759/1702 CE; Jeth Vadi 1, VS 1761/1704 CE; Chait Vadi 4, VS 1761/1704 CE; Mangsir Sudi 3, VS 1760/1703 CE; Mangsir Vadi 10, VS 1760/1703 CE.

27 *Arzdasht*, Vaishakh Sudi 7, VS 1769/1712 CE.

28 *Arzdasht*, Bhadva Vadi 3, VS 1741/1684 CE.

29 *Chithi* to the *amil*, *pargana* Khohri, Asadh Vadi 4, VS 1797/1740 CE.

30 *Arzdasht*, Asadh Sudi 5, VS 1766/1709 CE; Asadh Vadi 14, VS 1766/1709 CE.

Coercive measures were, however, not the only means to weaken the Meo zamindars. It appears that a systematic campaign was launched by the Amber Raja to destroy their socio-economic base so that they could not offer any effective resistance to the growing ambitions of the Kachhwaha Rajputs in the region.

We do not have much information about the zamindari rights of the Khanzadas in the region during the late 17th and early 18th centuries. However, the Khanzadas as Mughal allies were in a slightly better position than were the Meos, as regards their zamindari rights. Many Khanzadas had been associated with the land revenue assessment and management at *pargana* level during emperor Akbar's reign. According to the *arsattas* of the early 18th century, prominent Khanzadas such as Firoz Khan, Vazid Khan, and Azmat Khan enjoyed both *bhomi* and *jagirdari* rights for a long time in the region.[31]

The Meo zamindars, on the other hand, could not muster sufficient political support either from the Mughal court or from other rebel zamindars (such as the Jats) to meet the onslaught of Rajput *bhomias*. Economically too, the lack of material resources weakened their hold on the rural society. The growing heterogeneous composition of the zamindar class in Mewat further eroded the social base of the Meo zamindars. Although there are occasional references in the Rajasthani records to their seditious activities against the tyrannical attitude of the Amber Raja and other imperial *jagirdars*, they could not mobilize requisite support from local peasants, as the Jat rebels were able to do.[32] Unlike the Jats and Naruka Rajputs, the small Meo zamindars had meagre resources and, therefore, could not induce a large number of peasants to support their cause against the state. Their other weakness was that they did not possess *garhis* in their villages to organize better defence. Without the requisite political, socio-economic, and military might, they failed to withstand the onslaught of Rajput *bhomias*, who were, in all these respects, far more powerful. Further, they could not even match the Jat rebels in manpower and material resources.

31 *Arsatta*, *pargana* Pahari, VS 1783/1726 CE; *pargana* Khohri, VS 1769/1712 CE.

32 R. P. Rana, 'Agrarian Revolts in Northern India during the Late 17th and Early 18th Century', *Indian Economic and Social History Review*, nos 3–4 (1981): 281–326.

According to the *Ain-i-Akbari*, the Jats held zamindaris in the *parganas* of Alwar, Sahar, and Tijara *sarkars*.[33] Numerically, they were not as significant as the Meos and Khanzadas. But by the mid-17th century, they managed to carve out new zamindaris in many more *parganas* in Alwar, Sahar, and Tijara *sarkars*. The rising power of Jat zamindars in this region indicates that the Mughal administration and the Amber Raja were either indifferent to or unable to restrict the expansion of Jat zamindaris as well as their social base. The rise of Jats as a political force began with their revolt in the Mathura region in 1669 under the leadership of Gokula and Raja Ram Jat during the reign of Aurangzeb.[34] Raja Ram fought many battles against the Amber Raja as well as the Mughals. After the death of Raja Ram, the leadership of the Jats passed on to Churaman Jat, the son of Bhajja, zamindar of Sinsini (Bharatpur district, Rajasthan).

Being a shrewd leader, Churaman knew that a direct confrontation with the Mughal state would mean meeting the fate of Fateh Singh and Jorawar Singh, the two sons of Raja Ram who died fighting the Mughals,[35] and would only cause harm to the rising Jat power. So, apparently, Churaman did not involve himself in any confrontation with the Mughals, barring a few skirmishes, till Aurangzeb's death (1707) and rather followed a policy of conciliation. In fact, even during Aurangzeb's reign, Churaman tried to impress upon the emperor that he was different from (i.e., more trustworthy than) his predecessor Raja Ram and, if given a chance, would fulfil his responsibilities like a loyal Mughal soldier. But Aurangzeb never trusted Churaman and his loyalty towards the Mughal state. After Aurangzeb's death, Churaman sided with Bahadur Shah in the war of succession.[36] After the decisive Battle of Jajau in 1707 against his rival Azam Shah and upon becoming the emperor, Bahadur Shah rewarded Churaman by

[33] Abul-Fazl, *The Ain-i-Akbari*, vol. 2, 202–6.

[34] Irfan Habib, *The Agrarian System of Mughal India*, 340–1.

[35] G. C. Dwivedi, *The Jats: Their Role in the Mughal Empire* (Delhi: Arnold Publishers, 1989), 48–9.

[36] After the death of Aurangzeb in 1707, the war of succession started between prince Muazzam (Bahadur Shah) and prince Azam. The rivals faced each other in the battlefield of Jajau. In this battle, Churaman helped Bahadur Shah with 2,000–3,000 *sawars* (horsemen) (Dwivedi, *The Jats*, 54).

making him a *mansabdar* with the rank of 1,500/500 *zat* and *sawar*[37] and giving him the responsibility for the security (*rahdari*) of Agra–Delhi route. Subsequently, he took part in Bahadur Shah's campaigns against the Sikhs, notably the sieges of Sadhaura and Lohgarh.[38] At the same time, he continued his plundering activities whenever such an opportunity rose. Under Churaman's leadership, the Jat power increased considerably, as he succeeded in uniting the Jat zamindars under his leadership. A major and long-awaited diplomatic success came when Churaman's plea to the emperor for the grant of the *faujdari* of Mathura was accepted.[39] All this brought about a change in Churaman's image from one of a plunderer to that of an imperial *mansabdar*. This elevation in status, in turn, enabled him to establish cordial relations with other imperial *mansabdar*s at the Mughal court. Further, Churaman also improved his relations with Munim Khan, *diwan* of the Mughal state, who helped him in getting the *ijara* and zamindari rights from the other imperial *mansabdar*s in the Agra and Mewat regions. Moreover, he himself tried to persuade the imperial *mansabdar*s to assign him the *ijara* and zamindari rights, in the place of the Amber Raja, for the collection of land revenue (*hasil*) from their *jagir*s. Consequently, he secured the *ijara* of a number of *pargana*s in the Agra and Mewat regions between 1707 and 1720.

On the other hand, the political atmosphere of the Mughal court, from 1707 to 1720, that is, from the beginning of emperor Bahadur Shah's reign till the end of the Sayyid brothers' dominance, was not quite favourable to the Amber Raja. Churaman, on the other hand, received open support of the Sayyid brothers and Nawab Khan-i-Daura in consolidating his position vis-à-vis the Amber Raja in the Agra and Mewat regions. In the late 17th and early 18th centuries, the latter as an imperial *mansabdar*, too, secured, from other imperial *mansabdar*s the *ijaradari*, *thanedari*, and zamindari rights of many *pargana*s in Mewat that constituted their *jagir*s but were contiguous to his own *watan jagir*. This he did on the pretext of maintaining law and order in the region, since the collection of land revenue from the

37 Satish Chandra, *Parties and Politics at the Mughal Court, 1707–1740* (Aligarh: Aligarh Muslim University Press, 1959), 123.

38 Chandra, *Parties and Politics at the Mughal Court*, 124.

39 *Vakil*'s Report, Bhadva Vadi 2, VS 1764/1707 CE.

jagirs was heavily disrupted by agrarian revolts. For instance, in 1702, the Amber Raja secured the zamindari and *thanedari* of 14 *parganas* of Mewat from the Mughal authority. Next year, he got six more *parganas*[40] even as his position at the Mughal court was turning shaky.

Underlying these moves of the Amber Raja were crucial politico-economic calculations. For one, taking the *ijara* of the *parganas* in the vicinity of his *watan jagir* was motivated by his desire to expand his *watan* areas. Second, the Kachhwaha Rajputs were speedily growing in strength during the 17th century and organized themselves into 12 *khaps* (septs) by the end of the century. But the Amber Raja's income from his *watan jagir* was not sufficient to serve their economic interests. Thus, taking the zamindari, *thanedari*, and *ijaradari* rights of the imperial *jagirs* was meant to provide the Kachhwaha Rajput *khaps* and their *sardars* (chiefs) with a larger and stable source of income (by way of sub-assignment of these rights) and thereby secure their loyalty to him. But this move of the Amber Raja came into direct conflict with the politico-economic interests of the Jats in Agra and Delhi *subas* who had emerged as a formidable force to reckon with during the latter part of Aurangzeb's reign. Further, as mentioned earlier, the rising influence of Churaman at the Mughal court impaired the economic interests and political status of the Amber Raja. A fierce competition between the duo over the possession of the *parganas* of Mewat that formed the imperial *jagirs* was inevitable.

Churaman's patience dried up when Amber Raja took the zamindari and *thanedari* rights of *parganas* Khohri and Mojpur in 1712.[41] Khohri, a *pargana* with 342 villages,[42] formed more than half of the land in Alwar *sarkar* and was more fertile than other *parganas*. Besides, the two *parganas* were contiguous to the Jat territories. So, Churaman, in order to buttress his claim over Khohri and Mojpur removed all the *thanas* of the Amber Raja in the villages of these *parganas* and set up his own *thanas*.[43] By 1714, he had established his control over a number of villages in the two *parganas*. The *amil* of the Amber state complained of physical assaults on the Amber's

40 *Arzdasht*, Mangsir Sudi 3, vs 1760/1703 CE; Jeth Vadi 1, vs 1761/1704 CE.

41 *Arzdasht*, Vaishakh Sudi 7, vs 1769/1712 CE.

42 *Arsatta*, *pargana* Khohri, vs 1769/1712 CE.

43 *Arzdasht*, Asadh Sudi 3, vs 1769/1712 CE.

land revenue officials by Churaman's men.[44] The *vakil* (the agent of Amber Raja at the Mughal court), too, reported that Churaman had collected the entire land revenue of these two *parganas* by force.[45] By 1718, Churaman established his control over many *parganas* of Mewat, such as Devati-Sachari, Baroda Meo, Sonkhar-Sonkhari, Harsauli, Naharkhoh, Todathek, Hodal, Kot-Qasim, Sogar Pahari, Khohri, and Mojpur.[46]

These acts of Churaman threw an open challenge to the Amber Raja. The challenge can be understood from a letter written by the *vakil* to the Amber Raja. In his letter, the *vakil* professed that he kept his master well informed of Churaman's activities at the Mughal court and that he was extremely careful about protecting their interests at the Mughal court. He further informed the Raja that Churaman had sent a request to Nawab Khan-i-Daura for assigning him the zamindari of *pargana* Khohri, and Khan-i-Daura, being his supporter, had recommended Churaman's letter of request and sent it to Rairaya Gujjar Mal. The *vakil* claimed to have reasoned with Gujjarmal that the *pargana* demanded by Churaman had been part of the Amber Raja's *watan jagir*, and thus its zamindari could never be given to anybody, especially Churaman, who was a *mufsid* (rebel).[47]

The *vakil* of the Amber Raja tried his best to prevent the grant of zamindari and *ijara* of *pargana* Khohri to Churaman, but the latter enjoyed the patronage of Khan-i-Daura and the Sayyid brothers and tried to convince the imperial *mansabdar*s at the Mughal court that he could manage the land revenue collection better than the Amber Raja. Such an open support to Churaman at the Mughal court infuriated the Amber Raja and he complained against Churaman to the Mughal emperor. At the same time, the emperor also received complaints of those imperial *mansabdar*s whose *jagir*s Churaman's men had plundered since he had not got their *ijara* or zamindari rights.[48] In spite of these complaints, there was no change in Churaman's behaviour and

44 *Arzdasht*, Bhadva Vadi 1, VS 1771/1714 CE.

45 *Vakil*'s Report, Asadh Vadi 7, VS 1771/1714 CE.

46 *Vakil*'s Report, Jeth Sudi 11, VS 1771/1714 CE.

47 *Arzdasht*, Sawan Sudi 15, VS 1775/1718 CE.

48 *Vakil*'s Report, Asadh Vadi 7, VS 1771/1714 CE; *Vakil*'s Report, Jeth Sudi 11, VS 1771/1714 CE.

his armed struggle with the Amber Raja continued. The Rajput army suffered defeats at the hands of the Jat army in many battles.[49]

The power of Churaman can be gauged from the fact that in 1714 he forcibly collected the land revenue of the entire *pargana* of Khohri over which the Amber Raja had zamindari rights.[50] The *diwan* of Amber Ramchander expressed his anxiety at the growing audacity and might of the Jats in his letter to the Raja:

> The Jats have become very powerful in the entire region. They have demolished our *thana*s in the villages of *pargana*s Khohri, Sahar, Harsana, Sonkhar-Sonkhari and Aau and set up their own *thana*s in these *pargana*s. The Jats are also constructing their *garhi*s in these areas. In every fortress, they keep *sawar*s [horsemen] and *masala* [ammunition]. The fortress of Mojpur alone has 1000 men and ammunition: 600 *topchi*s [gunners], 2 *rahakalla*s [small cannons], 400 *pala-nafar*s [foot soldiers], 40 *ramchangi*s [muskets] and 200 *sawar*s. Thus, every fortress has men and ammunition and every village of the *pargana*s is occupied by their *thana*s. And our men have been shunted out from the villages and at many places beaten up.[51]

The *diwan* further wrote: 'Whenever we fight against the Jats, their army increases in numerical strength. At times when we are about to score a victory over the Jats, suddenly their ranks swell, which enables the Jats to win over us. In many instances they have taken away our flag, emblem and drum from us.'[52] The *diwan* chiefly blamed the weaknesses of Rajput chieftains and the lack of resources for such reverses:

> The fault lies with the Rajput *sardar*s who, as has been the case previously, do not perform their military duties and many Rajputs do not go to their *kotari*s [fortresses]. Earlier, they performed their duties well, but these days they do not go out of their homes. All of them have become greedy and selfish. Everyone considers himself a Rao [*bhomia*]. All this provides enough time to the Jats to fortify themselves. The second cause is that they are in trouble due to non-payment [of remuneration]. Sometimes there is

49 *Arzdasht*, Bhadva Vadi 1, vs 1771/1714 CE; Sawan Vadi 6, vs 1772/1715 CE.

50 *Vakil*'s Report, Jeth Sudi 11, vs 1771/1714 CE; *Arsatta*, *pargana* Khohri, vs 1772/1715 CE.

51 *Arzdasht*, Sawan Vadi 6, vs 1772/1715 CE.

52 *Arzdasht*, Kartik Vadi 4, vs 1766/1709 CE; Sawan Vadi 3, vs 1772/1715 CE; Asadh Vadi 15, vs 1766/1709 CE.

> no money for salary. We need a big army and weapons to defeat the Jats and all this requires lot of money.[53]

Time and again, the *diwan* pressed on the Amber Raja to teach a lesson to Churaman:

> Churaman Jat is our enemy ... [He] is a rascal ... totally unrealistic and unreliable. Acquiring land is his main target ... he requires a severe punishment ... I do not consider it a small matter ... It is a serious problem for us. If you do not take action against him in time then we have to make more efforts to control his wicked activities because [he] is becoming more and more aggressive.[54]

The *diwan* was particularly troubled by the fact that the revenue officials of Amber were often beaten up by Churaman's men in the presence of peasants and put to flight. While this ignominy of state officials dented the image of Amber, these acts of Jats increased Churaman's popularity as a valiant man. Referring to Churaman as a lion, the *diwan* complained that, inspired by the valour of Jat rebels such as Churaman, ordinary peasants had also turned 'treacherous and refused to pay the land revenue to our officials'.[55] Therefore, to punish the peasants of *pargana* Khohri, Mukand Ram Vakawat and Raj Singh Kilanot and others were sent with an army to the disaffected villages, but they found the villages deserted because the peasants had run away to the *thoon* (fortress) of Churaman.[56] However, they managed to capture and imprison some peasants of Rampur Khurd, Jainadipur, and Sithadheri villages. The Amber troops also attacked the villages of *pargana* Mojpur where the peasants were instigated by the Jats and Kishan Naruka's men not to pay land revenue to the officials.[57]

Upon receiving the news that the Jats were fortifying their villages in *parganas* Mojpur and Bharkol, the *diwan* immediately ordered Shyam Singh Khangrot and Jodha Singh Kilanot to march with an

53 *Arzdasht*, Sawan Vadi 6, vs 1772/1715 CE; Chait Sudi 4, vs 1769/1712 CE.

54 *Arzdasht*, Kartik Vadi 4, vs 1766/1709 CE; Posh Sudi 13, vs 1766/1709 CE; Asadh Sudi 3, vs 1769/1712 CE; Sawan Vadi 6, vs 1772/1715 CE.

55 *Arzdasht*, Asadh Sudi 3, vs 1769/1712 CE.

56 *Arsatta*, *pargana* Khohri, vs 1773/1716 CE.

57 *Arsatta*, *pargana* Khohri, vs 1773/1716 CE.

army to the Jat villages. The army occupied most of the Jat villages where Churaman was building his fortresses. In Vanahni village, the army destroyed the Jat fortifications; removed the *thanas* of Jats and set up the *thanas* of Amber; and arrested many peasants. The peasants of seven villages of *pargana* Mojpur, contiguous to the territories of Jats, ran away to the *thoon* fearing assault by the Amber army.[58] However, in *pargana* Sahar (Braj region) and in many villages of *pargana* Hodal, Bhikho Jat, Churaman's nephew, and Jait Singh, zamindar of Kama, joined hands to construct fortresses. They even replaced the *thana* of Amber in Vichhor village with their own *thana*.[59] In *pargana* Pahari too, the Jats removed the Rajput *thanas* even as the *faujdar* of Amber expressed his inability to protect the *thana* against the Jats residing in the vicinity of Kama.[60] The Jat villages in *parganas* Hodal and Palwal joined hands with the Jats of Sansanwal *gotra*, and by the time the *faujdar* of Mathura reached these villages with his army, the peasants had already fled to Sinsini.[61] The Jat peasants of Deswal and Sansanwal *gotras* as well as the Meena peasants belonging to *pargana* Kathumber also joined the army of Jats.[62]

In this context, it is to be noted that caste-based unity between the Jat zamindars and Jat peasants was found not only in Braj, Bharatpur, and Mewat regions, but also in *pargana* Kol (Aligarh), where 183 out of 442½ villages were under the control of the Jats. Bhopat Ram, the *amil* of *pargana* Kol, informed the Amber raja that the peasants of these 183 villages had not paid their land revenue to the Amber state, since they were under total control of Nanda Jat. They could only be taken to task by a large army.[63] The Jats kept blacksmiths (*lohars*) in their fortresses to manufacture weapons. For instance, in one report, the Amber Raja was informed that Churaman had captured some blacksmiths and taken them to his *thoon* to make *ramchangis* and *rahkallas*.[64] In response, the Amber state issued an order that if any

58 *Arsatta, pargana* Mojpur, VS 1774/1717 CE; *Arzdasht*, Asadh Vadi 6, VS 1772/1715 CE.

59 *Arzdasht*, Asadh Vadi 15, VS 1766/1709 CE.

60 *Arsatta, pargana* Mojpur, VS 1773/1716 CE.

61 *Arzdasht*, Sawan Sudi 15, VS 1775/1718 CE.

62 *Arzdasht*, Kartik Vadi 7, VS 1751/1694 CE.

63 Dwivedi, *The Jats*, 47.

64 *Arzdasht*, VS 1747/1690 CE.

blacksmith was found helping the Jats, strict action would be taken against him.[65]

From the foregoing account of Jat–Rajput conflict centred on the appropriation of agrarian surplus, it is evident that the Jat revolts, in fact, were essentially agrarian revolts against the state—revolts that drew not only peasants, zamindars, and artisans (i.e., blacksmiths), but also castes other than Jats, such as the Meos and Meenas. In the course of these protracted revolts, many Jat peasants turned into zamindars who provided a strong social base for the rise of the Bharatpur state.

A singular inspirational force behind the mobilization of several peasant castes in these revolts was their perception of Churaman Jat's activities. The 'heroic' exploits of Churaman and his men—beating up of Amber land revenue officials, removal of the Amber Raja's *thanas*, and establishment of their own *thanas*—fired the imagination of peasants who looked upon Churaman as their liberator from the oppressive rule of the Mughals and the Amber state. The number of peasants flocking to his *thoon* increased day by day. As mentioned earlier, impressed by Churaman's image as a 'manly' warrior, fearless of the state power and lording over the region like a lion, they mustered the courage to refuse the payment of land revenue, steal grains, or consume the standing crops. For the Amber state, however, Churaman was a cunning, crafty, and unreliable rascal; a notorious freebooter, traitor, seasoned plunderer, and robber-chief; and, most importantly, its chief enemy. Nobility at the Mughal court also considered Churaman a rogue and a crook, but reasoned that a courageous Jat zamindar, when required, could be used like a notorious *daroga*. So, the Sayyid brothers and Nawab Khan-i-Daura continued to support him against the Amber Raja. Even Churaman was well aware of the fact that he was being used as a weapon against the powerful Amber Raja and hence had been given the *ijara* of so many *parganas* in the Agra and Mewat regions. But Churaman made the most of

[65] *Arzdasht*, Chait Vadi 7, VS 1751/1694 CE. The Amber *faujdar* Shyam Singh informed the Raja that the blacksmiths of *qasba* Shavri who had made 11 *rahakallas* and *ramchangis* for the Jats had been arrested and compelled to give a written undertaking that in future they would not supply arms to the Jats (*Arzdasht*, Jeth Vadi 1, VS 1761/1704 CE).

this opportunity to create a strong socio-economic base for the Jat movement.

Here, Churaman's strategy of dealing with enemy villages, that is, those that opposed his authority, merits an explanation. The enemy villages were plundered and set on fire, the domestic animals were taken away, the *patel*s were held captive, and standing crops were destroyed. All these violent methods were aimed at intimidating the peasantry of the enemy villages and coercing them into submission. In the medieval society, loot and plunder during military campaigns were not considered unethical. Rather, they were regarded as a legitimate means of asserting a zamindar's or a ruler's politico-military authority over the recalcitrant subject-peasantry.[66] In fact, the *diwan* of Amber, in his letters, did not condemn Churaman's acts of loot and plunder, but rather expressed his anxiety at the growing strength of Churaman that posed a grave danger to the economic interests of the Amber state.

The Rajput–Jat conflict in the course of these revolts not only adversely affected the agricultural production, but also led to the over-exploitation of peasantry, as both Amber officials and the Jats forcibly collected land revenue from them. In 1712 when Churaman forcibly collected land revenue from the villages of *pargana* Khohri, the Amber state reacted sharply and many peasants were taken as prisoners because it was alleged that they had willingly paid land revenue to the Jats. In the words of the Amber *diwan*: 'The *raiyati* of the villages contiguous to the Jat territory have fled to the *thoon*. [But] the *raiyati* of many villages have been captured and put into prison as they had paid their dues to the Jats.' The *diwan*, however, admitted that the Meo peasantry had pleaded their helplessness: land revenue was being extracted from them by both the Jats and the Amber state. The Meo peasants

[66] In *Tarikh-i-Ahmad-Shahi* (Dwivedi, *The Jats*, 89), a significant remark of the 18th-century Maratha *subedar* of Malwa, Malhar Rao Holkar, reflects the general tendency of the soldiers after victorious campaigns. On the plunder carried out by the Maratha soldiers in 1754, Malhar reportedly said, 'These soldiers, they always do it.' Hence, Churaman's depredations in the course of military campaigns were in keeping with the general practice of the age. The examples of Mughal, Maratha, and even Rajput troops indulging in plunder can easily be multiplied. Much of the criticism of Churaman by his contemporaries reflected the Amber state's point of view.

had further argued that they could not pay land revenue twice on the same crop, since they had already paid land revenue to the Jats, and that they were being persecuted unnecessarily.[67] On the other hand, the Amber state claimed that the peasants should have paid the revenue to the Amber officials only, as the Amber state had the legitimate right to collect land revenue in the *parganas* of Mewat. For the Amber state, paying land revenue to the Jats meant supporting them and amounted to disloyalty for which the peasants deserved punishment. In desperation, the Meo peasants threatened that if they continued to be harassed for land revenue, they would be forced to leave the villages. Indeed, caught up in the bitter contention between the Amber state and Churaman, many peasants were forced to become deserters or rebels, that is, many either left their villages or fled to the Jat *thoon*.

In 1716, the *amil* reported that the peasants of 127 villages out of 342 villages in *pargana* Khohri had deserted their villages fearing an armed assault by the Amber state. The *amil* further complained that land revenue could not be collected from many villages because the entire harvest had been consumed by the peasants in defiance of the state.[68] Similar were the conditions in *pargana* Pahari comprising 209 villages. There, according to the *arzdasht* of 1716, the standing crops of 24 villages were destroyed by the peasants out of the fear of Amber army.[69] The *amil*'s report of 1718 from *pargana* Sahar lamented the decrease in agricultural production of many villages of the *pargana* due to Jat revolts.[70] The *amil*'s detailed report of 1716 from *pargana* Khohri shows that in the wake of the Jat revolts, the peasants of 28 villages did not deposit the land revenue for various reasons: the Amber army destroyed the harvest of one village; the peasantry of three villages consumed their entire harvest before the arrival of the Amber army; the peasants of two villages, discontent with the Amber state, fled to the *thoon*; the peasantry of 20 villages, many of which were contiguous to the Jat territory, took away the share of produce payable as land revenue to the *thoon*; and two villages were completely deserted due to the high-handedness of the land revenue officials.[71]

67 *Arzdasht*, Jeth Vadi 3, vs 1761/1704 CE.

68 *Arsatta*, *pargana* Khohri, vs 1773/1716 CE.

69 *Arzdasht*, Asadh Sudi 3, vs 1769/1712 CE.

70 *Arzdasht*, Sawan Sudi 5, vs 1777/1720 CE.

71 *Arsatta*, *pargana* Khohri, vs 1773/1716 CE.

The Jat revolts also affected the agricultural production and revenue collection in *pargana* Kol (Aligarh), apart from Mewat and Braj regions. Bhopat Ram, the *amil* of *pargana* Kol, informed the Amber Raja that 183 out of 449½ villages were under the control of the turbulent Jats; that the state's revenue officials managed to collect a meagre 1,300 rupees out of the total revenue of 97,729 rupees due from these villages; and that it would be difficult to collect the revenue from these villages until and unless the Jats were overpowered.[72]

However, Churaman's influence at the Mughal court gradually declined, particularly after the fall of the Sayyid brothers. His plundering activities in the *parganas* of the imperial *jagirdars* also made him unpopular at the Mughal court which continued to receive complaints that he and his henchmen were collecting *rahdari* and secretly manufacturing arms.[73] The Jat power had reached its peak under the leadership of Churaman, but after his death in 1721, the Amber Raja seized the *thoon* and razed it to ground. The Jat power ultimately suffered such a setback that Churaman's nephew Badan Singh Jat became a feudatory of the Amber Raja.[74] The process by which the Jats had acquired their zamindari rights in the Mewat region was different from the manner in which the Naruka Rajputs had carved out their zamindaris. However, it is evident from the Rajasthani documents that the Jats had built up their socio-political base in the region through the *ijara* system. They acquired the *ijara* of many *parganas* from the imperial *jagirdars* by intimidatory tactics. Gradually, the Jat peasants were encouraged to settle in these *parganas*. Ultimately the Jat zamindars constructed their *garhis* in the villages numerically dominated by the Jat peasants and stationed armed guards to protect these *garhis*. To avoid confrontation with the Narukas who could have been their potential rivals, they aligned themselves with the Narukas who, too, were openly defying the authority of the Amber Raja. The confrontation between the Narukas and the Amber Raja provided the Jats enough ground to establish their zamindari rights over many *parganas* of Mewat. Like the Narukas, the Jats could also organize themselves in a better way than did the Meos. Economically too, the Jats were more

72 *Arsatta, pargana* Pahari, VS 1773/1716 CE.

73 Chandra, *Parties and Politics*, 123.

74 Chandra, *Parties and Politics*, 178.

prosperous than the Meos. The Jats and Narukas thus succeeded in consolidating their military strength and social base in many *parganas* of Mewat, thereby greatly undermining the position of the Meos.

The creation of new caste/clan zamindaris in the region had a threefold effect on the rural society. First, the new zamindars sought to extend their hereditary territorial rights and, in the process, depressed the position of the small zamindars, who happened to be mainly Meos. Second, this development eroded the traditional caste relationship between the peasants and the zamindars. The new zamindars in some villages encouraged the settlement of a composite rural population in order to deprive the Meos of their numerical advantage, since they had been in majority among the peasants. The third consequence of the creation of new zamindaris was the conversion of a large number of hitherto *raiyati* villages into zamindari and the further imposition of new taxes and cesses on the peasantry. This increasingly oppressive tax burden on the peasantry reduced them to a state of bare subsistence.

The reshuffling in the territorial jurisdiction of the zamindars not only altered the caste/clan composition of the zamindar class, but also led to its growing heterogeneity. The stratification within the zamindars of Mewat was also governed by the customary forces of the caste and clan networks. On the one hand, in some *parganas*, the position of the Jats improved as many dominant Jat peasants became small zamindars and many Jat zamindars were able to expand their territorial jurisdiction by suppressing the petty zamindars belonging to other castes. On the other hand, the Narukas, who had gained zamindaris in various pockets and enclaves of the region in the course of the 17th century, consolidated their position further by the early 18th century and eventually carved out an independent principality of Alwar by the end of the century. Nevertheless, the Amber Raja and his clansmen also managed to retain their *bhom* rights in parts of the region. Overall, the Kachhwaha Rajputs emerged as the most influential and powerful class of zamindars followed by the Jats. The worst sufferers at all levels were the Meos. The process of the contraction of Meo zamindaris reached its peak in the mid-18th century. By then, they were almost totally subjugated by the Kachhwaha Rajputs and Jats and thenceforth had to accept a subordinate status vis-à-vis the Jats and Kachhwaha Rajputs.

The zamindar as a class gained considerable political, economical, and social dominance during the Mughal period. The Mughal empire was heavily dependent on their support and cooperation in the collection of the enormous surplus generated by the subject-peasantry. The imperial policy towards them was shaped by local conditions and the extent to which they could be roped in the task of revenue administration. The continuance or discontinuance of their customary superior rights in land largely depended on their attitude towards the imperial administration in a particular region. Those who cooperated with the administration were allowed to enjoy their customary privileges, whereas the hostile ones were punished, subdued, or replaced by the loyal ones. The Mughal emperor conferred zamindari rights (in some *parganas* of Mewat) on the Amber Raja and the Jats who were bitter rivals and entrusted them with the task of maintaining law and order and extracting land revenue from the recalcitrant sections of peasantry. In a way, the Mughals thus tried to cash in on the mutual rivalries of the zamindars belonging to different castes (Rajputs, Jats, Meos) with the objective of weakening their position vis-à-vis the imperial state. However, in practice, many zamindars took advantage of the imperial support extended to them, to enhance their territorial rights and appropriate for themselves a greater share of the land revenue. In periods of stress, they even sought to expand their hereditary territorial rights at the cost of the imperial authority. Most of the administrative difficulties that the Mughal emperor and other authorities (such as the Amber Raja) had to face were caused by a section of seditious zamindars. Despite the best efforts on the part of the imperial administration, neither all the zamindars could be conciliated nor could they be completely overawed.

The majority of Naruka Rajput and Jat zamindars refused to accept a subordinate status vis-à-vis the state, whether Mughal or Amber, and thus could not be integrated into the state administrative machinery. That many Jats and Naruka *bhomias* in the region became restive and openly defied the imperial authority in the second half of the 17th century is amply attested by the Rajasthani documents, although the reasons for their discontent with and hostility towards the imperial authority are not mentioned. Their hostility and recalcitrance found an overt manifestation in the forcible misappropriation of land revenue that belonged to the imperial *jagirdars*. The latter's inability to collect revenue from their *jagirs* due to the acts of embezzlement and plunder resorted to by the Jat and Naruka zamindars is also well documented. For instance, the Naruka *taluqdars* of *parganas* Banawar, Sonkhar, and Mandawar were charged with not sending the revenue arrears amounting to 180,000 rupees.[75] In another instance, the Naruka *bhomias* robbed four lakh rupees from 14 *parganas* of Alwar *sarkar*, while the imperial *jagirdar* could hardly collect 3,000 *maunds* of foodgrains.[76] In yet another instance, the Naruka *bhomias* misappropriated the entire land revenue of 13 villages in *pargana* Hasanpur.[77] Rao Hathi Singh Naruka, *taluqdar* of *pargana* Jalalpur and Bharkol that were part of the *jagir* of imperial *jagirdar* Vakil Khan, embezzled the entire land revenue of two *parganas*.[78] The Jat zamindars, too, were very active in plundering the peasants of Alwar, Sahar, and Tijara *sarkars*. An imperial *jagirdar* sent a petition to the Mughal court complaining that the Jat zamindar Churaman and his allies had not deposited the land revenue of *pargana* Khohri.[79] He further alleged that the Jat zamindars were involved in plundering activities in the entire region from Akbarabad (Agra) and Shahjahanabad (Delhi).[80] Interestingly, at about the same time, the growing encroachment upon their zamindari rights forced a number of Meo zamindars to embezzle land revenue from the villages of *parganas* Khohri and Pahari.[81]

The helplessness of the imperial *jagirdars* in the face of such depredations is evident from their repeated complaints against the rebel zamindars, each one of whom was in possession of his own *garhi* and armed forces. In 1686, the *amil* reported to the Amber Raja that when the *ijara* of the *jagirs* of nawab Shiphedar Khan and Bahadur Khan was given to the Raja, the Chauhan and Panchnot Rajput *bhomias* occupying these *jagirs* removed all the *sahnas* of the Amber state from the villages, cut the standing crops, and carried them to the villages

75 *Arzdasht*, Asadh Sudi 14, VS 1760/1703 CE.
76 *Arzdasht*, Asadh Vadi 5, VS 1742/1685 CE.
77 *Arsatta, pargana* Hasanpur, VS 1747/1690 CE.
78 *Arzdasht*, Kartik Vadi 6, VS 1759/1703 CE.
79 *Arsatta, pargana* Khohri, VS 1772/1715 CE.
80 *Arzdasht*, Mangsir Vadi 2, VS 1744/1687 CE.
81 *Arsatta, pargana* Khohri, VS 1772/1715 CE; *pargana* Pahari, VS 1788/1731 CE.

of other *parganas*, where they prepared the grains in the fields and distributed them among themselves. The Chauhan *bhomias* took away the entire *rabi* harvest to their own *garhis* in the villages Bagri, Mandawari, Meharaware, and so forth. The Panchnot *bhomias* also carried the *rabi* harvest into their *garhis* in the villages Vachhochh, Phoolwara, Jharoda, and so on. Further, the *bhomias* imprisoned in their *gharis* the peasantry (*raiyati*) and *patels* of some villages that did not support them. They even killed Dayaram Patel. The *raiyati* was terribly frightened of the oppression of the *bhomias*.[82] Other reports too mention that the *bhomias* had overrun the entire region of Mewat, forcibly collecting food grains, looting the merchants and collecting the *rahdari* tax from them, and charging *bhomi* and *faujdari* taxes from the peasants in contravention of the customary practices. Whenever the agents of the *jagirdars* asked the peasants to pay the land revenue, the latter submitted that the zamindar had already extracted it from them. The *jagirdars*, in turn, repeatedly pleaded at the Mughal court that unless the defiant zamindars were overpowered, it would be impossible to collect revenue from their respective *jagirs*.[83] It was a general complaint at the Mughal court that whenever the imperial *faujdar* was transferred, disturbances caused by the rebel zamindars and peasants increased.[84]

It seems that the imperial authority could not exert enough military pressure on the rebel zamindars after the death of emperor Aurangzeb, leading to a further deterioration in the situation. The growing conflict between the zamindars and the state weakened the administrative authority and military power of the Mughals. The rapid breakdown of law and order, in turn, rendered the peasants helpless and placed them entirely at the mercy of the rebel zamindars, tilting the balance of power more and more in favour of the latter. The peasant's response to these developments, however, was not uniform. In some areas, they joined hands with the rebel zamindars. Elsewhere, they merely surrendered to the diktats of the zamindars.

[82] *Arzdasht*, Posh Vadi 7, VS 1743/1686 CE.

[83] *Arzdasht*, Chait Sudi 7, VS 1751/1694 CE; Asadh Sudi 2, VS 1752/1695 CE; Asadh Sudi, VS 1739/1682 CE; Vaishakh Sudi 7, VS 1755/1698 CE; Chait Vadi 9, VS 1746/1689 CE.

[84] *Arzdasht*, Asadh Vadi 5, VS 1742/1685 CE.

The unstable conditions also forced many peasants to leave their villages and migrate to relatively peaceful areas.

It is also essential to examine the pattern of inter-relationships between the different sections of zamindars, in terms of their caste/clan affiliations, stratification within their ranks, the state of economy, and the nature of administrative control in the region. First, as discussed earlier, the growing power of the Narukas and Jats in the region threatened the political and economic interests of the Amber Raja who wanted to increase his politico-economic base in Mewat by securing the *ijaradari*, zamindari, or *thanedari* rights of as many *parganas* as possible. Hence, he tried his best to prevent the emergence of the Naruka and Jat zamindars as rival centres of power in Mewat. However, due to his clan ties with the Narukas he could not afford to be as harsh to them as he was to the Jats. Second, since the Rajputs considered themselves socially and militarily superior to the Jats, the Amber Raja was not prepared to tolerate the rise of Jat power in the very neighbourhood of his *watan jagir*. The growing antipathy of the imperial *jagirdars* against the Jats also tilted the balance of power in favour of the Amber Raja. Henceforth, the Mughals sided with the Amber Raja in his struggle for power with the Jats except during the period of the ascendency of Sayyid brothers. He was also favoured by the other imperial *jagirdars* who found it more convenient to farm out their *jagirs* to him under the *ijara* system.

The more fundamental changes in the relationship between the Narukas and the Jats on the one hand and the Amber Raja on the other are discernible after the foundation of the Bharatpur state by Rao Badan Singh Jat in Deeg in 1724. Thereafter, the struggle of the Jats and Narukas against the Amber Raja and other *jagirdars* became negligible. It seems that the Amber Raja succeeded in controlling them, by either force or conciliatory tactics. However, he, as also the imperial *jagirdars*, did not give up their hostile attitude towards the Jats and the Meos, as is discernible from several instances. The Amber Raja issued an order (*parwana*) to the effect that the Jats and Meos should not be allowed to get the *ijara* of *jagirs* from the imperial *jagirdars*.[85] He also ordered his *faujdar* and *amil* to ensure that the Meo zamindars were not allowed to keep horses in their possession.

85 *Arzdasht*, Asoj Sudi 12, VS 1761/1704 CE.

Those Meos who were already in possession of horses were ordered to surrender them immediately.[86]

The Rajasthani sources clearly demonstrate that the Meos in particular, irrespective of their class status, were persecuted and downgraded in the village society more than the other middling castes. The Raja of Amber perhaps considered this as an appropriate step to put a permanent stop to the plundering activities of the rebel Meos and to reduce their capacity to resist.

Examining the relationship between the various groups of zamindars and the peasants is also important in order to understand the nature of agrarian relations in the region. The peasantry of the Mewat region was heterogeneous, comprising castes such as the Meos, Jats, Gujjars, Ahirs, Malis, and Meenas. The social bases of the different groups of zamindars among the peasants of the region were quite variable. The Jat and Meo zamindars had their social base among the peasants of their castes. On the other hand, the Narukas who did not have caste links with the peasants were looked upon as more oppressive than the Jats. Unlike abundant references in the Rajasthani documents to oppressed peasants seeking refuge with the Jat zamindars, there are no instances of peasants ever fleeing to the Naruka zamindars for protection.

It is evident that caste affinity was quite strong between the Jat peasants and zamindars. But it is striking to note that the Meo and Meena peasants also considered it worthy to take refuge with the Jat zamindars. For instance, in 1715, when the *faujdar* of Mewat sent his army to the villages of *pargana* Khohri to collect the land revenue, the Meo and Meena peasants of seven villages ran away to the Jat *thoon*.[87] In another instance, the *amil* reported to the Amber Raja that the Meo and Meena peasants of 16 villages in *pargana* Khohri had refused to pay revenue at the instigation of the Jat zamindars.[88] In yet another instance, in 1690, the Jat zamindars raised a huge army basically comprising Jat (of mainly Sansanwal and Deswal *gotras*), Gujjar, and Meena peasants.[89] In still another instance, the Amber Raja issued an

86 *Chithi* to the *faujdar*, Mangsir Vadi 6, VS 1784/1727 CE.

87 *Arsatta, pargana* Khohri, VS 1779/1722 CE.

88 *Dehai-ferhashti, pargana* Khohri, VS 1779/1722 CE.

89 *Arzdasht*, VS 1747/1690 CE.

order in 1727 to his *amils* in *parganas* Khohri and Pahari that the Meo and Jat peasants should not be allowed to settle in the newly founded villages as well as the old villages that were being rehabilitated. Those Jats and Meos who were already residing in these villages were asked by the administration to give an undertaking that they would not support the recalcitrant Jat and Meo zamindars.[90]

It was in order to erode the social base of the Jat and Meo zamindars, who had strong ties with the peasantry of their respective castes in the region, that the Amber Raja encouraged the settlement of Ahir peasants in the villages of Mewat. Although the relationship between the Meo peasants and their zamindars was cordial, the Meos could no longer defend their zamindaris from encroachment by the Amber Raja. The weak resistance offered by them was crushed by the *faujdar* of Mewat through periodic expeditions against them. It is this failure of the Meo zamindars to emerge as powerful class of zamindars and shelter the oppressed peasantry of their caste that explains the flight of many Meo peasants to the Jat-dominated areas, as the Jats could provide them with the necessary protection.

The position of the Naruka *bhomias* in the rural society of Mewat was more complex and merits some explanation. Since they lacked caste ties with the peasants, they derived their strength mainly from their superior military and economic power, thereby emerging as the most powerful class of *bhomias* in the region. However, later on, they also tried to reconcile the peasants to their rule by adopting an altogether different method by which the interaction between them and the peasants could be increased. In the villages where they constructed their new *garhis*, they organized community feasts (*nangals*) to celebrate the completion of these *garhis*,[91] and asked the peasants to join them and eat together. This generated a feeling of brotherhood between them and the peasants and won them, to some extent, the support of the peasants belonging to the *parganas* Bharkol, Naharkhoh, and Mojpur.[92] Even the blacksmiths of *pargana*

90 *Parwana* to *amils*, *parganas* Khohri and Pahari, Posh Vadi 6, VS 1784/1727 CE.

91 *Arzdasht*, Jeth Vadi 1, VS 1761/1704 CE.

92 *Arzdashts* Mangsir Sudi 15, VS 1759/1702 CE; Vaishakh Vadi 2, VS 1761/1704 CE.

Bahatri used to supply them guns and other weapons.[93] However, the social base of the Naruka *bhomias* among the peasants still remained weak, partly due to the lack of caste affinity and partly due to their high-handedness and harassment of the peasantry. This attitude of the Narukas was particularly manifest when they consolidated their position in their *bhom* territories.

The difficult relationship of the Naruka *bhomias* with the peasantry can be better understood in the larger context of the changing relationship between the Rajput *bhomias* of various clans (including Narukas) and the Amber state. The *mansab* of the Amber rulers fluctuated from time to time. The highest *mansab* was granted to them by Aurangzeb from 1658 to 1678. During this period, the Amber Raja got maximum number of *parganas* in Mewat as part of his *tankhwah jagir* which he further sub-assigned to his soldiers and clansmen. It was during this period that the Rajput sub-assignees endeavoured to consolidate their strength on the basis of their clan ties with the Raja and began to claim hereditary rights to lands assigned to them. They even attempted to combine the *jagirdari* and *bhomi* rights into one.

But thereafter, the Amber Raja's *mansab* was progressively reduced, leading to shrinkage in the size of his *tankhwah jagir*. Faced with the prospect of the loss of income from land, some of his sub-assignees, however, were not prepared to surrender their sub-assignments and instead tried to usurp the *bhomi* rights in the areas sub-assigned to them. Further, the Rajput troopers rendered unemployed by the reduction in the Raja's *mansab* took to plundering activities and openly defied the authority of the Amber Raja as well as that of the other imperial *jagirdars*. An *arzdasht* of 1689 addressed to the Amber Raja vividly captures this conflictual relationship between the Amber Raja and his *chakars* (Rajput servants). Therein, he was informed that the Rajput *chakars* who had in the past served the Amber state as sub-assignees with sincerity were left without a source of income as a consequence of the shrinkage in the Raja's *tankhwah jagir*. Hence, they became selfish, cunning, ungrateful, and least concerned with the interests of the state. They were openly creating disturbances, claiming *bhomi* rights, and agitating for the retention of the areas sub-assigned to them. These rebel Rajputs included the Rajawats,

93 *Arzdasht*, Jeth Vadi 1, vs 1761/1704 CE.

the Narukas, the Shekhawats, the Kilanots, and the Chauhans. The author of the *arzdasht* clearly stressed that it was the Raja who was the real zamindar of the whole area, not the sub-assignees. Finally, he appealed to the Raja to prevent his erstwhile sub-assignees from causing trouble and claiming any territorial rights.[94]

This increasingly grim situation is further described in a long letter of 1712 from the *vakil* to the Amber Raja. Therein, he complained that the Rajputs who earlier used to perform their duties honestly had become selfish, unfaithful, and cunning. They had begun to cause disturbances in the *jagir*s of the imperial *mansabdar*s and force the peasants to pay them the *bhomi* tax. They had forsaken their moral duty, as servants (*chakar*s) of the Amber state, to protect its economic interests. Instead, driven by the motive of making economic gains, they had begun to plunder the villages in the *jagir*s of the imperial *mansabdar*s and prevent the peasants from complaining against them at the Mughal court. Nevertheless, according to the letter, the imperial *mansabdar*s who held *jagir*s in Alwar *sarkar* had complained to the Mughal authorities that the Rajput *chakar*s of the Amber Raja had forcefully collected the land revenue they were entitled to and had harassed the peasants in their *jagir*s. There were a total of 27 *pargana*s that were part of the *jagir*s of the imperial *mansabdar*s in which the Rajputs had been creating disturbances. The *vakil* concluded the letter stating that the Mughal court had issued a strong warning that if the Rajputs did not cease to trouble the imperial *mansabdar*s, the latter would not assign the *ijara* of their *jagir*s to the Amber Raja.[95]

The Amber Raja's fall from imperial favour, particularly during the period of Sayyid brothers' ascendency (1707–20), is discernible from an another letter of 1712, wherein the *vakil* informed the Raja that Sarfaraz Khan Badshahzada, the *jagirdar* of Firozpur Jhirka, had received a letter from the *diwan* of Khan-i-Jahan Bahadur conveying that the *ijara* of Firozpur Jhirka should not have been given to the Amber Raja, as he had not deposited the arrears of the previous year worth 12,000 rupees. The *vakil* further informed that the peasantry of Firozpur Jhirka had also pleaded at the Mughal court that their villages be freed from the *ijara* rights held over them by the Amber Raja,

94 *Arzdasht*, Asadh Sudi 7, vs 1746/1689 CE.

95 *Vakil*'s Report, vs 1769/1712 CE.

since they were being forced to pay various non-customary taxes to him and also plundered by his men. According to the *vakil*, the peasants had heightened their plea by reminding the Mughal emperor that they are his *raiyati* (subjects), not that of the Amber Raja.[96] In another of his reports, the *vakil* informed the Raja that, despite his best efforts, he had not been able to impress upon the Mughal authorities the need to increase the Raja's *mansab* which had been substantially reduced in the last 30 years.[97] In the years following the reduction in their *mansab*, the Amber rulers were faced with a difficult situation wherein their military strength had to be maintained even as their financial resources were being considerably reduced.[98] Having failed to secure an increase in the size of his *tankhwah jagir*, the Amber Raja and his *vakil* at the Mughal court endeavoured to regain some of the lost ground by securing the *thanedari*, *ijaradari*, and zamindari rights in those *parganas* of Mewat that had formed part of his *tankhwah jagir* a few decades ago.[99] The Amber Raja's efforts to increase his income from other sources in the face of his inability to expand his *tankhwah jagir* must be viewed in the context of increasing rivalries and factionalism among the Mughal nobles in the aftermath of the crisis of *jagirdari* system.

The Rajasthani documents suggest that the rural society of Mewat was in turmoil in the years following 1680 as a direct result of the growing power of the rebel Jat and Rajput zamindars, which led to a tussle between them and the imperial *mansabdars* holding *jagirs* in this region. In the process, two significant developments took place in the region: (a) the emergence of the Jats who strove to expand their zamindari in the Mewat region and (b) the Amber Raja's continuous attempts to establish his zamindari over many *parganas* of Mewat along with *thanedari* and *ijaradari* rights which he acquired from the imperial *faujdars* and *jagirdars* of the region. These attempts on the part of the Amber Raja brought him into direct conflict with his own clansmen (the Narukas) as well as the Jats. These two developments together aggravated the conflicts within the rural society. These

96 *Vakil*'s Report, Bhadva Vadi Amavash, VS 1769/1712 CE.

97 *Vakil*'s Report, Fagun Vadi 11, VS 1769/1712 CE.

98 *Vakil*'s Report, Fagun Vadi 11, VS 1769/1712 CE.

99 *Vakil*'s Report, Fagun Vadi 11, VS 1769/1712 CE.

protracted conflicts raged not only among the Rajputs, Jats, and Meos, but also among the various Rajput sub-clans.

The stage was set for a turbulent contention among multiple overlapping claims over the surplus produce of the peasantry. The situation had already been aggravated by the deepening crises of the *jagirdari* system. The worst weaknesses of the Mughal and Rajput *jagirdari* systems found manifestation in the multiple problems faced by the Amber chiefs and the other imperial *mansabdars*. The Amber Raja, who when compelled by the need to serve the economic interests of his own clansmen could not adhere to the imperial rules and regulations with regard to his *tankhwah jagir*, had to face the wrath of the Mughal state manifested in a reduction in his *mansab*. The depredations of the rebel Rajputs and Jats greatly diminished the revenue income from the affected *parganas*, and consequently the other imperial *jagirdars* also suffered a loss in their income. The ensuing tussle between the imperial *jagirdars* and the rebel *bhomias*, eventually, led to a decline in production and deterioration in the condition of the peasants.

CONCLUSION

THE GRADUAL BUT CONTINUOUS TRANSFORMATION of the Meo community from a tribal way of living to sedentary peasantry, often leading up to Islamization by the 18th century, is a history of contestations, negotiations, and adaptations. This process followed a see-saw pattern, sometimes gaining momentum, and, at other times, losing momentum with the establishment of a centralized state initially during the Sultanate period and subsequently under the Mughals. We have seen that right from the establishment of the Turkish rule in India in the 13th century, Mewat attracted the attention of the rulers of Delhi. In view of the strategic and economic significance of the region, the Delhi sultans always endeavoured to bring it under their effective control. However, despite stern action taken by Sultans Balban and Muhammad Shah against the Mewatis, they could not be brought under total subjugation for any considerable length of time. The perennial attitude of the Mewati chiefs towards the central authority was one of assertion of their autonomy. Chronicles of Delhi sultans have, most of the times, portrayed this assertion as hostility, although its intensity varied over time. The Khanzada chiefs of Mewat at times also took active part in the politics of the Sultanate on behalf of one faction of the nobility or the other. On numerous occasions, they joined hands with the chiefs of neighbouring principalities to confront the central authority.

Soon after the death of Sultan Firozshah Tughlaq, the Khanzada chiefs of Mewat, with the help of the former Firozi slaves, carved out a small principality in the vicinity of Tijara at Kotla. The last Khanzada chief, Hasan Khan Mewati, participated in the Battles of Panipat and Khanwa against the Mughals. The local perception of his role is reflected in the 16th-century ballad 'Hasan Khan ki Katha' whose author, Narsingh Meo, clearly accused Hasan Khan for taking part in these battles without any compelling reason and thereby accelerating the subsequent demise of his own state at the hands of the Mughals. The antagonism between the Khanzada chiefs and the central authority finally ended with the annexation of the region during Akbar's reign. We have discussed the two chief reasons why the incipient Khanzada chiefdom could not transform itself into a full-fledged state. First was the inability of the Khanzada chiefs to mobilize sufficient resources for building the requisite material base of a state. The most probable reasons for this have been examined in the first two chapters. Second and equally important was the unwillingness of the Mughal emperors to encourage the formation of a rival state in a region that was strategically located between the two Mughal centres of power, Agra and Delhi. This unwillingness of the Mughals to allow the Khanzada chiefs any degree of political autonomy within the region, perhaps, rested on their knowledge that the Khanzadas in the past had been a source of trouble to the Delhi sultans. Therefore, the Mughal emperor Akbar, while bringing the region under the direct purview of the imperial administration (the region was divided into five *sarkar*s of the Mughal *suba*s of Agra and Delhi), reduced the status of the Khanzadas to that of petty zamindars.

We have also traced the gradual process of the transformation of Meos from tribes to peasant castes. The Meo tribes inhabiting the Aravali hills, valleys, and dense forests of the region lived chiefly on cattle-lifting, plunder, and hunting, but their depredations adversely affected the conduct of trade through the region and constituted a serious law-and-order problem for both the Delhi sultans and the Khanzada chiefs. Consequently, as they took strong measures to control the Meo menace, the Meos seemed to have faced tremendous political pressure to abandon their predatory activities and semi-nomadic lifestyle, and take to agriculture. Although the process of their peasantization must have been quite prolonged and painful, it constitutes, by far, the most significant and almost revolutionary phase in their history. The state also seemed to have contributed to their peasantization in order to develop the region's agrarian economy and thereby its potential to generate more land revenue. The role of the Khanzadas in this process was definitely significant because a strong agrarian base was necessary for state formation. Second, the rising population of the Meos was also an important factor for their peasantization, as the limited resources of hills and their traditional occupations proved insufficient for their sustenance. And it was the plough-based sedentary agriculture that offered them a stable, assured source of livelihood. Thus, Meos abandoned their habitations in the hills and forest areas and began to settle down in the plains, whilst carrying out cultivation. This changed state of affairs is discernible from the references in the *Ain-i-Akbari* to the Meos not only as peasants but also as zamindars with landholdings in more than half of the region. Thus, one can see the gradual emergence of a highly stratified peasantry, extending up to the status of landlords.

The *Ain-i-Akbari* and other contemporary Indo-Persian sources further inform us that one section of the Meos was absorbed into the Mughal postal and espionage system as Dak Meoras who carried posts to remote areas of the empire even in adverse weather conditions, and *khidmatiyyas* who served as personal bodyguards of the emperor and as security guards in the imperial palace and forts. The *Ain-i-Akbari* even lauds these Dak Meoras and *khidmatiyyas* as the most loyal and efficient servants of the Mughal state. Thus, the Meos was transformed from tribes to peasants, post carriers, and soldiers by the end of the 15th century, and to zamindars by the end of the 16th century. Moreover, in the course of regular interaction with the Mughal court and officials, the Dak Meoras and the *khidmatiyyas* increasingly grew closer to the Islamic culture, and began to follow certain Islamic customs and rituals associated with the Mughal court. For instance, they started celebrating festivals such as Id-ul-fitr, Ramzan, Shab-e-barat, and the Urs of Khwaja Muinuddin Chishti in the Mewat region.

The agricultural regime of the region was marked by the cultivation of a multiplicity of food and cash crops in both *kharif* and *rabi* seasons, and was largely dependent on the bounty of monsoons, supplemented by well irrigation. As our analysis of the data on agricultural production in both seasons shows, the tendency initially was towards stability but later on one can see decline in output. The reasonably rich mineral resources of the region also enabled the production of a variety of non-agricultural items which became important articles of local and trans-regional trade and thereby diversified the region's economy. For instance, farmers of many villages in the periphery of *qasba* Nuh manufactured salt, while blacksmiths manufactured a variety of items, such as agricultural tools, swords, knives, small guns (*ramchangis*), and canons (*rahkallas*), from iron and copper, extracted from the Aravali hills and smelted in furnaces. As late as the late 19th century, the ethnographic accounts of British land settlement officers and the Urdu work *Arzang-i-Tijara* testified to the presence of old, ruined smelting furnaces, most of which had been active in the pre-colonial times, at places such as Tijara, Firozpur Jhirka, Akbarpur, Parthipura, Baleta, Nayagaon, Tehala, Gola ka Baas, and so on. The non-agricultural, particularly artisanal, production gave impetus to trade, both intra- and trans-regional. So did the location of Mewat, through which passed several trade routes linking the region to big cities such as Delhi, Agra, and Ahmedabad. The *mahajans*, *sarrafs*, *bohras*, and *banjaras* were actively involved in various commercial activities, such as moneylending, issuing *hundis*, insuring and transporting merchandise, and so forth. A mercantile economy, shaped by thriving artisanal production and trade, led to the emergence of a large number of *qasbas* and towns. To further add to Mewat's importance, the horses of Mughal cavalry were trained at places such as Nuh, Ghasera, Ujina, Indori, Kot-Qasim, and Firozpur Jhirka, according to the *Ain-i-Akbari*.

The transformation of agrarian relations in the Mewat region accompanied by significant changes in the economy and society during the late 17th and early 18th centuries has been the central theme of this study. The changing caste composition of the zamindars and consequent upheavals in the rural society were intricately linked to the emergence of multiple conflicting claims over the surplus produce of the peasantry. The Meo zamindars and the Khanzadas began to lose their position of pre-eminence in the wake of the emergence of Kachhwaha ruling family of Amber as a powerful political force in the region during the reign of Akbar.

Further dissolution of the Meo and Khanzada zamindaris occurred during the second half of the 17th century as a consequence of the combined onslaught of the Kachhwaha Rajputs and Jats, both of whom made determined attempts to expand the area under their respective zamindaris. Unable to match their Rajput and Jat adversaries in resources and military strength, most of the Meo and Khanzada zamindars were reduced to the status of either primary zamindars or peasant proprietors.

The twin process of the constriction of the Meo and Khanzada zamindaris and the expansion of the Rajput and Jat zamindaris disrupted the pre-existing caste nexus between the peasants and the zamindars in areas hitherto dominated by these zamindars. This brought about a significant change in the pattern of agrarian relations, as it placed the relationship between the zamindars and the peasants in such areas on a new pedestal. The Rajput *bhomias* and the Jat zamindars now established their hold over villages inhabited by the Meos, Khanzadas, and peasants belonging to other middle castes. The new breed of strident zamindars, in order to strengthen their hold on the rural society, also encouraged the settlement of peasants belonging to different castes including their own castes/clans in their zamindari areas. The growing heterogeneity in the caste affiliations of the zamindars and peasants weakened the position of the Meo peasantry. The peasants belonging to other dominant middle caste groups, such as the Ahirs and Jats, were encouraged to undermine the status of the Meo peasants in the village society.

The momentum that the emergence of the new groups of zamindars in the rural society generated ultimately culminated in agrarian turmoil and upheavals. In the wake of the growing crisis of the *jagirdari* system, the Amber Raja lost many *parganas* of the region that he held in *tankhwah jagir*, in around 1680 CE. Consequent upon a reduction in his *mansab*, he tried to make good the loss by acquiring the zamindari, *faujdari, thanedari*, and *ijara* rights from various Mughal authorities in areas that he had so far held in *tankhwah jagir*. This move of the Raja brought him into direct confrontation with the members of his own sub-clans who by now were deeply entrenched in these areas and had sought to convert their sub-assignments into permanent *bhomi* rights. Besides, the Raja had to deal with the recalcitrant Jat zamindars in other areas. The Kachhwaha troopers of the Amber Raja who had legally lost their sub-assignments resorted to defiance of the state authority by not moving from the areas which were now assigned to other imperial *mansabdars* in *jagir*. They asserted their *bhomi* rights over these areas without any legal sanction to that effect, and even prevented the peasants from paying revenue to the imperial *jagirdars* or to the Amber state. Most powerful among these Kachhwaha sub-clans were the Narukas whose rebellions often assumed alarming proportions. At the political and administrative levels, the rural scenario in the region during the ensuing four decades was characterized by armed revolts of the Rajput *bhomias* and the Jat zamindars on the one hand and the Amber Raja's efforts to suppress them on the other. The politico-administrative crisis was further aggravated as more often than not the *bhomias* got entangled in mutual feuds as well. Furthermore, the rebellions *bhomias* and zamindars often indulged in pillage and brigandage. It is thus clear that in the years following 1680 CE, the Mewat region was in a widespread political and administrative tumult. Normal functioning of the land revenue administration was seriously impaired, as the Amber Raja, other imperial *jagirdars*, the Rajput *bhomias*, and the Jat zamindars—all clashed over the surplus produce of the peasants and flouted the imperial rules and regulations with impunity.

However, it must be stressed that at a deeper level, the crisis was socio-economic as well. The basic cause of the conflict between the various sections of the ruling class was their desire to control the larger part of the surplus produce at the cost of each other. It has already been shown that the magnitude of the land revenue demand was quite high and, in addition, various other customary cesses were levied on the peasants. The regressive nature of the land revenue system also implied that the underprivileged middle and small peasants who constituted the bulk of the rural population were liable to endure more hardships on this count than their relatively richer brethren. In addition, the ruling class, in order to maximize its share in the surplus or to compensate the loss of revenue caused by one section to another, subjected the peasants to various illegal extortions. Thus, even in normal (i.e., drought- or famine-free) years, the pressure of the total revenue demand on the peasantry was constantly increasing. However, the agrarian turmoil of the late 17th and early 18th centuries led to further oppression of the peasantry when conflicting claims staked by different sections of the ruling class over the surplus produce increased the pressure on the primary producers to a point where this pressure became unendurable. Added to this pressure was the misery resulting from droughts and famines that visited the villages at regular intervals. All these developments ultimately provoked peasant protests in various forms.

In many other parts of the Mughal empire, peasant protests were organized and led by dominant zamindars who belonged to the same caste or sub-caste as the rebellious peasants. The Jat rebellions in the region seemed to conform to this pattern. However, the theory of zamindar-led peasant revolts[1] does not apply in the majority of cases of agrarian upheavals in the region. More often than not, the Meo peasants were at the receiving end of the revolts of the Rajput *bhomias* and Jats. The defiant Rajput *bhomias* and Jat zamindars imposed many new cesses on the peasants who did not belong to their castes. They indulged in plunder and pillage and forced the peasants to leave their villages or seek the intervention of the Amber Raja or the Mughal authorities. As the Meo zamindars were replaced by the Rajput *bhomias* or Jats, the Meo peasantry became an easy prey to the marauding retainers of the new zamindars. The Meo zamindars, now reduced to an insignificant position, could not mobilize sufficient resources to organize the peasants of their caste against the high-handedness of the Rajput and Jat zamindars and various other local authorities.

Growing conflict within the various sections of the ruling class, military campaigns of the Rajput *bhomias*, the Jats, the Amber Raja, and the Mughal forces, and finally the extortion of an unprotected peasantry already afflicted by recurrent droughts and famines presented symptoms of deep social malaise and economic decline. The cumulative effects of excessive revenue demand, illegal exactions, growing anarchy, pillage, and crop failures were agricultural devastation and depopulation. The downward trend in the agrarian economy is clear from changes in the pattern of production. First, there was a decline in the total cropped area under both the *kharif* and the *rabi* crops. The area under cultivation of such major cash crops as cotton, sugarcane, and indigo and superior *rabi* food crops also declined. The decline in the overall production, including that of superior crops, is also indicated by a decline in the volume of *mal*

[1] Irfan Habib, 'The Form of Class Struggles during the Mughal Period', in *Essays in Indian History: Towards a Marxist Perception* (London: Anthem Press, 2002), 233–58.

(revenue). The middle and poor peasants who mainly produced food crops for self-consumption were affected more adversely than the rich peasants who commanded sufficient resources to produce lucrative cash crops. For the former, it became difficult to maintain the cycle of production in the face of growing oppression at the hands of the ruling class and the devastations caused by the natural calamities. The cumulative effect of these factors was not confined to one agricultural season but could invariably spill into the next season as well, especially when credit provided by the state or the moneylenders was either non-existent or meagre. The decline in the cultivation of cash crops, too, soon began to adversely affect the income of the richer section of the cultivators.

While the region was characterized by semi-aridity of soil, low crop yields, and recurrent droughts and crop failures, growing oppression by the state/*jagirdar*s, the Rajput *bhomia*s, and the Jats ultimately led to the exhaustion of the peasantry. The prevalent conditions provoked, from sheer desperation, mass peasant migration. Destitution of peasantry and depopulation of villages drained the system of its essential life-blood and provoked a crisis in the agrarian economy which had a bearing on all sections of the rural society.

This crisis reinforced the source of rural unrest, that is, the turbulent interplay of multiple overlapping claims over the surplus produce of the peasantry. The imperial *mansabdar*s, who were assigned *jagir*s in the region, were unable to collect land revenue from the peasants in these conditions and began to farm out their *jagir*s under the *ijara* system to various powerful bidders, notably the Amber chiefs and the Jat zamindars. The *ijara* system led to further rack-renting of the peasants. The *bhomia*s, especially the Naruka Rajputs, became more and more assertive and consolidated their gains at the expense of the Meos, the Mughal state, and the Amber Raja. The worst sufferers were the peasants, most of whom became destitutes and migrated to other areas. Many of the migrating peasants who had earlier enjoyed permanent land tenure rights (*palti*s) were now reduced to the position of wandering peasants (*pahi*s).

Towards the end of the period under study, the political scenario in the Mewat region had considerably changed. While the Meos continued to remain oppressed at the hands of the Rajputs and Jats, the relations between the Amber Raja, the Naruka *bhomia*s, and the Jats acquired a degree of stability. This was mainly due to the appointment of the Amber Raja as the *subedar* of the Agra in 1722 and his victory over the Jats. The latter accepted his overlordship. On the other hand, the Raja accepted the consolidation of the power of Naruka *bhomias* as a fait accompli and recognized their *bhom* rights in exchange of their acceptance of his overlordship. The disintegration of the Mughal empire placed the Raja in an increasingly advantageous position in the region.

Further political changes occurred in the region during the course of the 18th century in the wake of the expansion of the Kachhwaha state of Amber (later designated as Jaipur) and the emergence of the Jat state of Bharatpur. While many *parganas* of Tijara *sarkar* in Mewat became part of the Jat state, Alwar *sarkar* formed the stronghold of the powerful Naruka *bhomias*. Many *parganas* of the region were also taken over by the Amber Raja. In the wake of the changing political scenario in the 18th century, the Mughal authority slowly eroded in Mewat. Nevertheless, despite the steady erosion of the Mughal administrative authority, the de facto independent Jat and Naruka states demonstrated remarkable tenacity in retaining the imperial revenue and administrative structure. The Jat and the Naruka chiefs did not attempt to modify the existing administrative framework. This fact is clearly borne out by the revenue records pertaining to the second half of the 18th century.

The only notable change was the waning control of the Mughals which ultimately led to the growing dependence of the Rajput chief on clan solidarity. This development had a definite impact on the working of the zamindari and *jagirdari* institutions in the region. Growing conflict between emerging powers of Amber and Bharatpur on the one hand and the declining fortunes of the Mughals on the other encouraged all of them to stake claim to revenue from the peasantry. The oppression of peasantry resulting from conflicting claims staked by different sections of the ruling class, that is, the Amber Raja and the Jats, over the surplus produce, as also the misery caused by the incidence of droughts and famines in the villages of Mewat at regular intervals, ultimately provoked peasant protests in various forms in Mewat. The whole notion of '*pal* polity', thus, seems untenable for this region during this time. Assertions of autonomy and self-sufficiency appear to be a fiction, as one witnesses enhanced contestations among the appropriators of surplus who were often outsiders, and in the process local peasantry gradually lost its say.

APPENDIX

'HASAN KHAN KI KATHA'

'HASAN KHAN KI KATHA' is a historical ballad composed by Narsingh Meo. This work was found transcribed in *gutka* no. 213, kept in the Digambar Jain temple of Neminath Swami in Tonk district, Rajasthan. The year of composition is Posh Vadi 14, VS 1639 or 1582 CE. Its untranslated original version was published in Devanagari script by Mahavir Prasad Sharma in October–December issue of *Shodh Patrika* (Sahitya Sansthan, Rajasthan Vidyapith, Udaipur) in 1970. The work is in verse and has a mix of words from old Mewati dialect and Persian. From a historical perspective, it is an important source, since it conveys a bard's folk perception about the historic Battles of Panipat and Khanwa; their key players, namely Ibrahim Lodi, Rana Sanga, and Hasan Khan Mewati; and the nature of state and ruling class in medieval India. Instead of offering a line-by-line translation of the text, I have transilterated the original in Roman script and summarized the content, focusing on the historic substance of the work.

Atha Hasan Khān kī kathā prārabhyate

Nārāyaṇ syo vīnatī karau | hāth jori mani akhir dharau |
auvali surau eka khudāi | paigambar ke lāgau pāi ||1||
Baṛā pīr khwāje Ajmeri | jin Turkāṇā kī sā pheri |

seh goh khāte bukhār | khwājai baiṭhā mān kuphār ||2||
Sauro śārad mahā māi | bhūlyo akhiru dehi samjhāi |
vināig ākhiru dai mohi | gahau kān sir nāū tohi ||3||
Kathā kahat mat lāvahi khoḍi | akhiru dehi jam karyo joḍi |
Nagar kajhautā uttim thān | narsigu meu kathai tah jñān ||4||
Tau baikuṇṭhah vāsau lahau | jaiso vīti taisai kahau |
dhur Vaisākh vapāsī aḍe | Ivrāhimu aru Vāvaru laḍai ||5||
Hūn to kahu hūwā sanmān | dekhau kisau kathahigau jñān |
lok mahājan baiṭhe āi | narsighu bhaṇai laḍai kyau rāi ||6||
Rāj rāj nitarāhe hue | bhai kāraṇi kau raukhyau gae |
bhairu mihālū byāhī joi | auḍī paḍai aur kī hoi ||7||
Etar dūnau dījahi hāri | saval hoi so lesai māri |
jasarath rahai saṃvāī rauki | vaharu jalā so bhai mahi ṭhoki ||8||
Rāvaṇ hau Laṅkā kau rāu | aurahi deṇ na detī pāu |
chāri chaukaḍī mo varu diyo | mai hī mulaku savāyo liyo ||9||
Garav kiye Sītā le gayo | śrī Rām kopantar bhayo |
bandar khiḍe aṭhārah koḍi | daśagir māre daśagir toḍi ||10||
Laṅkā Rāmu le gayo māri | kañchan phaili gae saṃsāri |
paradukh bhañjan rāi ajītu | rājā vaḍau Vikramjītu ||11||
Paradukh bhānai yāko karai | tākau āku dunī mahi phirai |
kite kite hue bhauvāl | bhai upari jhāḍe karavāl ||12||
Bhairumihālū vyāhī joi | maratī verā sāthi na soi |
takhati vaiṭhi Ibrahamu rajyo | bhai kahu Vāvaru kāvil sajyo ||13||
Deś nāś kī chintā nāhi | pāse khelai harman māhi |
pāse khelai rā (ḍā) lai sār | Hindu deś liyo sab māri ||14||
Tāi ṭhāi ke thāne phire | Hindū āi chau (pau) lī utare |
makanu vaḍhau thau khāke rāji | sāgā āgai chālau bhāji ||15||
Iharu vāt kāvil mahi gaī | tavahī tahi alavāī bhaī |
Jambū deś paḍyo tav soru | Mugalan māri liyau Lāhauru ||16||
Māri kūḍhi (ṭi) vāhuḍi ghar ga (yau) e | māḍhi diṭhu kari dāu diyau |
madhi desu Lodī kau rāju | mati hīṇau kachhu nāhī sāju ||17||
Tākai koi karāvag nāhi | ghar phūṭe te ukhyo jāhi |
jasan akhāḍe upari chāu | makanu kahai do dījahi pāu ||18||

Navā rāju navā taṇāu | ā (la) damu lei koṭ mahi chiṇāi |
jav tav to syo dūjī karai | vaisī Gwaliyar dāvo diyo ||19||
Māryo ā (la) damu kiyo kuphāru | vākai sāthī satrah hajār |
pakaṛilyā bahu khān Jalāl | kāḍho āṅki up upāḍau khāl ||20||
Māke jāe māre vīr | gardan vahutap jaisah tīr |
vaiṭhau rahai chhatra kai pāsi | bhau (dā) vākhā māriyo visāsi ||21||
Mantru apar chhanakīyo rāti | Saudokhān māryo parbhāt |
toḍī vāh udhā (dhā) ṛī pīṭhi | tuhare gale rāj kī ūṭhi ||22||
Gayau ubhārau bhājīvāu | dāvādaru na dījo dāu |
tav Vāvaru kāvil tahi chaḍhyo . . . . . ||23||
Paigambar dīyo phurmān | pakaḍi khāḍau gahī kamān |
dīnī jimī mulak saṃsār | tokahu koī nāhi juhyāru ||24||
pu ṣu rāsān kāvil tahi chaḍhyo | tav Vāvaru ghāṭī nīkalyo |
. . . . ||25||
Koī Rāmu ko japai khudāi | tav kāphar melechurī vulāī |
vaḍḍemuu peṭ mānthaṇī | tin dekhai āvai kāpaṇī ||26||
Syālkoṭ mārau Lāhauru | sunai uḍe savāyo mo (so) ru |
hāki laḍan Daulati Khā gayo | kaṭaku sametī nadī mahi vaho ||27||
Insau laṛai hoi garakāvu | phiri māryo meharyo Kusāv |
tav umre hue savai makhmūl | Vavar pātisāh kī paṛī kabūl ||28||
Ko vast (tu) ne leī kāledām | jar lūṭe sīhanand samān |
laskar āe vahut visār | Hāsī lūṭī aur Hisār ||29||
Kāphir āe asīte mol | Pāṇīpath jo (jā) pahuche lol |
laskar ṭikyo Dillī syo āi | karahu phirādi Āgrai jāi ||30||
Tūtau rahau mahal mahi vaisi | kāphar phaile tere des |
tavahi tamaki uṭhau bhauvālo | tīni lākh ghoḍe karachhāl ||31||
Suṇat phirād vāragahadīya | des des kī sākhatī kīya |
pūkh paṇḍvādes vihār | laśkar utari āyo pār ||32||
Desu baṅgālā baḍā mukām | āvahu ros huvā sultānu |
pachhim des khiḍī Gujarāt | khiḍiyā vāgaḍu aru Mewāt ||33||
La (śa) tvākar juḍikari āe ṭhāṭ | phauj juḍī Mathurā kai ghāṭ |
raī uṛi chhāe asmān | sāhi alam kahu bhae salām ||34||
pāṅsai ko hoi vākuḍi ghar nāi | āṭh sahas kau pāvai ṭhāi |

ruv-uḍe uvare pāvahi pān | sākhat karahu kahai sulitān ||35||
khāhu paragane rākhahu desu | ivakai mārhu dher dares |
kūch huvo ḍere upaḍe | laśkar āi dilīsihu aḍe ||36||
Dilī pīr kā vaḍā mukām | tinakī sev karahi sulitān |
ālādaitu ulūkhān | vaibhī mālu deti Khurāsān ||37||
Suṇi Ivrāimu khwāje kahe | līk ā (gi) Dilī iv kyau rahai |
deh mālu jyo vai ghar jāhu | tū phiri vaiṭhi Dilī hī māhī ||38||
Hūn rāī etī leṇe na deu | inhahi māri kāvil jyā (yo) leu |
tavahūn na (la) ī dahūdhān ḍhāl | un vich lāgī phir narasāl ||39||
Kahai riśāl ju men kahun laḍo | pāuhu rabhist mahi paṛau |
ausar dīno hūr vulāī | jasan akhāḍai rachyo khudāī ||40||
Juḍahi suhar palah Hisār | kautigu jovai sirjaṇahār |
chāḍhi Ivrāhimu āyo chūri | Vāvar phāṭik kīyo dūri ||41||
Kai mainrī kai tairī āju | alahudei so kari hai rāju |
phāṭik kholi paḍe tavadāki | huī dhośatah ādhīrāti ||42||
Taḍke gole bhaḍkī nāli | hāthī gaye avārī rā (ḍā) li |
Hidustānī laśkar muḍau | to pīchhe tahi vāvak chaḍau ||43||
Vāvai dāḍhī jhāḍai hāth | huye uvare vārah vār |
vahatai kīnī malik nawāj | chhāḍi khasam uḍi chali bhāji ||44||
sahankamahi je khāte khān | ubhe chhoḍi gaye sulitān |
saidu kahai thāmotahi koṇ | vahu āṭe mahi huvau lauṇu ||45||
pahar doi Ivrāhimu laḍau | āyo nāhī raṇmahi paḍau |
nālikarī sab chhāḍau desu | lūṭaṇ lāge rabhist dares ||46||
Khaṛag teg vādhate kākh | ujah māgate do do lāl |
śvāmi kāj doi kari gaye | choṭ paḍat tav lolī bhaye ||47||
Karate sañjo ghar ke chāri | hamahi maṇsanū dekhahi nāri |
galiyāre mahi bhūle phirāhi | hāki diye chhoḍe tahi girāi ||48||
Pāṇīpath kai ḍerai aḍe | ghoḍe marad garaṭ hoi paḍe |
etī samudar jīyā jauṇi | āī kaṭak chhatīsau pauṇi ||49||
Laskar log karahi vyāpār | kakhe antu na jāṇahi sār |
laskar āe vaṇij vakāl | māre khūndi huye paimālu ||50||
Laskar bhūl āpu bhī gaye | je uvare te ghar tahi liye |
tinakau khasam paṛau bhovāl | mālī kolī kīrak hār ||51||

Darajī lūṭe auru sunār | . . . . |
Turak tavolī bakar kasāb | antravedhamahi bhae garakāv ||52||
Ik māre ik ghāil bhae | ik vādhi gargaḍī ghar kahu gae |
gurujan dekhi khare kadarāhi | lolī hohi laṭki paḍi jāhi ||53||
utarau saidu Vavar kai kāji | ḍarapī paṭṭaṇ chāle bhāji |
kahar nām tav likhyo khudāi | antravedhamahi vīdhe āi ||54||
nāgī teg karīh jharkār | Hajarat tahi āe asavār |
chhūṭahi chaṇā havāī āgi | jīvate rahahi mue si (ru) u lāgi ||55||
ghusi ghusi rahahi silah savu rāli | upari chhoḍahi muradauṭāli |
apnau lohī a ṅga lagāi | khaivahi pavan rahahi muhavāi ||56||
kāmiṇ jaise sej khilāi | hīyau de muradesyo milā (i) ha |
ik vādhe sir bhāre die | je uvare te Jamunā lie ||57||
Utare Mugal Jamunā peli | Dilī daravāje dīe kholi |
gaḍamahi hoi na dhīrī dharai | Hindū hoi tau sākau karai ||58||
kābil tahi āe viḍnūp | tinke kān jisehahi sūp |
ākhi mīchurī nāk chhīparī | bandarmuhī kāvil vurī ||59||
Dilī mi simahi dīe meli | vādhi kavar jisīhahi veli |
Juvāhahi vai mīchahi ānkh | sundari marīh jībh dai dānt ||60||
Apachhar aṅgi vahat kaulādhi | laī hūr hajarat kī veli |
daī vigāḍī pahilī joṭ | huī valadh bhaise kī joṭ ||61||
bhogī desu logu bhovāl | tinakau sāthī Ivrāhim mugvālu |
liyo Āgrau bhājī āu | Lodī paḍī Hasan Khā lākh ||62||
vahu bhai kāriṇ Mugalan syo laḍe | bhāgi Āgrau Alvar chaḍe |
Alvar Meu Hasan Khān | Dilī kau sahnā pardhān ||63||
Dilī Mev kī vāndhī līk | ṭakā lākh ghoḍe chālīś |
jite Dilī ho gae rāj | Mevātī kī rākhī ān ||64||
Khān kā lūṇ halālu na karai | bhisti chhoṛi dojig mahi pa (ḍai) ḍau |
pūt Alāval Khān ko jaṇyo | sūrvīr khatrī ati vaṇau ||65||
kie kaulu nivāhai sarai | kyon navalu jīvai Ivrāhamu marai |
iv tharpau Rāmādūṇ taṇau | kāḍhau vairu Ivrāhimu taṇau ||66||
śvāmi kāji bhiri bhaethu (bhārathu) karau | Mugal māri ghāṭī had dharau |
kīyau mantra Alvar āi | mantrī līe mahal vulāī ||67||
mālik Karamchandu sāntal saidu | Ser Khān Nāgaurī sedu |

dekhau mantru karahu kiś bhānti | karahu sākhatī vāndh kuñj(ñjā) ti ||68||
kahai na kīv sunahu suvihān | ham pahle chhuḍāv (hi) ḍi Nāhar Khān |
aisi vat kahai mat koī | khāṇḍe dāni vilumb na hoī ||69||
kai melidei mere man kī kāṇi | kai lyāu khāṇḍe kai pāṇi |
tum kāṅgad likhi bhejahu Chītauḍ | mudhanā haraṣā kīnā hī dauḍ ||70||
sāgā tāi joḍī sār | līyo desu daresan māri |
ham tum vīchi isī kyo hoi | madhi des kī mukdam hoi ||71||
suṇi sāgā Hasan Khān kahai | mo āgai ko Bāvaru rahai |
phero Dilī duhāī āi | mohi pūchhi Kāvil ka (bu) phu jāī ||72||
Hindu kahai garav ke vol | vākahu āe hākim gol |
vihu Khurīsān kau Vāvaru vidu | tai jāṇau Khalachī Mahmudu ||73||
dou utari chale gaḍh chhoḍi | . . . . . |
gaḍh vai hoi kari vāhuḍi laṛai | tākī matī narā (yu) suṇ haṛau ||74||
e dou bhovāl mile man jog | kiyo mantru mile man thog |
kī laśkarī vāndhī ṭhāṇ | duhūn ṭoḍai kiyo milāṇu ||75||
Hindū utare karat kilol | Khān kahu bhejai rāihi gol |
āihi gol Alvar utarau | dekhi Khān man rañjyo kharo ||76||
huvau gah gahau khākai ritu | jāṇ nausah chale janet (tu) |
karai navalu (su) laśkar kī dauḍu | Mevātī siru vādhyo mauḍu ||77||
Alvar khiḍī amīto kheḍ | karai Meu Mugalan syo chheḍ |
unke āt savāhī hāth | rājai khān varaḍ ko chhātu ||78||
ajahū Vāvaru hue rai nāhi | sevā karahu paragane khāhu |
Dilī lok kyon khāte Mev | avahi ek tum do kari lehu ||79||
sīv Mev kī Mathurā pār | Vāvaru meli na sakaī kār |
khet chaḍhai naru dei na jāṇu | mānīh Mugal Mev kī kāṇi ||80||
isā Mukdam huvā na hoi | tākī khaichai na ḍhāṅkarī koī |
Nāharṣā kahu pān magāi | kahī vāt jāmu vaisāi ||81||
Vāvaru karm isau hai kiyo | desu dīnau hāthu sir diyo |
Khurāsān kau Vāvaru dhaṇī | deṇ kahī potī āpaṇī ||82||
syo pargane payānau lehi | sīkh vāp kahu āpaṇu dehi |
melyo Nāhar Khān navī (vā) ja | chhatra tanau vaisārau rāj ||83||
rahai nāhi kyo muhya syo āi | us kahu lyogān Alvari jāī |
mānai Vāvaru virājan vaḍai | tyaun tyaun Khān apūṭhau paḍai ||84||

Mugal valavai volī āi | ukhali (Alāvali) Khān khuṭ mat khāī |
aisī vāt kahai mat pheri | laṛai Khān Lodī kai vair ||85||
Vāvaru itnī kiś kahu karai | Khān sūt it aurai dharai |
Duhilaut sīṅgal kī nāli | Khān sakerī vārah pāl ||86||
Lev (mu) drā vaiṭhau daravār | dhaulī pīlī mahur pasāri |
khās malikae lie vulāi | lāgyau ghoḍe deṇ kuvā (dā) i ||87||
kholi kharachu auh kiyo jihānu | a (jī) vatājī vāraṇ lāgyo Khān |
chāri hajār gaṇat ke gaṇe | jīṇ lagg mahā sulevaṇe ||88||
chakhādār duvāge vāndhi | pilachi pahuchahi tinakai kādhi |
jaṇ kāgad ke kari rākhe kān | chautā khelehi chaugān ||89||
vādhe jāte inasyon laḍe | hāṅki hāṅki hāthīn syon laḍe |
kohyu kin sakai karaṛau kari hiyo | pahle ek ḍhakūkau diyau ||90||
kautal pheri maggae pān | choṭā paḍ dekhie nidān |
charai kaṭaku huvo asavār | Khān vāṭaṇ lāgyau hathiyār ||91||
vaḍai damāmai ḍākau huvo | hāthi khaḍagu āpaṇu liyo |
ulagaṇe ubhe sav vār | kholi kivāḍ dehu taravār ||92||
jāti chagālau āchhī julī | hyalakahi jyo āvari vījulī |
magg silah khaḍag nauhāṇ | unkahu dījahi vāṭikā māṇ ||93||
jaisī lāgat taisā dehu | tīr dāya galai kī lehu |
garucho chāhiv jahar gambhīru | bhari bhari tarakas vārai tīru ||94||
vagatar ṭopā rāg sameti | duvakai laṛau Vavar syo kheti |
sāhiv chaḍhau rahis kyau kauṇ | duv khāḍai māgaṇ lāgau sauṇ ||95||
dīnau tamaki pāvaḍai pāu | liyo nāhi Mahamad nāu |
kīyo garvu manī vahu dharī | Mahamad sumirau na kalmā bharī ||96||
kahai joisī jī mahagyān | khā kahu kāl des kahu jyānu |
vāī vājū bhadrā khaḍī | hāthi khaparu paināvai chhurī ||97||
jūs karaṇ Vāvar sihujāi | pīyo chāhahi ragatu aghāi |
dharatau pāg tau dhaṛī | huvo vinā sumatī savy haṛī ||98||
chhatīsyo bhūlyo bhovāl | Khān kahu paḍau aras kau jāl |
naujovanā madodarī mūdh | kāmakandalā phūl sugandh ||99||
Laṅkā jāṇahār jav huī | tav daśgir Sītā haḍilai |
Itī tiskaro Dilī kahu Khān | vā kahu varajai jagat jihān ||100||

Varajyo kahyo na suṇaī navalu | jāṇahār āi pūjyo kavalu |
jākau kutavā Alavīr paḍai | tā upari khā auru na chaḍai ||101||
varajau the khāje iv muḍai | ihu sahatīru so gagdan paḍai |
Khān varai jīsmah dosu | uchai gāv karai man rosu ||102||
Said Chhajosih kahau vulāi | tū gaḍh rākhahi nāl chaḍhāi |
man mah khān gyān jai gharai | duhun laḍai tai eku tau paḍai ||103||
itnī kahi Khān chālo uṭhi | pairi chale tandurai ṭūṭi |
vovatai ādi tu jav jav khilau | yau sauṇāhai Nāhar Khān milau ||104||
utare sauṇāhe kai vāgi | bāp pūt bheṭe gal lāgi|
kahahi pūt tū unkī vāt | leṇ kahahi merī Mevāt ||105||

Nāhar Khān uvāch—

Muhya kahu desu vayānau diyau | to kahu ghoḍau musghar kiyau |
līk hamārī rākhai nāhi | Khān jī un upari gat jāhi ||106||
Nāhar Khān kau rahai na mān | ḍartā hai Lauḍī nādān |
pātisāhi kī paḍī kavūl | Alvarī chhoḍ vasāu kūl ||107||
hāthī tahān chale kilkāri | phauj Khān kī vīs hajār |
koī chhāh ko utaro dhūp | pahalau ḍerau huvo dhasūk ||108||
huvao kusauṇ Khān khavari na paḍī | Khān utarau rītī Vāvaḍī |
pahar rāti dūjai din chaḍau | dīnī tara-u chhoḍai jāi paḍau ||109||
laskar āe ṭūṭi Khandhār | chahun vojya (u) sare vājār |
duhu voḍ melai kī māl | milahi umāhe dui bhovāl ||110||
Sāṅgā sadā lobh kī khoḍi | māge jīvatājī muh phoḍi |
sirī gardanī upari chaur | ān kiye jīvatājī do auru ||111||
bhalī suagati mele kahu chale | khusī Khān Rāṇā sihu mile |
Hindū Turkan kīya pichhāṇi | dargah vaiṭhi rāle paravāṇ ||112||
Likhi likhi kāgad karte vād | mulaki milāi lah pah hāthi |
sīsyodisā aru govalvāl | karahi mantra dūnau bhovālu ||113||
kai hārahi Alvar Chītauḍ | kai mārahi kāvil jyon dauḍ |
rāṇī mīṇī ke do juḍe | bhai kāraṇ dūnau uḍi chaḍe ||114||
itar Sāgā ut khatrī navalu | khudāi vīchi de kiyo kavalu |
upaṭhe laśkar kiyo uphāṇ | kiyo khāṇu vai ek milāṇ ||115||

phān mūl kau karte bhog | ṣaṭnāvalī vigūtau logu |
vāmbhaṇ māre kiya kusākh | sirjyo Rāṇā vuṛau pāp ||116||
rahai nāhi āpaṇau kaul | Sāgā dīe bhambhaḍ meli |
isī mat kar hit pahi khyo jāhi | lūṭahi kaṭak āpaṇe māhi ||117||
agaḍī lūṭahi ḍere mahi paisi | suṇī Hasan Khān huvo ros |
sochī ghaṇī vār daśvīs | māri mūḍ toḍe chālīś ||118||
Hindū kai mani kucharak paḍī | pheri chhāni tini audhe dharī |
Khatrī khaḍag ughāḍai laḍai | vahasu-Rāṇā nark mahi paḍai ||119||
laī akoḍ Vāvar pahi bhāgi | dojig paṛai lagāī dāgi |
Turak Musarmā hohu sahīd | duhūn bhājī jāu jaūd ||120||
phiṭu phiṭu karai vasīḍhuhi gol | Hindū bhaijai dūjī pol |
Hindū sāthi sāthi jāti hī jāti | khiḍi āī Rāṇā kai sāth ||121||
Kulīn māhi vaḍe Chauhāṇ | ṭhāne vādhi chaḍhe Nauhāṇ |
chāvahi pān phirahi vājār | dhaule gae janma savuhāri ||122||
Kachhvāhai sav āe kāchh | vīdhe āi . . . . . |
vānhī khaim kamar vadhu dehi | ne . . . gal kī lehi ||123||
unkī kulah dekhi kandarāhi | sūn sūn karahi Mugal mili khāhi |
karahi chyant auru kul sudh | ropyo satu pīvate dūdh ||124||
teu bhāge pākhar kāṭi | sūvar huve kheḍai rākhi |
Solaṅkhī āe savu chūri | kapaḍ koṭ kīe bharipūrī ||125||
Rāṇā sau hau karahu salām | ek mūṭh deh saṅgrām |
vaḍ gūjar kai khāṇḍau sadā | nyālī kānī utarau judā ||126||
ghaṇau karī varāduh leḍ | kahā karahi Rāṇā vahi kheḍi |
dīno pān vulāi pavār | chaḍhahu rāghalatahi hohu asavār ||127||

In the beginning of his *katha* (story), the bard Narsingh Meo pays his obeisance to the Hindu deity Narayan and Prophet Muhammad: he prays to the former with folded hands and bows at the latter's feet. He says that their divinity (*khudai*) is the same. In other words, although known by various names, God is one. He further says that the greatest saint (*pir*) of the Turks is the Khwaja Sahib (Muinuddin Chishti) of Ajmer. His tomb is visited by people from far, and he knows the distress of all who come to his tomb and wishes well for them. The bard then introduces himself as the resident of Kajhauta village in *pargana* Mojpur of Alwar *sarkar*, that is, in the region of

Mewat. He claims that the events that he is going to narrate in his *katha* are based on folk perception; therefore, he is applying his wisdom and best thoughts to this exercise.

A key event of this account is the battle that took place in Panipat between Ibrahim Lodi and Babur in the month of Vaishakh, VS 1583. Narsingh Meo prefaces his narration of the historic event and the characters associated with it with a discussion of his conception of rulership. He says that there have been different rulers in different ages, but we do not know about all of them. Rather, we know and remember only a few who have helped their subjects in times of distress and have been just rulers. The greatest of all is Vikramaditya who is known for his benevolence and justice. On the other hand, Ravana, king of of Lanka, is reviled for his misdeeds and his propensity to cause pain to others. With his misdemeanor and undue interference in others' affairs, he made many enemies. Out of sheer hubris and foolishness, he abducted Sita and did not even heed his wife Mandodari's good counsel. He thus incurred the enmity of Rama (Sita's husband). As a result, Rama's army (of monkeys) wrecked havoc on his prosperous city of Lanka. The consequences of his misdeeds destroyed his wealth and well-being.

Returning to the chain of events in his narrative, the bard says that Ibrahim Lodi, who occupied the throne of Delhi, was busy playing dice in his palace all the time, while Babur, marching from Kabul, had attacked Hindustan. On the other hand, Rana Sanga had also instigated Babur to launch this attack, and the people of Kabul were aware of this. But Ibrahim Lodi was not worried about these developments at all. Babur, having started from Kabul and having captured Lahore, Multan, Hansi, and Hissar on the way, was marching stridently. Only some powerful ruler could stop Babur's victorious march. But it seems that the entire Jambu *desh* (India) was slumbering. Ibrahim Lodi had made many enemies with his conduct. In the heat of youth, he had his opponents killed or buried alive in the walls of his fort. In this way he had made many enemies in his 'home'. As if seeking to arouse the ruler from his apathy and warn him of the impending danger, the bard makes a passionate plea to Ibrahim:

> O Sultan, come out of your palace and confront Babur, (for) he has attacked your country. You have three lakh horsemen at your command. The *rais* (chieftains) of Bihar, Bengal and Gujarat are with you. Besides, Mewat and

> Bangad[1] are with you. Fight your enemies! Your army has grown so formidable that the dust raised by the marching horses and elephants clouds the sky.

Finally, Ibrahim woke up to the situation. The bard recounts that Ibrahim's army halted at Delhi, home to the tombs of 'great' Sufi saints (*bade pir*), namely Nizamuddin Auliya and Nasiruddin Chirag. He bowed before them and declared to his generals that they would not allow Babur to march towards Delhi, would defeat him, and force him to retreat to Kabul. Filled with rage, Ibrahim then proceeded to confront Babur. At midnight Ibrahim's army reached Panipat. In the morning, Babur's artillery started firing cannonballs at Ibrahim's army. Elephantry and cavalry of both armies clashed. Soon, however, the Indian army panicked at facing Babur's army and started fleeing from the battlefield. Even many of the *sardar*s (Afghan nobles), who had sworn their loyalty to Ibrahim, their sultan, deserted him. Ibrahim fought for two hours and finally fell, never to return. Thereafter, his army was routed. The enemies fell upon his army and went on a pillaging and killing spree. Ibrahim Lodi's army, as vast as an ocean, was being mercilessly butchered. Dead bodies of soldiers and horses piled up on the field of Panipat. While local traders (*bania*s and *baqqal*s) profited from trading with the army, local artisans like florists (*mali*s), tailors (*darji*s), skinners (*koli*s), palanquin-bearers (*kori*s), goldsmiths (*sunar*s), *turak*s, stablemen (*taboli*s), and butchers (*bakar-kasai*s)—all were ruined. Both Hasan Khan's and Ibrahim Lodi's armies fell helplessly before the mighty Mughal army. While many died in the battle, the rest fled to Agra.

The Lodi dynasty was virtually extinguished except the dim-witted Muhammad Lodi (Ibrahim's son), who was still alive. Now the task of retrieving the lost honour of the dynasty rested on Hasan Khan, the king of Alwar. In other words, he was the protector of the throne of the Lodis. All the sultans of Delhi had recognized the position of Hasan Khan. An able son of Alawal Khan Mewati, Hasan Khan Mewati knew well to discharge his responsibility (towards the Lodis). After Ibrahim

[1] Bangad literally means an arid, less fertile area. Though its connotation varies from region to region, it generally refers to an area which is considered economically and culturally inferior. Here, specifically, it refers to southern Haryana and parts of western Rajasthan (Shekhawati).

Lodi's defeat in the Battle of Panipat, Hasan Khan made his fullest efforts to bring back the Lodis to power. He called an assembly of his ministers and aides. Among those invited were the chiefs (*chaudharis*) of 12 Meo clans (*pals*). In this assembly, he devised a strategy to fight Babur with Karamchand Khatri (the commander-in-chief of Hasan Khan's army) and other generals, such as Santal, Saiyyad Chaju Khan, and Sher Khan Nagori. All those attending the assembly reached a consensus: first, Hasan Khan's son Nahar Khan, who had been taken prisoner by Babur in the Battle of Panipat, would have to be freed from Babur's captivity. Hasan Khan told his associates not to make any further delay in preparing for a war with Babur. Hasan Khan then sent Harna and Sukha Khan with a message to Rana Sanga. In the message, Hasan Khan sought an alliance with Rana Sanga and promised him the middle country that was part of Ibrahim Lodi's empire in the event of their victory over Babur. In response, the Rana assured Hasan Khan that he would defeat Babur and send him back to Kabul. He further stated that he would march to Khanwa with a big army to join him in the impending battle. The poet says that both the rulers assured each other with proud words. This was how a military alliance against Babur was forged between the two.

Both Hasan Khan and Rana Sanga set off for Khanwa with their respective armies. Brimming with great gusto, both armies assembled near Todabhim from where they marched towards Khanwa. Bent upon achieving his object, Hasan Khan was preparing, in the poet's words, like a groom decking up for his wedding procession. To take on Babur, he had put together a huge army with great warriors. Fighting Hasan Khan's army was like stirring up a hornet's nest for Babur, for the Meos were fiercely brave and unafraid of death in battle. Heedless of their own safety, they inflicted heavy damage on the enemies. That is why even Babur was hesitant to fight the Meos and tried to dissuade Hasan Khan from taking part in the battle and even tried to tempt his son Nahar Khan by offering him 100 *parganas* in and around Bayana and his own granddaughter in marriage. However, in the poet's words, Hasan Khan's mind worked in the opposite direction; he was bent on destroying his kingdom.

When Nahar Khan, having escaped from Babur's captivity, told his father about the inducement offered and the honour accorded to him by Babur, Hasan Khan became livid with rage. He looked at his son with anger and rebuked him, saying, 'Your speech reeks of (subservience to) the Mughals. I, the able son of Alawal Khan, live on my honour, not on anyone's pity. I have built the kingdom of Mewat with my great prowess. Do not ever speak such words or bring such thoughts to your mind. Such words lower my head in shame. Compromise with Babur is unthinkable.' According to the poet, Hasan Khan had no concrete reason to fight with Babur except that he wanted to bring back the Lodis to power. In other words, he was taking others' hostilities upon himself; he was set to ruin his own house (for the sake of putting others' house in order). On the one hand, Babur, the ruler of Delhi and Khurasan, had not offered to any other Indian ruler the honour and inducements that he offered to Hasan Khan. On the other hand, the latter landed with his cavalry and elephantry on the battlefield of Khanwa to fight the Chagatais (Mughals). He had with him the chiefs of 12 Meo clans, of which Duhlot and Singal clans led his army.

On the battlefield, the Meo clan chiefs wore big turbans that covered their ears and kept stroking their yellow-and-black moustaches and beards with pride. They were fully armed with weapons; their chests and arms were covered by a variety of defensive accoutrements. Carrying quivers on their shoulders, some fought with bows and arrows; others fought on elephants and horses; yet others fought while running on foot; and still others fought by striking blows with their fists. There was great commotion in the battlefield. Hasan Khan, astride on a horse and with unsheathed sword in hand, was trying to lift his soldiers' morale. On the other hand, the Chagatais, too, conducted themselves bravely as arrows rained down on them from the right side. Poisoned arrows were striking soldiers dead. Hasan Khan was mortally wounded and died on the battlefield itself. The poet links the outcome of the battle, especially the tragic fate of Hasan Khan, to the handiwork of bad omens. He recounts that on their way to Khanwa, Hasan Khan and his army had camped near a dry stepwell—this augured ill for him. He also compares Hasan Khan with Ravana. Just as the latter had made Rama his enemy without any concrete reason and caused his city to be destroyed by Rama, Hasan Khan, too, had incurred Babur's enmity and caused the destruction of his kingdom. Like Ravana, Hasan Khan, too, was out of his mind in that he ruined his own home for the sake of others. In his last moments, Hasan Khan asked his son to take care of Mewat.

In the last few lines of the ballad, the poet uses the conversation between the dying Hasan Khan and his son to mount a trenchant critique of Rana Sanga's role in the whole affair. In the poet's words, Nahar Khan said to his father:

> When I conveyed Babur's message, you did not honour my word or heed my counsel (for alliance with Babur). Babur had promised to give us the area of Bayana and send me back with full honor, but you fought for the sake of that silly child (Mahmud Lodi). Further, you wanted to fight Babur in alliance with Rana Sanga who is seeped in treachery from head to toe. He always puts others in trouble to serve his own ends. Bad company brings destruction. My twin sons borne of my Meena wife have died in the battle. We have suffered heavy casualties. Rana Sanga has deceived us: he fled from the battlefield and went over to Babur's side, as he had already struck an alliance with him. Rana Sanga has the blood of innocent Brahmins on his hands. How would he who could not get along with his own people be loyal to your cause?

At the end, explaining Rana Sanga's deceit, the poet says that while leading the army from the front he was being defeated at the hands of Babur. When Hasan Khan was informed of his defeat, he got angry and began to realize the folly of making an alliance with the Rana. Then, suddenly, something crossed the Rana's mind and he left the battlefield without telling anyone. In fact, he met Babur secretly. While most of the Hindu (Rajput) rulers like Chauhans, Kachhwahas, Solankis, Pawars, and Badgujars who had joined the battle with their armies died, Rana Sanga chose to blemish his honour with this act of perfidy. On the other hand, Hasan Khan held his ground till death and became a martyr on death.

GLOSSARY

amil	revenue officer at the *pargana* level
amin	revenue officer at the *pargana* level
arsatta	a monthly treasury account of receipts and disbursements under different heads
arzdasht	written petition or memorial
asami	cultivator, revenue payer
asli	original (used for a village)
padshah	emperor
banjar	wasteland
banjara	itinerant tribes transporting and trading in various commodities
baqaya	arrears of revenue
barani	rain-fed land
batai/batai-jinsi/ ghalla-bakshi	crop-sharing
bhara	cess to meet the expenses of transportation of grain
bhent	regular gifts paid by the villages to the officials
bhom	zamindari tenure
bhomi/dastur bhomi	non-customary cess paid to the *bhomia*
bhomia	holder of a *bhom*
bigha	unit of land equal to 2/5 of an acre
bohra	moneylender

chahi	well-irrigated land
chakar	literally, servant; Rajput employee of the Amber Raja
chak-sehna and *ghughri/ghughri-sehna*	cess levied to remunerate watchmen employed to look after the crops assessed under the *batai-jinsi* system
chamar	cobbler
chappar	thatched hut
charai/ghas charai/ hasil ghas charai	grazing tax
charas	leather bucket
chaudhari	hereditary headman of a *pargana*
dahri	flooded land
dak chowki	postal station
Dak Meoras	Meo post carriers
dakhali	dependent village or a newly colonized village
dam	a copper coin
dastur	custom; customary revenue rate; also land revenue rates for different crops
dastur-al-amal	documents containing schedules of land revenue rates or *dasturs* for different crops for the guidance of revenue officials
dastur-chaudharai	customary share of the *chaudhari* in the yield
dehai-ferhashti	descriptive list of villages
dhanuk	weaver
dhenkhli	wooden scoop, a means of irrigation
dhol	cess paid by peasants to the *bhomias*
diwan	chief minister of a state
diwan-dasturi	cess levied on peasants to meet expenses on maintaining the office of *diwan*
dohnimi zabti	a *jihat* cess assessed at the rate of 5 per cent of *mal* under *zabti* system
farah	*jihat* cesses under *jinsi* system
farah-dahaani	a *farah* cess assessed at the rate of 10 *annas* per 100 rupees of *mal* under *jinsi* system
farah-sarina	exactions collected in *sers* and appropriated by officials under the *batai-jinsi* system
faujdar	chief police officer at the *pargana* level

gara tax on cart
garhi fortress constructed usually by zamindars
gharecha or *gharijna* remarriage of an already married woman
gharuhalla *khudkashta* peasants who possessed their own ploughs, bullocks, seeds, and other agricultural implements
gharujot personal holding
ghiwai cess levied in the event of non-payment of *taqavi* forwarded by the state to the needy peasants
gotra clan based on descent from common male ancestor
hali ploughman
hasil aghori cess on the hides of dead animals
hasil chak-chithi tax levied to meet the expenses incurred by the *amil*'s office in its administrative duties
hasil farohi penalties imposed by the *amil* or *faujdar* on offenders
hasil ghanna teli cess paid by oilmen (*telis*) operating oil crushers (*ghanna telis*) in the *qasbas*
hasil gharecha cess on remarriage
hasil ghas cess on grazing
hasil gur ganna cess on operating sugarcane crushers
hasil jhupari house tax
hasil kotwal cess collected from every village to remunerate the *kotwal* (police chief) of the *pargana*
hasil lakri cess on wood taken from the forest
hasil actual realization of revenue; state's share of the produce of land
hundi bill of exchange
ijara farming out of revenue of any given source
ijaradar holder of *ijara* rights on land
iqta grant of revenue of a piece of land
jagir assignment of revenue in lieu of salary
jagirdar holder of a *jagir*
jama revenue payable or assessed revenue
jamabandi total assessment of revenue
jama-i-dah-sala *jama* of 10 years

jamiyat	military contingent
jaribana	cess to meet expenses incurred on the measurement of land
jhupri	house; hut
jihat, sair-jihat, or *siwai-jamabandi*	miscellaneous extra cesses levied over and above *mal*
jihat	taxes levied in order to meet the expenses incurred in assessment and collection of land revenue
jihati-zabti	*jihat* tax levied on *zabti bigha*
jizya	tax on non-Muslims
karkhana	royal factories/workshops/enterprises for producing commodities required by the state
kawayara	a *virar* tax
kayali	*jihat* tax collected to meet expenses on weighing of grains under the *batai-jinsi* system
khalisa	land whose revenue went to the state exchequer
khap	sept of a clan
kharch or *minzalik*	total expenditure in the *parganas*
kharif	autumn harvest
khatoot ahalkaran	written report of a spy to the ruler
khera	settlement
khidmatiyyas	personal bodyguards of the Mughal emperor or palace guards
khorei	Meo settlement
khudkashta	peasants belonging to upper castes, that is, Brahmins, Rajputs, *mahajans*, and other members of the rural aristocracy (*patels*, *patwaris*, *qanungos*, and *chaudharis*). They possessed their own ploughs, bullocks, seeds, and other agricultural implements; and had to pay land revenue to the Mughal state at the rate of 25–33 per cent of their gross produce.
kotri	establishment of a *bhomia*
kotri bhomi ki	cess paid by the peasants to the *bhomia*
lao-charas	rope of a *charas* or leather bucket
lata-kharach	*jihat* tax collected to meet expenses on crop division under the *batai-jinsi* system

lawazima	a *jihat* cess collected to meet the expenses incurred in the assessment and collection of *mal* mainly under *zabti* system
lehari	sugarcane crusher
lohar	blacksmith
magro	hilly terrain
mahajan	moneylender and/or trader
mahal	*pargana*
mal	land revenue
malba	common financial pool of a village
malikana	special allowance assigned to a zamindar
mal-o-jihat	*mal* and *jihat* taxes merged into one head
mansab	military rank conferred on each official by the Mughal state
mansabdar	holder of a *mansab*
masala	ammunition
maund	28 *sers*
mauza	village
Mirasi	a caste involved in composing and reciting bardic compositions and also training cavalry horses
muafiq-jamabandi	revenue realized in accordance with assessment
muchalka	bond
mufsid	rebel; a term applied to peasants and zamindars who defaulted in revenue payment or defied state orders
mufti	tax-free land revenue grant
muqadam	hereditary village-level revenue official
muqaddami	cess belonging to the categories *sair-jihat* and *siwai-jamabandi* levied to meet expenses on remunerating *muqaddams*
muqararajama	total revenue collection in the *parganas*
mutsadi	a clerk/scribe
naib faujdar	deputy *faujdar*
nangal	communal feast organized by a Rajput *bhomia* to celebrate the inauguration of his *garhi*

neel	indigo
nehri	canal-irrigated land
nyota or *hasil nyota*	literally, invitation (for marriage ceremony); cess on royal marriage
pahi/pahikashta	migratory peasants who usually cultivated the arable wastelands or the lands abandoned by the *paltis* in the neighbouring villages. However, they could not become permanent residents of these villages or proprietors of the lands they cultivated.
pal	basic unit of Meo social organization
pal chaudhari	chief of a Meo *pal*
pala-nafar	foot soldier, infantryman
palti or *gaveti*	formed the single largest stratum, as also the majority, of the peasantry, and mostly belonged to the intermediate castes, namely Jats, Meos, Gujjars, Ahirs, Meenas, and Malis. They were inferior in social status to the *khudkashta* peasants and had to pay land revenue at the rate of 40–50 per cent of their gross produce—much higher than that charged from the *khudkashtas*—as well as several other cesses.
pargana	administrative sub-division of a *sarkar* under the Mughals
parwana	state order
patel	village headman
patta	document given to a revenue payer, indicating his obligations
patwari	cess belonging to the categories *sair-jihat* and *siwai-jamabandi*; also, village accountant
peshkash	tribute paid to higher-ups
polachh/polaj	land under continuous cultivation and never left fallow
qabuliyat	acceptance
qanungo	village-level revenue official; cess belonging to the categories *sair-jihat* and *siwai-jamabandi*

qasba	town
qazi	a Muslim judge
rabi	spring harvest
rahakalla	small locally made cannon in Mewat
rahdari	transit duties
raiyat	cultivators in general
raiyati	ordinary peasant, synonymous with *palti*
ramchangi	small locally made gun or musket
riyayati	*khudkashta* cultivators who had their personal holdings assessed for the purpose of revenue collection at concessional rates
rozina zabti	*jihat* tax levied under the *zabti* system
rozina-batai	*jihat* tax collected to meet expenses on crop sharing under the *batai-jinsi* system
rozina-tappadari	cess belonging to the categories *sair-jihat* and *siwai-jamabandi* and levied to recover the daily allowances paid to the *tappadar*
sadir-o-warid	cess to entertain those who visited the village as travellers, pilgrims, or strangers in general
sair-jihat	taxes other than *mal* or land revenue
salami	salutation fee paid by villages to officials
sarhi	*jihat* tax collected to meet expenses on the assessment of crops under the *zabti* system
sarkar	territorial subdivision of a Mughal province (*suba*)
sarraf	money changer, banker
sawar	cavalryman
sehna	village watchman
sehngi	cess paid to the watchman
ser	a measure of weight that varied from region to region
serino	customary cess levied at the rate of half-a-*ser* per *maund* of crop yield under the *batai-jinsi* system; changed to one *ser* per *maund*
Sharia	Islamic law
sikka-mabarak	cess on the celebration of the Urs of Khwaja Muinuddin Chishti

siwai-jamabandi	revenue realized from a variety of taxes other than the *mal-o-jihat*
suba	province under the Mughals
subedar	chief administrator of a *suba*
taka	silver coin
takhfif	abatement or remission of revenue
takina	*jihat* tax collected in *taka* under the *batai-jinsi* system
talabi	tank-irrigated land
taluqa	a zamindari territory
taluqdar	holder of a *taluqa*
tankhwah jagir	*jagir* assigned in lieu of salary
tappa	sub-division of a *pargana*
tappadar	revenue officer of a *tappa*
taqavi	agricultural loan
tawai-parkhai	a cess on weighing of grain assessed at the rate of 8 *annas* per 1,000 rupees of *mal* under *jinsi* system
tehsil	collection, especially of land revenue; an administrative sub-division of a district
tehsildari	tax levied to pay the allowances of the *tehsildar* or tax collector
thana	police station
thanedar	officer-in-charge of a *thana*
thoon	Jat fortress
topchi	gunner/musketeer
tulai	*jihat* tax collected to meet expenses on weighing of grains under the *batai-jinsi* system
vakil	agent of the Amber Raja posted at the Mughal court
vamsha	clan or lineage
van	cotton
var	sugarcane
vasi	*bhomia* settlement and residence
vasidar	tenants of a *jagirdar* or a *bhomia* working in the *vasi*
virar	a broad category of various specified and unspecified taxes collected from the peasants,

	mahajans, and hereditary village officials (e.g., *patels* and the *patwaris*) by the authorities to meet miscellaneous expenses
virar waqia-nawis	cess paid to the news writer (*waqia-nawis*)
watan jagir	*jagir* held hereditarily by a chief
yaddashti	memoranda written by revenue officials
zabitana	cess collected to pay to the measuring parties
zabti	method of land revenue assessment involving the measurement of land and payment of revenue in cash
zamindar	landlord
zirayati	standing crops
zortalab	rebellious/recalcitrant, that is, non-revenue-paying

BIBLIOGRAPHY

PRIMARY SOURCES

Rajasthani[1]

I. Archival Records, Jaipur Records, Historical Section and Daftar Diwan Huzuri, Rajasthan State Archives, Bikaner

Amber Records, vs 1721/1664 CE to vs 1776/1719 CE
Arzdashts, 1641–1749 CE, Jaipur Records, Historical Section
Arsattas, Mujmil, Jaipur Records, Historical Section

Pargana Alwar: vs 1768/1711 CE
Pargana Atela Bhabra: vs 1721/1664 CE to vs 1806/1749 CE
Pargana Bharkol: vs 1722/1665 CE to vs 1806/1749 CE
Pargana Gazi ka Thana: vs 1787/1730 CE to vs 1807/1750 CE
Pargana Harsana: vs 1722/1665 CE to vs 1806/1749 CE
Pargana Hasanpur: vs 1722/1665 CE and vs 1747/1690 CE
Pargana Jalalpur: vs 1722/1665 CE to vs 1797/1740 CE
Pargana Khilohra: vs 1775/1718 CE
Pargana Khohri: vs 1721/1664 CE, to vs 1806/1749 CE
Pargana Kotla: vs 1722/1665, CE to vs 1773/1716 CE
Pargana Mandawar: vs 1722/1665 CE to vs 1806/1749 CE

[1] All the documents are dated in the Vikrami Samvat (vs) which is ahead of the Common Era (CE) by 57 years. I have converted the years of Vikarmi Samvat into the years of Common Era.

Pargana Mojpur: vs 1747/1690 CE to vs 1806/1749 CE
Pargana Naharkhoh: vs 1774/1717 CE to vs 1806/1749 CE
Pargana Pahari: vs 1723/1666 CE to vs 1807/1750 CE
Pargana Pindayan: vs 1722/1665 CE to vs 1806/1749 CE
Pargana Piragpur: vs 1782/1725 CE to vs 1802/1745 CE
Pargana Ramgarh, vs 1820/1763 CE
Pargana Sahar: vs 1746/1689 CE, vs 1747/1690 CE and vs 1749/1692 CE
Pargana Todathek: vs 1774/1717 CE, vs 1778/1721 CE, vs 1779/1722 CE, vs 1783/1726 CE, vs 1786/1729 CE, vs 1787/1730 CE, vs 1789/1732 CE, vs 1800/1743 CE and vs 1806/1749 CE
Pargana Wazirpur: vs 1723/1666 CE to vs 1806/1749 CE

Chithis, Jaipur Records, Daftar Diwan Huzuri. *Parganas* Khohri, 1665–1757 CE; Pahari, 1724–47 CE; Jalalpur, 1728–9 CE; Atela Bhabra, 1712–44 CE; Piragpur, 1725–49 CE; Gazi ka Thana, 1754–68 CE; Alwar, 1726–32 CE; Bharkol, 1729 CE; Bairat, 1727–9 CE; Sonkhar, 1726 CE; Jaitpura, 1728–34 CE; Pawta, 1730–8 CE; Chatsu, 1738–46 CE; Averi, 1726–32 CE; Hindaun, 1722–57 CE; Narnol, 1746 CE; Bahatri, 1746 CE; Banawar, 1737 CE; Khilohra, 1727 CE; Mojpur, 1692–1738 CE

Dastur-al-amals, Jaipur Records, Historical Section. *Parganas* Khohri, AH 1049/1639–40 CE, vs 1723/1666 CE; Atela Bhabra, vs 1767/1710 CE, vs 1791/1734 CE; Sonkhar Sonkhari, vs 1773/1716 CE; Mojpur, vs 1770/1713 CE; Narnol, vs 1803/1746 CE; Piragpur, vs 1789/1732 CE

Dehai-Ferhashtis, Jaipur Records, Historical Section. Khohri, 1710–50 CE

Jamabandis, Jaipur Records, Historical Section. *Parganas* Atela Bhabra, 1664–65 CE; Khohri, 1665–1747 CE; Pindayan, 1666–1729 CE; Jalalpur, 1691–1714 CE; Bawal, 1665–6 CE; Kotla, 1664 CE; Baroda Rana, 1665 CE; Chalkaliyana, 1665–66 CE; Mojpur, 1729 CE; Harsana, 1729 CE

Yaddashtis Hal Bail, Jaipur Records, Historical Section. *Parganas* Chalkaliyana, vs 1721/1664 CE, vs 1722/1665 CE; Kotla, vs 1723/1666 CE; Pindayan, vs 1783/1726 CE; Pahari, vs 1784/1727 CE; Mauzabad, vs 1723/1666 CE

Vakil Reports, Jaipur Records, Historical Section, 1693–1715 CE

Khatoot Ahalkarans, Mah Vadi 6, vs 1740/1683 CE; Asoj Vadi, vs 1771/1714 CE; Mah Vadi 4, vs 1775/1718 CE; Asadh Sudi 4, vs 1780/1723 CE; Mah Vadi 4, vs 1775/1718 CE

Dastur Komwar, Tozi Dastur Komwar, bundle no. 3, vs 1774–1790/1717–33 CE

Farmans, trans. Shujawat Khan Naksbandi (Hindi), vol. 1, Rajasthan State Archives, Bikaner, 2010

II. Non-archival Records of Alwar State, Rajasthan State Archives, Bikaner

Bandhak no. 3, *Granthank* nos 66, 81
Bandhak no. 4, *Granthank* nos 43, 83
Bandhak no. 5, *Granthank* no. 89
Bandhak no. 6, *Granthank* nos 71, 83
Bandhak no. 11, *Granthank* no. 112
Bandhak no. 12, *Granthank* nos 10, 89
Bandhak no. 13, *Granthank* no. 1
Bandhak no. 66, *Granthank* nos 3, 7
Bandhak no. 67, *Granthank* nos 4, 6
Bandhak no. 68, *Granthank* nos 4, 5
Bandhak no. 71, *Granthank* nos 6, 7, 12

III. Jagga records, *Pothi* nos 1, 2 in personal possession of Jagdish Jagga, son of Shri Ghasi Ram Jagga, village Khuteta Kalan, Tehsil Ramgarh, District, Alwar, Rajasthan.

Persian

Abdullah.'Tarikh-i-Daudi'. In *History of India as Told by Its Own Historians*, vol. 4, edited by H. M. Elliot and John Dowson. Allahabad: Kitab Mahal, 1975.

Abul-Fazl. *The Ain-i-Akbari*, vol. 1, trans. H. Blochmann, 3rd ed. Calcutta: Royal Asiatic Society, 1977.

———. *The Ain-i-Akbari*, vol. 2, trans. Col. H. S. Jarrett; corr. and ann. Sir Jadunath Sarkar, 3rd ed. Calcutta: Royal Asiatic Society, 1978.

———. *The Akbarnama*, vols 2 & 3, trans. H. Beveridge. Delhi: Low Price Publications, [1902–39] 1993.

Afif, Siraj. 'Tarikh-i-Firozshahi'. In *History of India as Told by Its Own Historians*, vol. 3, edited by H. M. Elliot and John Dowson. Delhi: Low Price Publications, 2001.

Ahmad, Khwajah Nizamuddin, *Tabaqat-i-Akbari*, 3 vols, edited and translated by B. De and M. Hidayat Hossain. Calcutta: Bibliotheca Indica, 1913–35.

Babur. *Baburnama*, vol. 2, trans. A. S. Beveridge. London: E.J.W. Gibb Memorial Trust, 1921. Reprint, New Delhi: Low Price Publications, 1995.

Barani, Ziauddin. 'Tarikh-i-Firozshahi'. In *History of India as Told by Its Own Historians*, vol. 3, edited by H. M. Elliot and John Dowson. Delhi: Low Price Publications, 2001.

Chisti, Abdur Rahman. 'Mirat-i-Masudi'. In *The History of India as Told by Its Own Historians*, vol. 2, edited by H. M. Elliot and John Dowson. Delhi: Low Price Publications, 2001.

Juzjani, Minhaj Siraj, *Tabaqat-i-Nasiri*, trans. H. G. Raverty. Delhi: Oriental Books Reprint Corp., [1881] 1970.

Khusrau, Amir. 'Khazaina-i-Futuh and the Kiranu-i-Sadain' (The Poem of Amir Khusrau). In *History of India as Told by Its Own Historians*, vol. 3, edited by H. M. Elliot and John Dowson. Delhi: Low Price Publications, 2001.

———. 'Tuzuk-i-Baburi'. In *History of India as Told by Its Own Historians*, vol. 4, edited by H. M. Elliot and John Dowson. Allahabad: Kitab Mahal, 1975.

Khan, Inayat. *The Shahjahannama*, translated by A. R. Fuller, edited and compiled by W. E. Begley and Z. A. Desai. Delhi: Oxford University Press, 1990.

Khan, Khafi. 'Muntakhab-ul-Lubab'. In *History of India as Told by Its Own Historians*, vol. 7, edited by H. M. Elliot and John Dowson. Delhi: Low Price Publications, 1993.

Khan, Muhammad Habibur Rahman. *Tazkirah-i-Sufia-i-Mewat: Islami Hind ki Tarikh ka Bhula Hua Ek Aham Bab*. Gurgaon: Mewat Academy, 1979.

Khan, Muhammad Hashim Khafi. *Muntakhab-al Lubab*, vol. 1, trans. Anees Jahan Syed as *Aurangzeb in Muntakhab-al Lubab*. Bombay: Somaiya Publications, 1977.

Khan, Nawwab Samsam-ud-daula Shah Nawaz and Abdul Hayy. *The Maathir-ul-Umara*, vol. 1, trans. H. Beveridge. Revised, annotated, and completed by Baini Prasad. Patna: Janaki Prakashan, 1979.

Khan, Saqi Mustad. *Maasir-i-Alamgiri*, trans. Jadunath Sarkar, 2nd ed. Delhi: Munshiram Manoharlal, 1986.

Khan, Zain, *Tabaqat-i-Baburi*, trans. S. Hasan Askari. Delhi: Idarah-i Adabiyat-i Delli, 1982.

Minhaj Siraj. 'Tabakat-i-Nasiri'. In *The History of India as Told by Its Own Historians*, vol. 2, edited by H. M. Elliot and John Dowson. Delhi: Low Price Publications, 1990.

Mustaqi, Shaikh Rizqullah. *Waqiat-e-Mustaqi*, edited and translated by I. H. Siddiqui. New Delhi: Northern Book Centre, 1993.

Naimutulla. 'Tarikh-i-Khan-Jahan Lodi'. In H. M. *History of India as Told by Its Own Historians*, vol. 5, edited by H. M. Elliot and John Dowson. Delhi: Low Price Publications, 1990.

Qandhari, Muhammad Arif. *Tarikh-i-Akbari*, trans. Tasneem Ahmad. Delhi: Pragati Publications, 1993.

Sirhindi, Yahya bin Ahmad bin 'Abdullah'. *The Tarikh-i-Mubarakshahi*, trans. H. Beveridge. Delhi: Low Price Publications, 1990.

Timur. 'Malfuzat-i-Timuri'. In *History of India as Told by Its Own Historians*, vol. 3, edited by H. M. Elliot and John Dowson. Delhi: Low Price Publications, 2001.

Tughlaq, Firozshah. 'Futuhat-i-Firozshahi'. In *History of India as Told by Its Own Historians*, vol. 3, edited by H. M. Elliot and John Dowson. Delhi: Low Price Publications, 2001.

Yadgar, Ahmad. 'Tarikh-i-Salatin-i-Afghana'. In *History of India as Told by Its Own Historians*, vol. 5, edited by H. M. Elliot and John Dowson. Delhi: Low Price Publications, 1990.

Urdu

Makhdum, Sheikh Muhammad. *Arzang-i-Tijara*. Agra: Agra Akhbar, H. 1290/1873 CE, trans. (Hindi) Anil Joshi. Alwar, 1989.

Shakur, Abdul. *Tarikh Mev Chatri*. Nuh, Gurgaon: Chaudhuri Yasin Mev High School, [1919] 1974.

Hindi

Meo, Narsingh. 'Hasan Khan ki Katha', *Shodh Patrika* (Udaipur: Rajasthan Vidyapeeth), vol. 4 (October–December 1970): 53–62.

European Travelogues

Bernier, Francois. *Travels in the Mogul Empire, A. D. 1656–1668*, edited and translated by A. Constable. Reprint, Delhi: Munshiram Manoharlal, 1983.

Pelsaert, Francisco. *Jahangir's India: The Remonstratie of Franscisco Pelsaert*, translated by W. H. Moreland and P. Geyl. Cambridge: W. Heffere, 1925.

Colonial Reports

Channing, F. C. *Land Revenue Settlement of the Gurgaon District*. Lahore: Central Jail Press, 1882.

Cunningham, Alexander. *Report of a Tour in Eastern Rajputana in 1882–83*, Archaeological Survey of India Reports, vol. 20. Varanasi: Indological Book House, [1885] 1969.

Fraser, A. *Statistical Report of Zillah Gurgaon*. Lahore: n.p., 1846.

Ibbetson, D. *Panjab Castes: Being a Reprint of the Chapter on 'The Races, Castes and Tribes of the People' in the Report on the Census of the Panjab Published in 1883*. Lahore: Superintendent, Government Printing, 1916.

Powlett, Major P. W. *Gazetteer of Ulwur*. London: Trubner & Co., 1878.

Watson, J. Forbes and John William Kaye, eds. *The People of India*, vol. 4. London: W. H. Allen and Co. for the India Museum, 1869.

Wills, C. U. *A Report on the Land-Tenures and Special Powers of Certain Thikanedars of the Jaipur State, The Jaipur Gazette*, vol. 51. Delhi: I. M. H. Press, 1933.

SECONDARY SOURCES

Vernacular

Morwal, Bhagwan Das. 'Mewati Lok Sahitya Mein Jeevan Darshan' (Hindi). In *Shrijan*, edited by Changa Ram Meena. Alwar: Babu Shobharam Arts Government College, 2005–6.

Rajasthani-Hindi Sankshipt Shabdakosh, vol. 2, edited by Sita Ram Lalus. Jodhpur: Rajasthan Oriental Research Institute.

Ram, Munshi. 'Mewati Lok Sahitya evam Mewat ka Arthik Vishleshan' (Hindi). In *Shrijan*, edited by Changa Ram Meena, 99–102. Alwar: Babu Shobharam Arts Government College, 2005–6.

Rawat, Saraswat. *Meena Ithihas* (Hindi). Jaipur: Jhunthlal Nandala, vs 2025.

Sharma, Mahavir Prasad. *Mewati ka Udbhav aur Vikas* (Hindi). Kotputli, Jaipur distt: Lokbhasha Prakashan, 1976.

English

Aggarwal, Pratap C. *Caste, Religion and Power: An Indian Case Study*. Delhi: SRC, 1971.

Ali, Athar. 'Ethnic Character of the Army during the Delhi Sultanate (13th–14th Centuries)'. In *Medieval India 2: Essays in Medieval Indian History and Culture*, edited by Shahbuddin Iraqi, 165–72. Delhi: Manohar, 2008.

———. *The Mughal Nobility under Aurangzeb*. Bombay: Asia Publishing House, 1966.

Ali, Hashim Amir. *The Meos of Mewat*. Delhi: Oxford University Press, 1970.

Aziz, Abdul. 'Measurement of Agricultural Productivity: A Case Study of Mewat'. Unpublished PhD thesis, North Eastern Hill University, Shillong, 1981.

Banga, Indu. *Agrarian System of the Sikhs: Late Eighteenth and Early Nineteenth Century*. Delhi: Manohar, 1978.

Bhadani, B. L. 'The Mughal Highway and Post Stations in Marwar'. *Proceedings of the Indian History Congress*, 141–55. Delhi, 1990.

Bhardwaj, Surajbhan. 'Qasbas in Mewat in the Medieval Period: A Study of the Interface between the Township and the Countryside'. In *City in Medieval India*, edited by Yogesh Sharma and Pius Malekandathil, 567–85. Delhi: Primus, 2014.

Bhardwaj, Surajbhan. 'Migration, Mobility and Memories: Meos in the Processes of Peasantisation and Islamicisation in Medieval Period'. *Indian Historical Review* 39, no. 2 (2012): 217–50.

———. 'Myth and Reality of the Khap Panchayats: A Historical Analysis of the Panchayat and Khap Panchayat'. *Studies in History* 28, no. 1 (2012): 43–67.

———. 'Socio-economic Conditions in the Mewat Region, c. 1650–1750'. Unpublished PhD thesis, Centre for Historical Studies, Jawaharlal Nehru University, Delhi, 1990.

Bhargava, Meena, ed. *The Decline of the Mughal Empire*. Delhi: Oxford University Press, 2014.

Bingley, A. H. *History of Caste and Culture of Jats and Gujars*. Delhi: Ess Ess Publication, [1899] 1978.

Blok, Anton. 'The Peasant and the Brigand: Social Banditry Reconsidered'. *Comparative Studies in Society and Economy* 14, no. 4 (1972): 494–503.

Chandra, Satish. *Medieval India: Society, the Jagirdari Crisis and the Village*. Delhi: Macmillan, 1982.

———. 'Some Aspects of Indian Village Society in Northern India during the 18th Century: The Position and Role of *Khud-kasht* and *Pahi-kasht*'. *Indian Historical Review* 1 (1974): 51–64.

Chandra, Satish. *Parties and Politics at the Mughal Court, 1707–1740*. Aligarh: Aligarh Muslim University Press, 1959.

Chandra, Satish and Dilbagh Singh. 'Structure and Stratification in the Village Society in Eastern Rajasthan'. *Proceedings of the Indian History Congress*, 196–203, 33rd session, Muzaffarpur, 1972.

Dasgupta, Ashin. 'Trade and Politics in 18th Century India'. In *Islam and the Trade of Asia: A Colloquium*, edited by D. S. Richards. Pennsylvania: University of Pennsylvania, 1970.

Dwivedi, G. C. *The Jats: Their Role in the Mughal Empire*. Delhi: Arnold Publishers, 1989.

Fukuzawa, H. *The Medieval Deccan: Peasants, Social Systems and States, Sixteenth to Eighteenth Centuries*. Delhi: Oxford University Press, 1991.

Gopal, Lallanji and V. C. Srivastava, eds. *History of Agriculture in India up to c. 1200 AD*, *History of Science, Philosophy and Culture in Indian Civilization*, vol. 5, part 1. Delhi: Concept Publishing, 2008.

Grover, B. R. 'Land and Taxation System during the Mughal Age'. In *Collected Works of Professor B. R. Grover*, vol. 4, edited by Amrita Grover, Dr Anju Grover Chaudhary, and Dr J. C. Dua. Delhi: Low Price Publications, 2009.

———. 'Landed Hierarchy and Village Community during the Mughal Age'. In *Collected Works of Professor B. R. Grover*, vol. 1, edited by Amrita Grover, Dr Anju Grover Chaudhary, and Dr J. C. Dua. Delhi: Low Price Publications, 2005.

Grover, B. R. 'Mughal Land Revenue Apparatus'. In *Collected Works of Professor B. R. Grover*, vol. 5, edited by Amrita Grover, Dr Anju Grover Chaudhary, and Dr J. C. Dua. Delhi: Low Price Publications, 2010.

———. 'Nature of Land Rights in Mughal Indian History'. *Indian Economic and Social History Review* 1, no. 1 (1963): 1–23.

Gulati, G. D. *Mewat: Folklore, Memory, History*. Delhi: Dev Publishers, 2013.

Gupta, S. P. and Shireen Moosvi. 'Bhomi in the Territories of Amber c. 1650–1750'. *Proceedings of the Indian History Congress*, 353–9, 32nd session, Jabalpur, 1970.

———. *The Agrarian System of Eastern Rajasthan (c. 1650–1750)*. Delhi: Manohar, 1986.

———. 'Ijara System in Eastern Rajasthan'. In *Medieval India: A Miscellany* (Aligarh Muslim University) 2 (1972): 263–8.

Habib, Irfan. *An Atlas of the Mughal Empire*. Delhi: Oxford University Press, 1982.

———. 'Caste System in Indian History'. In *Essays in Indian History: Towards a Marxist Perception*, edited by Irfan Habib, 161–79. London: Anthem Press, 2002.

Habib, Irfan. 'Postal Communication in Mughal India'. *Proceedings of the Indian History Congress*, 236–52, 46th session, Amritsar, 1985.

———. 'Potentialities of Capitalist Development in the Economy of Mughal India'. *Enquiry*, New Series, 3, no. 3 (Winter 1971): 1–56.

———. *The Agrarian System of Mughal India 1556–1707*, 2nd rev. ed. Delhi: Oxford University Press, 1999.

———. 'The Form of Class Struggles during the Mughal Period'. In Irfan Habib, ed., *Essays in Indian History: Towards a Marxist Perception*, 233–58. London: Anthem Press, 2002.

———. 'The Social Distribution of Landed Property in the Pre-British India: A Historical Survey'. *Enquiry*, Old Series, no. 12 (1965): 21–75.

Habib, M. and K. A. Nizami. *A Comprehensive History of India*, vol. 5: *The Delhi Sultanat, A.D. 1206–1526*. Delhi: People's Publishing House, 1970.

Habibullah, A. B. M. *The Foundation of Muslim Rule in India*. Allahabad: Central Book Depot, 1961.

Hasan, S. Nurul. 'Further Light on Zamindars under the Mughals: A Case Study of (Mirza) Raja Jai Singh under Shahjahan'. *Proceedings Indian History Congress*, 497–502, 39th session, Hyderabad, 1978.

———. *Thoughts on Agrarian Relations in Mughal India*. Delhi: People's Publishing House, 1973.

———. 'Zamindars under the Mughals'. In *Land Control and Social Structure in Indian History*, edited by R. E. Frykenberg, 17–32. Madison: University of Wisconsin Press, 1969.

Hasan, S. Nurul, K. N. Hasan, and S. P. Gupta. 'The Pattern of Agricultural Production in the Territories of Amber (c. 1650–1750)'. *Proceedings of the Indian History Congress*, 244–64, 28th session, Mysore, 1966.

Hasan, S. Nurul and S. P. Gupta. 'Prices of Foodgrains in the Territories of Amber (c. 1650–1750)'. *Proceedings of the Indian History Congress*, 345–68, 29th session, Patiala, 1968.

Husain, A. M., *Tughluq Dynasty*. Calcutta: Thacker Spink, 1963.

Khan, A. R. *Chieftains in the Mughal Empire during the Reign of Akbar*. Shimla: Indian Institute of Advanced Study (IIAS), 1977.

Khan, Iqtidar Alam. 'The Nobility under Akbar and the Development of His Religious Policy, 1560–1580'. *Journal of the Royal Asiatic Society of Great Britain and Ireland* (1968): 29–36.

Kulkarni, A. R. 'The Indian Village with Special Reference to Medieval Deccan (Maratha Country)', General Presidential Address. *Proceedings of the Indian History Congress*, 1–62, 52nd session, Delhi, 1992.

Kumar, Dharma and Meghnad Desai, eds. *The Cambridge Economic History of India*, vol. 2: c. 1757–c. 1970. Cambridge: Cambridge University Press, 1982.

Lal, Kishori Saran. *History of the Khaljis, A.D. 1290–1320*. Delhi: Asia Publishing House, 1967.

Ludden, David. *An Agrarian History of South Asia*. Cambridge: Cambridge University Press, 1999.

Malcolm, Major-General Sir John. *The Political History of India from 1784 to 1823*, vol. 2. London: John Murray, 1826.

Mayaram, Shail. *Against History, Against State: Counterperspectives from the Margins*. Delhi: Permanent Black, 2004.

———. *Resisting Regimes: Myth, Memory and the Shaping of a Muslim Identity*. Delhi: Oxford University Press, 1997.

Mishra, Pratibha. *Soil Productivity and Crop Potentials: A Case Study (District Alwar-Rajasthan)*. Delhi: Concept, 1984.

Moosvi, Shireen. *The Economy of the Mughal Empire c.1595: A Statistical Study*. Delhi: Oxford University Press, 1987.

Moreland, W. H. *Agrarian System of Moslem India*. Cambridge: W. Heffer & Sons, 1929.

Mukhia, Harbans. 'Was There Feudalism in Indian History', Presidential Address. *Proceedings of the Indian History Congress*, 229–80, 40th session, Waltair, 1979.

———. 'Illegal Extortions from Peasants, Artisans and Menials in Eastern Rajasthan during the Eighteenth Century'. *Indian Economic and Social History Review* 14, no. 2 (1977): 231–45.

Pande, Ram. 'Raja Bishan Singh's Campaign against the Jats'. *Proceedings of the Indian History Congress*, 29th session, Patiala, 1968.

Rana R. P. 'Agrarian Revolts in Northern India during the Late 17th and Early 18th Century'. *Indian Economic and Social History Review* 18, nos 3–4 (1981): 287–325.

———. *From Rebels to Rulers: The Rise of Jat Power in Medieval India, c. 1665–1735*. Delhi: Manohar, 2006.

Rao, M. S. A. 'Rewari Kingdom and the Mughal Empire'. In *Realm and Region in Traditional India*, edited by Richard G. Fox, 79–89. Delhi: Vikas Publishing House, 1977.

Raychaudhuri, Tapan and Irfan Habib, eds. *The Cambridge Economic History of India*, vol. 1: c. 1200–c. 1750. Cambridge: Cambridge University Press, 1982.

Rizvi, S. A. A. *A History of Sufism in India*, vol. 2. Delhi: Munshiram Manoharlal, 1983.

Rizvi, S. H. M. *Mina: The Ruling Tribe of Rajasthan: Socio-Biological Appraisal*. Delhi: B. R. Publishing Corporation, 1987.

Sahai, Nandita Prasad. *Politics of Patronage and Protest: The State, Society and Artisans in Early Modern Rajasthan*. Delhi: Oxford University Press, 2006.

Scott, James C. *Weapons of the Weak: Everyday Forms of Peasant Resistance*. Delhi: Oxford University Press, 1990.

Sharma, G. D. 'Indigenous Banking and the State in the Eastern Rajasthan during the Seventeenth Century'. *Proceedings of the Indian History Congress*, 332–441, 40th session, Waltair, 1979.

Siddiqi, N. A. 'Land Revenue Demand under the Mughals'. *Indian Economic and Social History Review* 2, no. 4 (1964): 373–80.

Singh, Chetan. *Region and Empire: Panjab in the Seventeenth Century*. Delhi: Oxford University Press, 1991.

Singh, Dilbagh. 'Caste and Structure of Village Society in Eastern Rajasthan during the Eighteenth Century'. *Indian History Review* 2, no. 2 (1976): 299–311.

———. 'Local and Land Revenue Administration of the State of Jaipur (c. 1750–1800)'. Unpublished PhD thesis, Centre for Historical Studies, Jawaharlal Nehru University, 1975.

———. 'Rural Indebtedness in Eastern Rajasthan during the 18th Century'. *Proceedings of the Indian History Congress*, 83–93, 5th session, Jadavpur, 1974.

———. 'Tenants, Sharecroppers and Agricultural Labourers during the Eighteenth Century Eastern Rajasthan'. *Studies in History* 1, no. 1 (1977): 31–43.

———. 'The Position of the Patel in Eastern Rajasthan during the Eighteenth Century'. *Proceedings of the Indian History Congress*, 360–6, 32nd session, Jabalpur, 1970.

Singh, Dilbagh. 'The Role of the Mahajans in the Rural Economy in Eastern Rajasthan during the 18th century'. *Social Scientist* 2, no. 10 (1974): 20–31.

———. *The State, Landlords and Peasants: Rajasthan in the 18th Century*. Delhi: Manohar, 1990.

Sinha, Nandini. 'Reconstructing Identity and Situating Themselves in History: A Preliminary Note on the Meenas of Jaipur Locality'. *Indian Historical Review* 27, no. 1 (2000): 29–43.

Sinha, Surjit. 'State Formation and Rajput Myth in Tribal Central India'. *Man in India* 42, no. 1 (April–June 1962): 35–80.

Skaria, Ajay. *Hybrid Histories: Forests, Frontiers and Wilderness in Western India*. Delhi: Oxford University Press, 1999.

Spate, O. H. K. *India and Pakistan: A General and Regional Geography*. London: Metheun, 1957.

Temple, R. C. *The Legends of Punjab*, 3 vols. Bombay: Bombay Education Society, 1884.

Thapar, Romila. *Cultural Transaction and Early India: Tradition and Patronage*. Delhi: Oxford University Press, 1987.

Thapar, Romila. *From Lineage to State: Social Formations of the Mid-first Millennium BC in the Ganga Valley*. Delhi: Oxford University Press, 1990.

Tod, James. *Annals and Antiquities of Rajasthan*, vol. 2. London: G. Routledge & Sons, 1914.

Umar, Muhammad. *Muslim Society in Northern India during the Eighteenth Century*. Delhi: Munshiram Manoharlal, 1998.

Watson, J. Forbes and John W. Kaye, eds. *The People of India*, vol. 4. London: W. H. Allen and Co. for the India Museum, 1869.

INDEX

ABOUT THE AUTHOR

Suraj Bhan Bhardwaj is Associate Professor in the Department of History at Motilal Nehru College, University of Delhi, India. He obtained his PhD from the Centre for Historical Studies, Jawaharlal Nehru University, New Delhi, India, and has taught at the University of Delhi for over 20 years. He has published articles in leading journals such as *Studies in History* and *Indian Historical Review* and chapters in edited volumes. His research interests lie in areas such as socio-economic history of late medieval north India, history of community formation, contemporary issues in the articulation of community identity in north-western India, particularly in Rajasthan and Haryana, and socio-historical analysis of folklore.